ISO 9001:2000 Audit Procedures

ISO 9001:2000
Audit Procedures

Second edition

Ray Tricker

ELSEVIER
BUTTERWORTH
HEINEMANN

AMSTERDAM • BOSTON • HEIDELBERG • LONDON • NEW YORK • OXFORD
PARIS • SAN DIEGO • SAN FRANCISCO • SINGAPORE • SYDNEY • TOKYO

Elsevier Butterworth-Heinemann
Linacre House, Jordan Hill, Oxford OX2 8DP
30 Corporate Drive, Burlington, MA 01803

First published 2002
Reprinted 2003
Second edition 2005

British Library Cataloguing in Publication Data
A catalogue record for this book is available from the British Library

Library of Congress Cataloguing in Publication Data
A catalogue record for this book is available from the Library of Congress

ISBN 0 7506 6615 3

For information on all Elsevier Butterworth-Heinemann publications
visit our website at http://books.elsevier.com

Typeset by Charon Tec Pvt. Ltd, Chennai, India
www.charontec.com
Printed and bound in Great Britain by Biddles Ltd, King's Lynn, Norfolk

Working together to grow
libraries in developing countries

www.elsevier.com | www.bookaid.org | www.sabre.org

ELSEVIER   BOOK AID
            International   Sabre Foundation

Contents

Foreword

One of the requirements of ISO 9001:2000 (Section 8.2.2) is that:

> *'The organisation shall conduct internal audits at planned intervals to determine whether the quality management system:*
>
> *a. conforms to the requirements of the ISO 9001:2000 standard and to the quality management system requirements established by the organisation and,*
> *b. is effectively implemented and maintained.'*

To meet this requirement, organisations must continually review their system to ensure its continuing suitability and success, reveal defects, danger spots or irregularities, suggest possible improvements, eliminate wastage or loss, check the effectiveness of management (at all levels) and be sure that managerial objectives and methods are effective and that they are capable of achieving the desired result. Above all, organisations must be prepared to face up to an audit of their own quality processes and procedures from potential customers and prove to them that their Quality Management System fully meets the recommendations, requirements and specifications of ISO 9001:2000 – **and** that it is capable of meeting customer requirements.

The aim of this book, with its audit checklists, explanations and example questionnaires, is to assist auditors in completing internal, external and third party audits of newly implemented, existing and transitional ISO 9001:2000 Quality Management Systems.

Preface

ISO 9001:2000 and ISO 9004:2000 were developed as a '*consistent pair*' of Quality Management System (QMS) standards, based on eight quality management principles with a common process-oriented structure and harmonised terminology. In contrast to previous versions of these standards, they are designed to meet the requirements of service industries (as well as manufacturers) and may be used together, or as stand-alone documents. **Together**, they lay down requirements for incorporating the management of quality into the design, manufacture and delivery of products, services and software.

The aim of having a 'consistent pair' of standards, with an aligned structure, is to encourage organisations not only to look at their activities from a process standpoint, but also to look beyond certification to a system that will be truly beneficial in improving operational performance. In this respect, ISO 9001:2000 specifies the requirements for a QMS (which can be used by organisations for certification and/or contractual purposes) whilst ISO 9004:2000 provides guidance aimed at improving an organisation's overall quality performance. ISO 9004:2000 is **not**, however, meant as a 'guideline for implementing ISO 9001:2000' nor is it intended for certification or contractual use. Supporting both of these standards is ISO 9000:2000 (which superseded ISO 8402:1995) and which describes the fundamentals of Quality Management Systems and specifies their terminology.

To achieve its main objectives, ISO 9001:2000 requires manufacturing plants and service industries to possess a **fully auditable Quality Management System** consisting of Quality Policies, Quality Processes, Quality Procedures and Work Instructions. It is this Quality Management System that will provide the auditable proof that the requirements of ISO 9001:2000 have been and are still being met.

Since the introduction of ISO 9001:2000, however, certain sections of the industry see compliance auditing as no longer being 'fashionable' and performance auditing is the only way forward. Compliance auditing is, however, a mandatory requirement under clause 8.2.2 which clearly states that '*The organisation shall conduct internal audits at planned intervals to determine whether the quality* *management system **conforms** to the planned arrangements **to the requirements of this international standard** and the quality management system requirements established by the organisation.'*

This is amplified in clause 6.4.3 of ISO 19011:2002 ('*Guidelines for quality and/or environmental management systems auditing*') which states:

> *The **audit team members should** review information relevant to their audit assignment and **prepare work documents** as necessary for reference and for recording audit proceedings. Such documents may include*
>
> - ***Checklists and audit sampling plans**, and*
> - *Forms for recording information, such as supporting evidence, audit findings and records of meetings.*
>
> *The use of checklists and forms should not restrict the extent of audit activities, which can change as a result of information collected during the audit.*

Whilst not always required for all management system standards, audit checklists (composed of items relating to both compliance with the requirements of the standard and items that check the performance of the organisation's processes) are just one tool available from the 'auditor's toolbox'.

Most auditors usually find it beneficial to audit from the organisation's quality management system up to the ISO 9001:2000 requirements (as shown in the figure below) rather than start afresh.

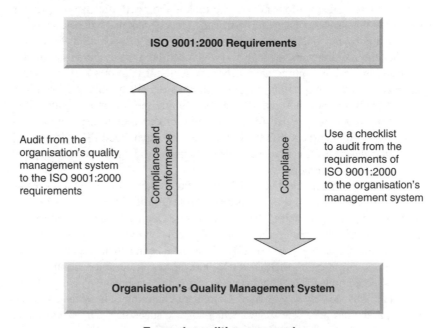

Example auditing approach

Alternatively, a checklist may be used to ensure that all the relevant ISO 9001:2000 requirements have been addressed in the management system.

Advantages of using an audit checklist

Checklists, if developed for a specific audit and used correctly, can:

- act as a sampling plan and time manager;
- be provided to the auditee ahead of the on-site audit;
- be used as an information base for planning future audits;
- ensure a consistent audit approach;
- ensure that adequate evidence is obtained;
- ensure that the audit scope is being followed;
- help an auditor to perform better during the audit process;
- help to ensure that an audit is conducted in a systematic and comprehensive manner;
- provide a means of communication and a place to record data for use for future reference;
- provide a repository for notes collected during the audit process (i.e. audit field notes);
- provide a record that the QMS was examined;
- provide objective evidence that the audit was performed;
- provide structure and continuity to an audit;
- serve as a memory aid.

Disadvantages of using an audit checklist

When audit checklists are not available, or poorly prepared, the following disadvantages can occur or be observed:

- checklists should not be a substitute for audit planning;
- generic checklists, which do not reflect the specific organisational management system, may not add any value and may interfere with the audit;
- poorly prepared checklists can slow down an audit due to duplication and repetition;
- the focus of the checklist may be too narrow in scope to identify specific problem areas;
- an inexperienced auditor may not be able to clearly communicate what he is looking for;
- checklists can be restrictive if used as the auditor's only support mechanism.

Note: As can be seen above, there are both advantages and disadvantages to using audit checklists. It depends on many factors, including customer needs, time and cost restraints, auditor experience and sector scheme requirements. Auditors should therefore assess the value of the checklist as an aid to the audit process and consider its use as a functional tool.

Historically this is the 2nd edition of 'ISO 9001:2000 Audit Procedures' and although the requirements of ISO 9001:2000 have not changed since publication of the 1st edition in 2002, it was felt that its predecessor (because it was written during the transitional stage between the 1994 and the full implementation of the 2000 standards) made far too much mention and comparisons with the old version of this standard. It also laid insufficient emphasis on the fact that ISO 9001:2000 has now become the industry accepted standard for international quality.

Consequently (and with the benefit of four years' field experience of the standard) this book has been completely updated and now includes:

- more detail concerning the actual structure of ISO 9001:2000;
- guidance on the mandatory written procedures required by the standard;
- more detail concerning the eight principles of management which are applied within the standard;
- more detail about the aims, benefits and requirements of ISO 9001:2000;
- reformatted diagrams drawn against a common template;
- an updated section providing advice about internal and external audit programmes;
- a new section concerning specific ISO 9001:2000 management responsibilities;
- a new section detailing ISO 9001:2000 organisational requirements;
- improved advice on how to comply with the requirements of ISO 9001:2000 and the likely documentation that an organisation will need to prove this compliance;
- thoroughly updated auditors' check sheets;
- an expanded list of Useful Addresses (containing details of all the members of ISO);
- updated Index, Glossary, References, Abbreviations and Acronyms sections.

 **Note:** For the benefit of Masters Degree students (and other interested parties) a reduced record of ISO 9000's development is still available in the text.

ISO 9001:2000 Audit Procedures, Edition 2, with its audit checklists, explanations and example questionnaires is designed to assist auditors in completing internal, external and third party audits of ISO 9001:2000 Quality Management Systems.

For convenience, this book is divided into three parts, with Part 1 describing the requirements of ISO 9001:2000, Part 2 providing background information for auditors – for example:

- how ISO 9001:2000 can be used to check an organisation's QMS;
- how internal and external audits should be completed (e.g. audit plan, supplier evaluation, surveillance or quality audit visits);

- how quality assurance can affect the product throughout its lifecycle;
- QMS requirements, principles and determinates;
- the manufacturer's, supplier's and purchaser's responsibilities;
- the benefits and costs of quality assurance;
- the type of documentation an organisation needs to satisfy the requirements of ISO 9001:2000;

and Part 3, containing a series of explanations, checklists and example questionnaires to assist auditors in compiling their own system and individual specific audit check sheets. These consist of:

- **ISO 9001:2000 headings etc.**
  A complete listing of the sections and subsections making up ISO 9001:2000 requirements together with a brief explanation of their requirements.
- **ISO 9001:2000 – explanation and likely documentation**
  A brief explanation of the specific requirements (i.e. the 'shalls') of each element of ISO 9001:2000 together with a description of the likely documentation that an organisation would need to have in place to meet the requirements.
- **ISO 9001:2000 – organisational requirements**
  A summary of how an organisation is expected to work in conformance with the requirements and recommendations of ISO 9001:2000.
- **ISO 9001:2000 – management requirements**
  Complete details of all the mandatory requirements listed in ISO 9001:2000 for top management (totalling 21) together with those (over 250) for the general management of an organisation.
- **ISO 9001:2000 audit questionnaire**
  An indication of areas of an organisation's QMS that could be looked at and possibly further investigated during internal, external and/or third party audits.
- **Additional (general purpose) audit checks**
  Lists of some of the most important questions that an external auditor would be likely to ask when assessing an organisation's QMS for conformance to ISO 9001:2000 and/or other management standards.
- **Stage audit check sheet**
  List of the most important questions that an external auditor is likely to ask when evaluating an organisation for their:
  - design stage;
  - manufacturing stage;
  - acceptance stage;
  - in-service stage.
- **Complete index for ISO 9001:2000**
  A listing of all the main topics and subjects covered in ISO 9001:2000.
- **ISO 9001:2000 crosscheck and correspondence form**
  The intention of this form is to show how and where the requirements of ISO 9001:2000 have been met in an organisation's quality management system.

- **Audit check sheet form**
  A list of the most important questions an auditor should ask.
- **Comparison between ISO 9001:2000 and ISO 9001:1994**
  A complete list of the sections and subsections making up ISO 9001:2000 requirements cross-referenced to the previous ISO 9001:1994 elements.
- **Counter-comparison between ISO 9001:1994 and ISO 9001:2000**
  A complete list of the elements making up ISO 9001:1994 cross-referenced to the sections and subsections of ISO 9001:2000.
- **A selection of audit forms**
  A selection of forms used by auditors.
- **ISO 9001:2000 – elements covered and outstanding**
  A checklist used by auditors to confirm that the client's QMS fully covers the requirements (i.e. clauses) of ISO 9001:2000.

And for assistance:

- **Acronyms and abbreviations used in quality**
  An extensive list of acronyms and abbreviations encountered by auditors.
- **Glossary of terms used in quality**
  An extensive list of terms and conditions used in quality management.
- **References**
- A guide to the most common publications, standards and documents concerning quality management.
- **Useful addresses.**

Note: To save you having to photocopy these checklists, explanations and questionnaires (and/or having to type them all out again), 'unlocked', fully accessible, non-.pdf, soft copies of **all** these files (**plus** copies of the generic example Quality Manual, Business Processes and Quality Procedures from the sister publication *ISO 9001:2000 for Small Businesses*, third edn) are available on a CD (for a small additional charge) from the author in Word format. He can be contacted at ray@herne.org.uk.

About the author

Ray Tricker (MSc, IEng, FIIE (elec), FCMI, FIQA, FIRSE) is the Principal Consultant of Herne European Consultancy Ltd – a company specialising in Integrated (i.e. Quality, Environmental and Safety) Management Systems. He served with the Royal Corps of Signals (for a total of 37 years) during which time he held various managerial posts culminating in being appointed as the Chief Engineer of NATO's Communications Security Agency.

Most of Ray's work since joining Herne has centred on the European Railways. He has held a number of posts with the Union International des Chemins de fer (Quality Manager of the European Train Control System (ETCS)) and with the European Union (EU) Commission (T500 Review Team Leader, European Rail Traffic Management System (ERTMS) Users Group Project Co-ordinator, HEROE Project Co-ordinator).

Currently (as well as writing books on ISO 9001:2000, Optoelectronics and Building Regulations for Butterworth-Heinemann) he is busy assisting small businesses from around the world (usually on a no cost basis) produce their own auditable Quality Management Systems to meet the requirements of ISO 9001:2000.

He is also consultant to the Association of American Railroads (AAR) advising them on ISO 9001:2000 compliance and has recently been appointed as a UKAS Technical Specialist for the assessment of Notified Bodies for the Harmonisation of the trans-European high speed rail system.

To my grandson Kenneth

1

Background to the ISO 9001:2000 standard

During the last few years of its life, it was recognised that the 1994 version of ISO 9000 (i.e. ISO 9001:1994, ISO 9002:1994 and ISO 9003:1994) was far too orientated towards manufacturing and that there was a need to revise the existing structure of the standard to try and suit **all** organisations, no matter their type or size.

Under existing international agreement, all International Standards have to be reinspected, 5 years after publication, for their continued applicability. In accordance with this agreement, the International Standards Organisation (ISO) contacted more than 1,000 users and organisations for their views on ISO 9000:1994 using a questionnaire covering:

- problems with the existing standards;
- requirements for new/revised standards;
- possible harmonisation and interoperability between quality management, environmental management and health and safety standards.

1.1 The revision process

The revision process was the responsibility of ISO Technical Committee (TC) 176 and was conducted on the basis of consensus among quality and industry experts nominated by ISO member bodies, and representing all interested parties. Initial specifications and goals were established following extensive user surveys and these were followed by a user verification and validation process to ensure that the standards that had been produced would actually meet the requirements of the user.

 Note: Once Draft International Standards have been adopted by the technical committees they are then circulated to member bodies for voting. Publication as an International Standard then requires a two-thirds majority of the votes.

The aims of the revision were (in the words of the International Standards Organisation (ISO)) to:

- *give users the opportunity to add value to their activities;*
- *continually improve their performance by focussing on the major processes within the organisation;*
- *guarantee the effectiveness (but not necessarily the efficiency) of the organisation;*
- *make sure the standards are applicable to all types of organisations;*
- *make the language used in the revised standards simpler, more userfriendly, and with less manufacturing bias;*
- *make the new standards equally appropriate to all sectors, including service providers;*
- *produce standards that will minimise any potential costs during a smooth transition.*

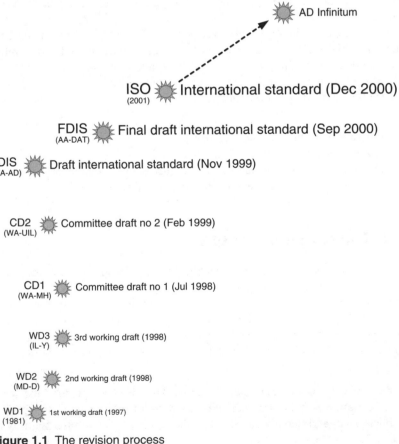

AD Infinitum

ISO International standard (Dec 2000)
(2001)

FDIS Final draft international standard (Sep 2000)
(AA-DAT)

DIS Draft international standard (Nov 1999)
(FA-AD)

CD2 Committee draft no 2 (Feb 1999)
(WA-UIL)

CD1 Committee draft no 1 (Jul 1998)
(WA-MH)

WD3 3rd working draft (1998)
(IL-Y)

WD2 2nd working draft (1998)
(MD-D)

WD1 1st working draft (1997)
(1981)

Figure 1.1 The revision process

1.2 The main changes

In providing the ISO 9000:2000 standards, TC176 took into account previous experience with quality management system standards such as the original BS 5750 series, the 1987 and 1994 editions of ISO 9000, as well as emerging generic management systems. This resulted in a closer alignment of quality management systems with environmental and safety standards and a more accurate method of reflecting the way organisations run their business activities.

Virtually all of the requirements from the previous 1994 standard have been included in the revised ISO 9001:2000 standard (but with clearer definition) and the addition of a lot of 'shalls' (totalling 141 in all!) as opposed to 'coulds' and 'shoulds'. The main changes have been that the new standard:

- is centred around a process-orientated structure with a more logical sequence of contents;
- includes a requirement for the organisation to monitor information on customer satisfaction as a measure of system performance;

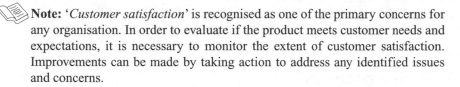**Note:** '*Customer satisfaction*' is recognised as one of the primary concerns for any organisation. In order to evaluate if the product meets customer needs and expectations, it is necessary to monitor the extent of customer satisfaction. Improvements can be made by taking action to address any identified issues and concerns.

- gives considerable emphasis on higher management issues (such as the need for defined (and auditable) quality targets and the need to include supporting activities within the system);
- includes a continual improvement process as an important step to enhance the quality management system;

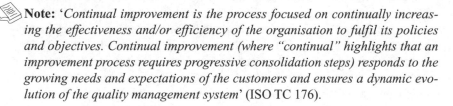**Note:** '*Continual improvement is the process focused on continually increasing the effectiveness and/or efficiency of the organisation to fulfil its policies and objectives. Continual improvement (where "continual" highlights that an improvement process requires progressive consolidation steps) responds to the growing needs and expectations of the customers and ensures a dynamic evolution of the quality management system*' (ISO TC 176).

- provides (in ISO 9004:2000) an additional concept of organisational self-assessment as a driver for improvement (further emphasising the need to monitor customer satisfaction);
- establishes measurable objectives at relevant functions and levels (monitoring of information of customer satisfaction as a measure of system performance);
- lays increased emphasis on the role of top management, including a commitment to the development and improvement of the quality management

system, consideration of legal and regulatory requirements, and establishment of measurable objectives at relevant functions and levels (see also 1.3.4);
- extends measurements to include system, processes, and product;
- increases attention to resource availability;
- emphasises the need to determine training effectiveness;
- considers the benefits and needs of all interested parties;
- assures consistency between quality management system requirements and guidelines;
- promotes the use of generic quality management principles by organisations (and enhancement of their compatibility with environmental and safety standards such as ISO 14001:1996, BS 8800:2000 and OHSAS etc.);
- significantly reduces the amount of documentation required;
- includes terminology changes and improvements that allow easier interpretation;
- provides increased compatibility with the environmental management system standard;
- makes specific reference to quality management principles;
- meets the need for more user-friendly documents;
- provides measures for the analysis of collected data concerning the performance of an organisation's quality management system.

1.3 Key changes

The 1994 ISO 9000 family of quality standards contained well over 27 standards and documents and this caused quite a lot of concern (not to mention confusion!) over the years. Thankfully the year 2000 quality management system standards now only consist of three primary standards, i.e. ISO 9000, ISO 9001 and ISO 9004 supported by a number of technical reports.

To the maximum extent possible, the key points in the other 1994 standards and documents (and sector-specific needs) have been integrated into the three primary standards. Over the next few years, all the other standards and documents from the ISO 9000 family will either be withdrawn, transferred to other Technical Committees, or replaced by technical reports, technical specifications or brochures (with the exception of ISO 10012 'Quality Assurance for Measuring Equipment', which will remain as an international standard).

1.3.1 Requirements

The main difference between ISO 9001:2000 and the previous version of the standard is that the 20 elements contained in section four of ISO 9001:1994 have now been replaced by four sections covering the management of resources, the quality of the product, the maintenance of quality records and the requirement for continual improvement.

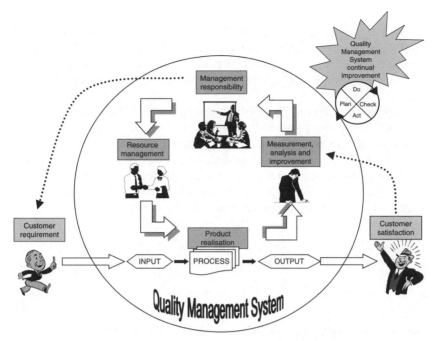

Figure 1.2 ISO 9001:2000 Quality Management System (QMS)

1.3.2 Revised title

Each of the three main standards (i.e. ISO 9000:2000, ISO 9001:2000 and ISO 9004:2000) now have a revised title, which no longer includes the term '*quality assurance*'. This has been done in order to reflect the fact that the QMS requirements specified in these standards address the quality assurance of a product as well as customer satisfaction.

1.3.3 Consistent pair of standards

ISO 9001:2000 and ISO 9004:2000 have been developed as a '*consistent pair*' of QMS standards, based on eight quality management principles (that reflect best management practices) with a common process-orientated structure and harmonised terminology. They are designed to be used together, or may be used as stand-alone documents.

The idea of a 'consistent pair' of standards is the very core of the revision process. The aligned structure of ISO 9001:2000 and ISO 9004:2000 is aimed at encouraging organisations not only to look at their activities from a process standpoint, but also to look beyond certification to a system which will be truly beneficial in improving operational performance.

Whilst ISO 9001:2000 specifies the requirements for a QMS (that can be used by organisations for certification or contractual purposes), ISO 9004:2000 provides guidance aimed at improving an organisation's overall quality performance. ISO 9004:2000 is not, however, meant as a 'guideline for implementing ISO 9001:2000' nor is it intended for certification or contractual use.

One specific change to ISO 9001:2000 and ISO 9004:2000 that was brought about late in the day concerned the usage of the term 'product'. During the Committee Draft stages, it became apparent that there was a need to have a single word that described an organisation's output as well as the service that it provided. Consequently in the new standards, 'product' has been defined as '*a system of activities, which uses resources to transform inputs into outputs*' and there are four agreed generic product categories, namely:

- hardware;
- software;
- services;
- processed materials.

 Note: Further details of the guidance provided for Transition Planning Guidance are available on BSI's website at http://www.bsi.org.uk/iso-tc176-sc2.

1.3.4 Top management

Top management is a new term in ISO 9001:2000 and is defined as '*a person or group of people who direct and control an organisation at the highest level*'.

In essence the standard is now no longer dealing with a Quality Management System but more with a system for management that can be used by the whole organisation. However, no organisation can function effectively without direction from top management, and in order for them to direct effectively, they will need to have at their disposal a wide range of information. The main pieces of information that they will need to have readily available is the needs and expectations of their customers, and knowledge of all the regulatory and legal requirements that are applicable to the organisation. This will enable top management to know what they need to do within the organisation to achieve customer satisfaction.

Management then needs to be able to show the workforce what the purpose of the organisation is, the perceived values of the organisation and their attitude and actions towards the customers. Through the mission and policy statements, management should try to produce unity within the organisation by enabling the staff to see clearly what the organisation is striving to achieve.

In the past, an organisation's Quality Policy was seen more as a piece of paper signed by a senior member of staff rather than an objective. With

ISO 9001:2000, the policy now needs to show a commitment to improvement, which will be measured throughout the organisation to make sure that the policy provides a framework for the setting of the objectives and is communicated and understood throughout the organisation.

Once the policies have been set, policy objectives will need to be established. These should be applicable to the various activities within the organisation and take into account the various functions of the organisation and how these fit into the strategic framework.

Top management should ensure that all staff know what the organisation's objectives are and know (and appreciate) the relevance and importance of how the staff can affect the overall objectives of the organisation. Through having a caring and open culture, the morale and motivation of the workforce will be improved and as a consequence, products and services supplied will improve as will customer satisfaction. They will also need to take into consideration the interested parties of the organisation (see also 1.5).

1.3.5 The process model

The whole concept of ISO 9001:2000 now revolves round a systematic process approach which uses eight quality management principles reflecting best practice which are designed to enable a continual improvement of the business, its overall efficiency and be capable of responding to customer needs and expectations.

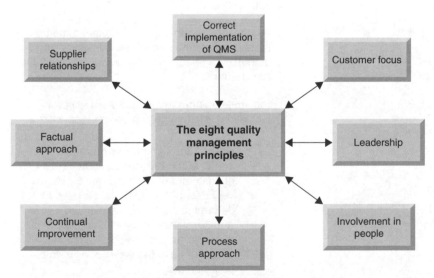

Figure 1.3 The eight quality management principles

The eight principles contained in ISO 9001:2000 are of primary concern to an organisation, as they will affect an organisation's overall approach to quality. They are:

1. Customer focused organisation

Organisations depend on their customers and therefore should understand current and future customer needs. They should meet customer requirements and should strive to exceed customer expectations. Customer communication is the method used to enable customers to interact with the organisation.

The table below identifies the clauses within the ISO 9001/9000/9004 standards that relate to customer satisfaction and customer communication.

Requirements and recommendations

ISO 9001	ISO 9000	ISO 9004	
5.1			requires top management to communicate the importance of meeting customer as well as statutory and regulatory requirements
5.2			requires top management to ensure that customer requirements are determined and are met with the aim of enhancing customer satisfaction
5.5.2			requires the organisation to appoint a member of management who has the responsibility and authority for ensuring the promotion of customer requirements
5.6.2			requires the input to management review to include information on customer feedback
			Note: Although there is no requirement in ISO 9001:2000 for customer surveys or customer questionnaires, these are very useful tools that can be used to determine customer satisfaction levels. A full explanation about customer surveys and customer satisfaction is contained in the sister book to this publication.

ISO 9001	ISO 9000	ISO 9004

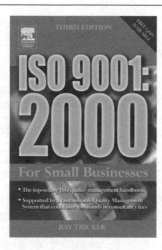

ISO 9001:2000 for Small Businesses, third edn

6.1		requires the organisation to determine and provide the resources needed to enhance customer satisfaction
7.2.3		requires the organisation to determine and implement effective arrangements for communication with the customer in relation to product information, enquiries, contracts or order handling (including amendments), and customer feedback (including customer complaints)
7.5.4		requires the organisation to: • exercise care with customer property while it is under the organisation's control or being used by the organisation • identify, verify and safeguard customer property that has been provided for use with (or incorporation into) the product • report to the customer if any property is lost, damaged or otherwise found to be unsuitable for use
8.2.1		requires the organisation to monitor information relating to customer satisfaction as one of the measurements of the performance of the QMS

(*continued*)

ISO 9001	ISO 9000	ISO 9004	
8.4			requires the analysis of data to provide information relating to customer satisfaction
8.5.2			requires a documented procedure to be established to define requirements for reviewing non-conformities (including customer complaints)
	3.1.4		advises that customer complaints are a common indicator of low customer satisfaction but their absence does not necessarily imply high customer satisfaction
		7.2	recommends that management should ensure that the organisation has defined mutually acceptable processes for communicating effectively and efficiently with its customers and other interested parties
		8.2.1.2	suggests that sources of information on customer satisfaction include customer complaints
		8.5.2	suggests that sources of information for corrective action consideration include customer complaints

 Note: See also ISO 9001:2000 clauses 7.3 and 8.3 which have additional links to 'customer focus'.

2. Leadership

Leaders establish unity of purpose, direction, and the internal environment of their organisation. They create the environment in which people can become fully involved in achieving the organisation's objectives.

An organisation should ensure that its leaders:

- build trust and eliminate fear;
- consider the needs of all interested parties;
- establish a clear vision of the organisation's future;
- establish shared values and ethical role models at all levels of the organisation;

- lead by example;
- promote open and honest communication;
- provide people with the required resources and freedom to act with responsibility and accountability;
- set challenging goals and targets;
- set up a strategy to achieve these goals and targets;
- understand and respond to changes in the external environment.

Requirements and recommendations

The table below identifies clauses within the ISO 9000 standards that relate to leadership.

ISO 9001	ISO 9000	ISO 9004	
5.5.2			requires top management to appoint a member of management who, irrespective of other responsibilities has responsibility for the overall effectiveness of the QMS

Note: See also ISO 9001:2000 clauses 5.1, 5.2, 5.3, 5.4, 5.6, 6.1, 6.2, 6.3 and 6.4 which have additional links to 'leadership'.

3. Involvement of people

People at all levels are the essence of an organisation and their full involvement enables their abilities to be used for the organisation's benefit.

An organisation should ensure that its leaders:

- accept ownership and responsibility to solve problems;
- actively seek opportunities to enhance their own competence, knowledge and experience;
- actively seek opportunities to make improvements;
- are enthusiastic and proud to be part of the organisation;
- are firmly focused on the creation of value for customers;
- are innovative and creative in furthering the organisation's objectives;
- derive satisfaction from their work;
- freely share their knowledge and experience with other members of the organisation;
- represent the organisation to customers, local communities and society in general.

Requirements and recommendations

The table below identifies clauses within the ISO 9000 standards that relate to the involvement of people.

ISO 9001	ISO 9000	ISO 9004	
5.5.1			requires top management to ensure that responsibilities and authorities are defined and communicated within the organisation
5.5.3			requires top management to ensure that appropriate communication processes are established within the organisation and that communication takes place regarding the effectiveness of the QMS

 Note: See also ISO 9001:2000 clauses 5.1, 5.3, 6.2 and 7.3 which have additional links to 'involvement with people'.

4. Process approach

A desired result is achieved more efficiently when related resources and activities are managed as a process.

An organisation should ensure that its leaders:

- are aware of the results the process is achieving;
- define the objectives of the organisation's processes;
- define a process that will achieve specific objectives;
- determine the stages in the process necessary to achieve the results;
- determine the activities required to accomplish each process stage;
- determine the competence required of the people performing these activities;
- determine the measurements required to verify process inputs and outputs;
- determine the measurements required to establish process efficiency and effectiveness;
- determine the information and resource requirements needed to achieve the process objectives;
- determine the sequence and interaction of activities within the process;
- evaluate possible risks, consequences and impacts of processes on customers, suppliers and other stakeholders of that process;

- establish clear responsibility, authority and accountability for managing the process;
- identify the customers, suppliers and other stakeholders of the process;
- identify the inputs and outputs of the process;
- identify the interfaces between the processes within the organisation;
- measure process outputs, efficiency and effectiveness;
- take action to prevent use or delivery of non-conforming inputs or outputs until remedial action has been effected;
- take action to eliminate the cause of non-conforming inputs or outputs.

Requirements and recommendations

The table below identifies clauses within the ISO 9000 standards that relate to the process approach.

ISO 9001	ISO 9000	ISO 9004	
7.1			requires the organisation to plan and develop the processes needed for product realisation

 Note: See also ISO 9001:2000 clauses 4.1, 4.2, 5.6, 7.2, 7.3, 7.4, 7.5 and 8.2 which have additional links to 'process approach'.

5. System approach to management

Identifying, understanding and managing a system of inter-related processes for a given objective contributes to the effectiveness and efficiency of the organisation.

An organisation should ensure that its leaders:

- continually improve the system through measurement and evaluation;
- define the organisation as a system that is established to achieve organisational goals;
- define the system by identifying or developing the processes that affect a given objective;
- establish resource constraints prior to action so that system integrity is maintained when changes are made;
- structure the system to achieve the objective in the most efficient and effective way;
- understand the interdependencies among the processes of the system.

Requirements and recommendations

The table below identifies clauses within the ISO 9000 standards that relate to the system approach to management.

ISO 9001	ISO 9000	ISO 9004	
5.3			requires top management to ensure that the quality policy includes a commitment to improve the effectiveness of the QMS continually
5.4.2			requires top management to ensure that the integrity of the QMS is maintained when changes to the QMS are planned and implemented
5.5.3			requires top management to ensure that communication takes place regarding the effectiveness of the QMS
5.6.3			requires the output from the management review to include any decisions and actions related to improvement of the effectiveness of the QMS
8.1			requires the organisation to plan and implement the monitoring, measurement, analysis and improvement processes needed to improve the effectiveness of the QMS continually
8.5.1			requires the organisation to improve the effectiveness of the QMS continually

 Note: See also ISO 9001:2000 clause 4.1 which has additional links to 'system approach'.

6. Continual improvement

Continual improvement is a permanent objective of any organisation.

Requirements and recommendations

The table below identifies clauses within the ISO 9000 standards that relate to continual improvement.

ISO 9001	ISO 9000	ISO 9004	
4.1			requires the organisation to continually improve the effectiveness of its QMS
5.1			requires top management to provide evidence of its commitment to the development and implementation of the QMS and to continually improve its effectiveness
5.3			requires top management to ensure that the quality policy includes a commitment to continually improve the effectiveness of the QMS
6.1			requires the organisation to determine and provide the resources needed to continually improve the effectiveness of the QMS
8.1			requires the organisation to plan and implement the monitoring, measurement, analysis and improvement processes needed to continually improve the effectiveness of the QMS
8.4			requires the organisation to evaluate where continual improvement of the QMS can be made
8.5.1			requires the organisation to continually improve the effectiveness of the QMS through the use of quality policy, quality objectives, audit results, analysis of data, corrective and preventive action and management review
		5.1.2	recommends that top management establish continual improvement as an objective for processes of the organisation and consider breakthrough changes to processes as a way to improve the organisation's performance
		6.6	recommends encouraging suppliers to implement programmes for continual improvement of performance and to participate in other joint improvement initiatives

(continued)

ISO 9001	ISO 9000	ISO 9004	
		8.5.1	recommends that improvements can range from small-step ongoing continual improvement to strategic breakthrough improvement projects

 Note: See also ISO 9001:2000 clauses 5.6 and 8.2 which have additional links to 'continual improvement'.

7. Factual approach to decision making

Effective decisions are based on the logical and intuitive analysis of data and information.

An organisation should ensure that its leaders:

- take measurements and collect data and information relevant to the objective;
- ensure that all data and information are sufficiently accurate, reliable and accessible;
- analyse the data and information using valid methods;
- understand the value of appropriate statistical techniques;
- make decisions and take action based on the results of logical analysis balance with experience and intuition.

Requirements and recommendations

The table below identifies clauses within the ISO 9000 standards that relate to the factual approach to management.

ISO 9001	ISO 9000	ISO 9004	
5.4.1			requires top management to ensure that quality objectives are established at relevant functions and levels within the organisation and that these objectives

ISO 9001	ISO 9000	ISO 9004	
			shall be measurable and consistent with the quality policy
5.6			requires top management to review the organisation's QMS at planned intervals to ensure its continued suitability, adequacy and effectiveness
7.3.1			requires the organisation to plan and control the design and development of a product
8.4			requires the organisation to determine, collect and analyse appropriate data to demonstrate the suitability and effectiveness of the QMS

 Note: See also ISO 9001:2000 clauses 4.1, 5.3, 6.2, 7.1, 7.2, 7.5, 7.6, 8.1, 8.2, 8.3 and 8.5 which have additional links to 'factual approach to decision making'.

8. Mutually beneficial supplier relationships

Mutually beneficial relationships between an organisation and its suppliers enhance the ability of both organisations to create value.

An organisation should ensure that its leaders:

- create clear and open communications with customers and suppliers;
- establish supplier relationships that balance short-term gains with long-term considerations for the organisation and society in general;
- identify and select key suppliers;
- initiate joint development and improvement of products and processes;
- jointly establish a clear understanding of customers' needs;
- recognise supplier improvements and achievements;
- share information and future plans.

 Note: See ISO 9001:2000 clause 7.4 which has additional links to 'mutually beneficial supplier relationships'.

The eight principles of ISO 9001:2000 detailed above, correlate to the following clauses in the standard:

	Customer focus	Leadership	Involvement of people	Process approach	System approach	Continual improvement	Factual approach to decision making	Mutually beneficial supplier relationship
4.1	X			(x)	(x)	X	(x)	
4.2	X			(x)				
5.1		(x)	(x)					
5.2		(x)				X		
5.3		(x)	(x)		X	X		
5.4		(x)			X		(x)	
5.5	X	X	X		X	X	X	
5.6	X	(x)		(x)	X		X	
6.1	X	(x)				(x)	X	
6.2		(x)	(x)			X	(x)	
6.3		(x)						
6.4		(x)						
7.1				X				
7.2	X			(x)			(x)	
7.3	(x)		(x)	(x)			(x)	
7.4				(x)			X	(x)
7.5	X			(x)			(x)	
7.6							(x)	
8.1	X				X	X	(x)	
8.2	(x)			(x)		(x)	(x)	
8.3	(x)						(x)	
8.4	X				X	X	X	
8.5	X					X	(x)	

X = Strong link; (x) = Tenuous link

1.4 Benefits of the revised standards

There are many, quite major benefits because of the revised quality management systems standard structure, such as:

- its applicability to all product categories (in all sectors and to all sizes of organisations);
- being simpler to use, clearer in language, readily translatable and more easily understandable;
- having a significant reduction in the amount of required documentation;
- providing a link between quality management systems and organisational processes;
- providing a natural move towards improved organisational performance;
- covering the requirement for continual improvement and customer satisfaction;
- its increased compatibility with other management systems (for example, ISO 14000);
- providing a consistent basis to address the needs and interests of organisations in specific sectors (e.g. medical devices, telecommunications, automotive, etc.);
- the concept of the consistent pair (ISO 9001 covering the requirements and ISO 9004 for going beyond the requirements in order to further improve the performance of the organisation);
- considering the needs of and benefits to all interested parties.

1.5 Other benefits

As shown below, the benefits of an organisation implementing an ISO 9001:2000 culture are far-reaching.

1.5.1 Customers

Customers and users will benefit by receiving products that:

- conform to the requirements;
- are dependable and reliable;
- are available when needed;
- are maintainable.

1.5.2 People in the organisation

People in the organisation will benefit by:

- better working conditions;
- increased job satisfaction;

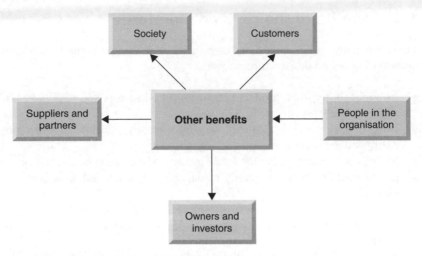

Figure 1.4 Other benefits of ISO 9001:2000

- improved health and safety;
- improved morale;
- improved stability of employment.

1.5.3 Owners and investors

Owners and investors will benefit by:

- increased return on investment;
- improved operational results;
- increased market share;
- increased profits.

1.5.4 Suppliers and partners

Suppliers and partners will benefit by:

- stability;
- growth;
- partnership and mutual understanding.

1.5.5 Society

Society will benefit by:

- fulfilment of legal and regulatory requirements;
- improved health and safety;
- reduced environmental impact;
- increased security.

1.6 Permissible exclusions

In order to make ISO 9001:2000 more applicable to different types of products and different types of organisations, the text of ISO 9001:2000 has been made far more generic than the previous 1994 version. Naturally, due to its generic nature, some industrial or commercial sectors might well identify additional requirements to those found in ISO 9001:2000 to satisfy their specific needs. Equally, some of ISO 9001:2000's requirements may not directly apply to a particular organisation and in this respect ISO allows for the **exclusion** of some requirements.

 Note: In the context of ISO 9001:2000, 'exclusions' are the requirements that are deemed to be outside the scope of an organisation's declared QMS.

ISO 9001:2000 requirements and recommendations

Clause 1.2 of ISO 9001:2000 states that:

(a) *All the requirements of the International Standard are generic and are intended to be applicable to all organisations, regardless of type, size and product supplied.*

(b) *Where any requirement(s) of this International Standard cannot be applied due to the nature of the organisation and its product, this can be considered for exclusion.*

(c) *Where exclusions are made, claims for conformity to this International Standard are not acceptable unless these exclusions are limited to requirements within clause 7, and such exclusions do not affect the organisation's ability, or responsibility, to provide products that meet customer and applicable regulatory requirements.*

Exclusions (usually referred to as 'permissible exclusions') are, therefore, limited specifically to Section 7 ('Product Realisation') and the ISO 9001:2000 requirements can **only** be left out if it can be shown that they do not have an effect on the organisation's capability of providing a product (or service) that will not only meet the customer's specific requirements but also satisfy the relevant statutory and/or regulatory requirements.

1.7 Cost

'An effective QMS should be designed to satisfy the purchaser's conditions, requirements and expectations whilst serving to protect the organisation's best interests' (ISO 9004:2000).

In practice, Quality Management Systems can be very expensive to install and operate, particularly if inadequate quality assurance and quality control methods were previously used. If the purchaser requires consistent quality he

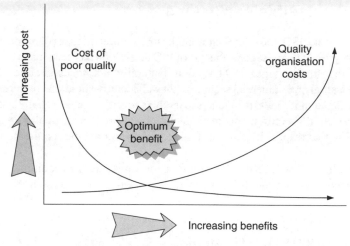

Figure 1.5 Quality Management System costs

must pay for it, regardless of the specification or order which the organisation has accepted. However, against this expenditure must always be offset by savings in rework, scrapped material and general problems arising from lack of quality.

From an organisation's point of view there is a business requirement to obtain and maintain the desired quality at an optimum cost. The following represent some of the additional expenses that can be incurred:

- implementation and maintenance of an organised document control system throughout the organisation;
- training for the quality assurance team;
- salaries for the quality assurance team, planners, quality supervisors, calibration/test equipment staff and Quality Managers;
- visits by the quality assurance staff to other organisations, subcontractors and the eventual consumer, for evaluation and audit of their facilities and products;
- test equipment of a recognised type, standard and quality; regularly maintained and calibrated by an accredited calibration centre;
- better storage facilities.

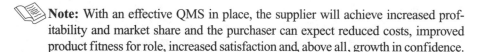**Note:** With an effective QMS in place, the supplier will achieve increased profitability and market share and the purchaser can expect reduced costs, improved product fitness for role, increased satisfaction and, above all, growth in confidence.

The cost of implementing any necessary changes in order to meet the requirements of ISO 9001:2000 will obviously vary from one organisation to another, depending on various factors such as the actual state of implementation of the Quality Management System, the size and complexity of the organisation, the attitude and commitment of the top management, etc. It is expected that the benefits to all organisations, however, will far outweigh eventual costs associated with the transition and any additional costs should be considered as a 'value-added investment'.

1.8 The ISO 9000:2000 family of standards

The ISO 9000:2000 family of standards consists of three primary standards supported by a number of technical reports. These are:

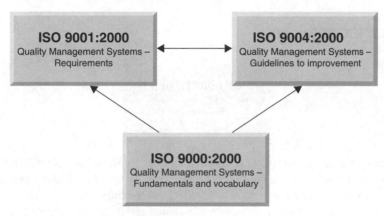

Figure 1.6 The ISO 9000:2000 family

1.8.1 ISO 9000:2000

Quality Management Systems – Fundamentals and vocabulary *(superseding ISO 8402:1995 'Quality Management and Quality Assurance – Vocabulary' and ISO 9000–1:1994 'Quality Management and Quality Assurance Standards – Guidelines for selection and use').*

ISO 9000:2000 includes a description of the basic approach to quality management as well as a revised vocabulary to reflect the usage of new and revised terms and associated definitions contained in ISO 9001:2000 and ISO 9004:2000.

The development of ISO 9000:2000 was completed in parallel with ISO 9001:2000 and ISO 9004:2000, the current (and future) environmental and safety standards plus all other existing and planned management standards – so as to (hopefully) ensure a harmonised approach to standardisation.

ISO 9000:2000 also includes a revision of the ISO 8402:1995 'Quality Management and Quality Assurance – Vocabulary' standard, provides a more formal approach to the definition of terms, specifies terminology for QMSs and will assist:

- those concerned with enhancing the mutual understanding of the terminology used in quality management (e.g. suppliers, customers, regulators);
- internal or external auditors, regulators, certification and/or registration bodies;
- developers of related standards.

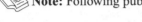 **Note:** Following publication of ISO 9000:2000, ISO 8402, was withdrawn.

1.8.2 ISO 9001:2000

ISO 9001:2000
Quality Management Systems –
Requirements

Quality Management Systems – Requirements *(superseding ISO 9001:1994 'Quality Systems – Model for quality assurance in design, development, production, installation and servicing', ISO 9002:1994 'Quality Systems – Model for quality assurance in production, installation and servicing' and ISO 9003:1994 'Quality Systems – Model for quality assurance in final inspection and test').*

The previous ISO 9001:1994, ISO 9002:1994 and ISO 9003:1994 standards have now been consolidated into a single revised ISO 9001:2000 standard. Organisations that previously used ISO 9002:1994 and ISO 9003:1994 are allowed to be certified to ISO 9001:2000 through a '*reduction in scope*' of the standard's requirements by omitting requirements that do not apply to their particular organisation.

ISO 9001:2000 is focused towards '*providing confidence, as a result of demonstration, in product conformance to established requirements*' and includes a section entitled '*permissible exclusions*'. This section allows organisations to formally '*exclude*' certain non-applicable requirements of the standard, yet still claim conformance to it. However, only those organisations that can **prove** that the nature of their products, customers and/or the applicable regulatory and statutory requirements do not need to meet the full requirements of ISO 9001:2000, are allowed these exclusions. For example, organisations whose products require no design activities (and who would have previously sought ISO 9002:1994 certification) can now claim to be in compliance with ISO 9001:2000 by excluding the requirements for design and development.

With the publication of ISO 9001:2000, there is now, therefore, a single quality management '**requirements**' standard that is applicable to all organisations, products and services. It is the only standard that can be used for the certification of a QMS and its generic requirements can be used by **any** organisation to:

- address customer satisfaction;
- meet customer and applicable regulatory and statutory requirements;
- enable internal and external parties (including certification bodies) to assess the organisation's ability to meet these customer and regulatory requirements.

For certification purposes, organisations will now have to possess a documented management system that takes the inputs and transforms them into targeted outputs. Something that effectively:

- says what they are going to do;
- does what they have said they are going to do;
- keeps records of everything that they do – especially when things go wrong.

The basic process to achieve these targeted outputs will encompass:

- the client's requirements;
- the inputs from management and staff;
- documented controls for any activities that are needed to produce the finished article;
- and, of course, delivering a product or service, which satisfies the customer's original requirements.

The implementation of a QMS has to be a strategic decision for any organisation and the design and implementation of their QMS will be influenced by its varying needs, objectives, products provided, processes employed and the size and structure of that organisation. As ISO are quick to point out, however, it is **not** the intention of ISO 9001:2000 to insist on a uniform structure for QMSs, or uniformity of documentation! Consequently, the QMS requirements specified in this standard should always be viewed as complementary to product technical requirements.

1.8.2.1 ISO 9001:2000's generic processes

The ISO 9001:2000 standard is the **only** standard within the 2000 edition to which an organisation can be certified. It includes all the key points from the previous 20 elements of ISO 9001:1994, but integrates them into four major generic business processes, namely:

1. Management responsibility

Policy, objectives, planning, system review including:

- management commitment;
- customer focus;
- quality policy;
- quality objectives;

- quality management system planning;
- responsibility, authority and communication;
- management representative;
- internal communication;
- management review;
- review input;
- review output.

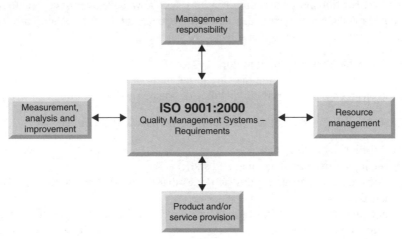

Figure 1.7 The four major generic business processes of ISO 9001:2000

Requirements and recommendations

The table below identifies clauses within the ISO 9000 standards that relate to management responsibility.

ISO 9001	ISO 9000	ISO 9004	
5.1			requires top management to provide evidence of its commitment to the development and implementation of the quality management system and continually improving its effectiveness
5.3			requires top management to ensure that the quality policy includes a commitment to comply with requirements and continually improve the effectiveness of the quality management system
7.2.2			requires the organisation to conduct a review of requirements related to the product prior to the organisation's commitment to supply a product to the customer

2. Resource management

Human resources, information, facilities including:

- provision of resources;
- human resources;
- competence, awareness and training;
- infrastructure;
- work environment.

Requirements and recommendations

The table below identifies clauses within the ISO 9000 standards that relate to resource management.

ISO 9001	ISO 9000	ISO 9004	
4.1			requires the organisation to ensure the availability of resources
5.1			requires top management to provide evidence of its commitment to the development and implementation of the quality management system and continually improve its effectiveness by ensuring the availability of resources
5.6.3			requires the output from the management review to include any decisions and actions related to resource needs
6.1			requires the organisation to determine and provide the resources needed to implement and maintain the quality management system, continually improve its effectiveness, and to enhance customer satisfaction by meeting customer requirements
7.1			requires the organisation to determine the need to provide resources specific to the product

3. Product realisation

Customer, design, purchasing, production, calibration including:

- planning of product realisation;
- customer-related processes;
- determination of requirements related to the product;
- review of requirements related to the product;

- customer communication;
- design and development planning (inputs, outputs, review, verification and validation);
- control of design and development changes;
- purchasing;
- purchasing process;
- purchasing information;
- verification of purchased product;
- production and service provision;
- control of production and service provision;
- validation of processes for production and service provision;
- identification and traceability;
- customer property;
- preservation of product;
- control of monitoring and measuring devices.

Requirements and recommendations

The table below identifies clauses within the ISO 9000 standards that relate to product realisation.

ISO 9001	ISO 9000	ISO 9004	
7.1			requires the organisation to plan and develop the processes needed for product realisation, and planning of product realisation to be consistent with the requirements of the other processes of the quality management system
8.2.4			requires the organisation to monitor and measure the characteristics of the product at appropriate stages of the product realisation

4. Measurement, analysis and improvement

Audit, process/product control, improvement including:

- monitoring and measurement;
- customer satisfaction;
- internal audit;
- monitoring and measurement of processes;
- monitoring and measurement of product;
- control of non-conforming product;
- analysis of data;
- improvement;
- continual improvement;

- corrective action;
- preventive action.

Requirements and recommendations

The table below identifies clauses within the ISO 9000 standards that relate to measurement, analysis and improvement.

ISO 9001	ISO 9000	ISO 9004	
4.1			requires the organisation to ensure the availability of resources and information necessary to support the operation and monitoring of the quality management system processes
4.1			requires the organisation to monitor, measure and analyse the quality management system processes
7.1			requires the organisation to determine the required verification, validation, monitoring, inspection and test activities specific to the product
7.5.1			requires controlled conditions to include the availability and use of monitoring and measuring devices, and the implementation of monitoring and measurement
7.5.3			requires the organisation to identify the product status with respect to monitoring and measurement requirements
7.6			requires the organisation to determine the monitoring and measurement to be undertaken to provide evidence of conformity of product to determined requirements
7.6			requires the organisation to establish processes to ensure that monitoring and measurement can be carried out and are carried out in a manner that is consistent with the monitoring and measurement requirements
8.1			requires the organisation to plan and implement the monitoring, measurement, analysis and improvement processes needed
8.1			requires the organisation to monitor information relating to customer perception as to whether the organisation has fulfilled customer requirements

(continued)

ISO 9001	ISO 9000	ISO 9004	
8.2.3			requires the organisation to apply suitable methods for monitoring of the quality management system processes
8.2.3			requires the organisation to monitor and measure the characteristics of the product to verify that product requirements are fulfilled
8.4			requires the organisation to determine, collect and analyse appropriate data, including data generated as a result of monitoring and measurement

1.8.2.2 Brief summary of ISO 9001:2000 requirements

ISO 9001:2000 consists of eight sections which are summarised below.

 Note: For a more complete description please see *ISO 9001:2000 for Small Businesses* by Ray Tricker from Butterworth-Heinemann's *ISO 9000:2000* series, http://books.elsevier.com.

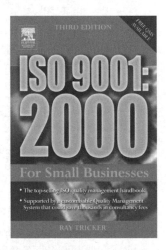

Figure 1.8 *ISO 9001:2000 for Small Businesses*

1.8.2.3 Section 1 – Scope

This is a short section explaining what the standard covers.

1.8.2.4 Section 2 – Normative reference

Another short section which contains details of other standards that form a **mandatory** input to ISO 9001:2000. In this instance the only reference is ISO 9000:2000 'Quality Management Systems – Fundamentals and vocabulary'.

1.8.2.5 Section 3 – Terms and definitions

The third section explains how the standard is based on a supply chain concept as shown in Figure 1.9.

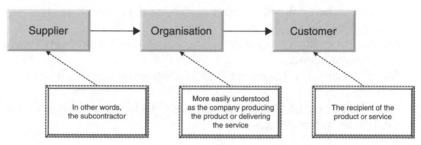

Figure 1.9 The supply chain

1.8.2.6 Section 4 – Quality Management System

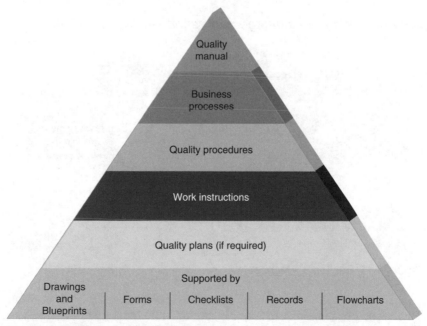

Figure 1.10 Documentation hierarchy

This basically states that an organisation **shall** have a documented QMS that defines the processes necessary to ensure that the product conforms to customer requirements. This QMS must be implemented, maintained and, most importantly, continually improved by the organisation.

This section also clearly states the types of documentation required to comply with the standard, as follows:

- **Quality Manual** – the main policy document that establishes the organisation's QMS and how it meets the requirements of ISO 9001:2000;
- **Core Processes** – business processes that describe the activities required to implement the QMS and to meet the policy requirements made in the Quality Manual;
- **Quality Procedures** – a description of the method by which quality system activities are managed;
- **Work Instructions** – a description of how a specific task is carried out.

 Note: The extent of the QMS documentation (which may be in any form or medium) is dependent on the:

- size and type of the organisation;
- complexity and interaction of the processes;
- competency of personnel.

1.8.2.7 Section 5 – Management responsibility

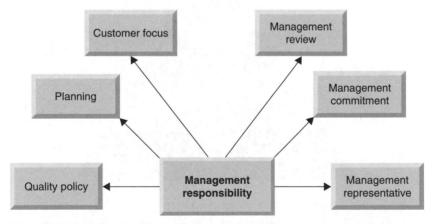

Figure 1.11 Section 5 – Management responsibility

This section contains the majority of the old ISO 9001:1994 management responsibility and quality requirements all rolled together. It is broken down into the following subclauses that cover the requirements for:

- **Management commitment** – top (i.e. senior) management committing, fully, to the development and improvement of the QMS (without their commitment the system will fall at the first hurdle);
- **Customer focus** – determining, fully understanding and documenting customer requirements; ensuring compliance with identified statutory legislation (e.g. EC Directives, other national and international standards, etc.);
- **Quality policy** – ensuring that it is appropriate for the purpose, understood by everyone and reviewed for continued suitability;
- **Planning** – clearly stating management's quality objectives and policy on quality in an established, fully documented, QMS;
- **Management representative** – appointing someone (or some people) to be responsible for the implementation and improvement of the organisation's QMS;
- **Management review** – carrying out regular reviews of the QMS to ensure it continues to function correctly (and to identify areas for improvement).

1.8.2.8 Section 6 – Resource management

This section covers resources with regard to training, induction, responsibilities, working environment, equipment requirements, maintenance, etc. It is broken down into the following subsections that cover the requirements for:

- **Provision of resources** – identifying the resources required to implement and improve the processes that make up the QMS;
- **Human resources** – assigning personnel with regard to competency, education, training, skill and/or experience;
- **Infrastructure** – identifying, providing and maintaining the required facilities (e.g. workspace), equipment (hardware and software) and supporting services to achieve conformity of product;
- **Work environment** – identifying and managing the work environment (e.g. health and safety, ambient conditions, etc.).

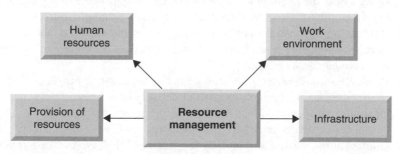

Figure 1.12 Section 6 – Resource management

1.8.2.9 Section 7 – Product realisation

This section absorbs most of the 20 elements of the old ISO 9000:1994 standard, including process control, purchasing, handling and storage, and measuring devices. This section is broken down into a number of subsections that cover the requirements for:

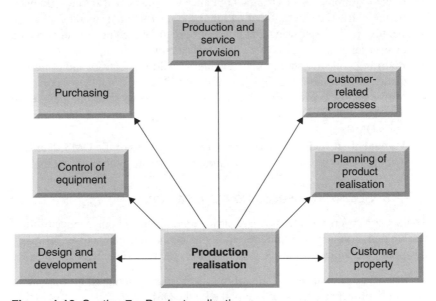

Figure 1.13 Section 7 – Product realisation

- **Planning of realisation processes** – clearly defining and documenting the processes used to ensure reliable and consistent products (e.g. verification and validation activities, criteria for acceptability and quality records, etc.);
- **Customer-related processes** – identifying customer, product, legal and design requirements;
- **Design and development** – controlling the design process (e.g. design inputs, outputs, review, verification, validation and change control);
- **Purchasing** – having documented processes for the selection and control of suppliers and the control of purchases that affect the quality of the finished product or service;
- **Production and service provision** – having documented instructions that control the manufacture of a product or delivery of a service;
- **Customer property** – identifying, verifying, protecting and maintaining customer property provided for use or incorporation with the product;
- **Control of measuring and monitoring devices** – their control, calibration and protection.

1.8.2.10 Section 8 – Measurement, analysis and improvement

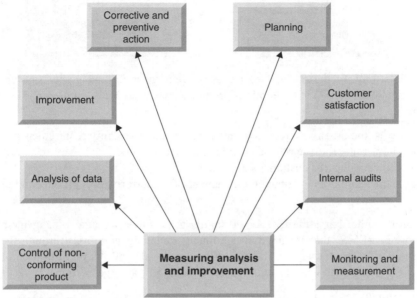

Figure 1.14 Section 8 – Measurement, analysis and improvement

This section absorbs the former inspection and measurement control sections of ISO 9001:1994. It includes requirements for:

- **Planning** – defining the requirements for measurement analysis and improvement (including statistical analysis);
- **Customer satisfaction** – monitoring customer satisfaction/dissatisfaction as a measurement and improvement of the QMS;
- **Internal audits** – conducting periodic internal audits to confirm continued conformity with ISO 9001:2000;
- **Measurement and monitoring of processes and product** – defining processes to monitor the performance of the QMS and the products and services delivered by the organisation;
- **Nonconformity** – controlling nonconformity and its rectification;
- **Data analysis** – collecting and analysing statistical data obtained from the organisation's measuring and monitoring activities to find areas of improvement;
- **Improvement** – planning for continual improvement of the QMS;
- **Corrective and preventive action** – having available procedures to address corrective and preventive action.

1.8.2.11 Relationship between ISO 9001:2000 and ISO 14001

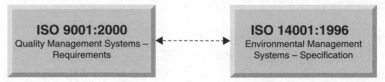

ISO 9001:2000	ISO 14001:1996
Quality Management Systems – Requirements	Environmental Management Systems – Specification

Whilst both of these standards are effectively 'generic management system standards', the ISO 9000 family is primarily concerned with 'quality management' and:

- what the organisation does to fulfil the customer's quality requirements;
- how it meets the applicable regulatory requirements;
- how it enhances customer satisfaction;
- how it achieves continual improvement of its performance, product and/or serve.

On the other hand, the ISO 14000 family is an Environmental Management System (EMS) that is aimed at continually reducing pollution (through the more efficient and responsible use of raw materials and the minimisation of energy usage and waste) and is concerned with how an organisation:

- minimises harmful effects on the environment caused by its activities;
- achieves continual improvement of its environmental performance.

Although ISO 14001 does not set performance requirements (such as emission limits), it does provide a mandatory, auditable, framework for an Environmental Management System. In quite a number of areas, these requirements are similar to those of ISO 9000 and other management systems (e.g. TL 9000, QS 9000, ISO 13485 and ISO/IEC 17025, etc.) and currently work is under way to produce an integrated management system involving quality, environmental as well as safety management.

The main difference between ISO 14001 and these other standards, however, is that organisations must have procedures to identify, examine and evaluate all the environmental aspects of its activities, products and services. Whilst the standard doesn't actually specify the depth of the evaluation or the methodology (the only requirement is that *the methodology should be appropriate*!) it does, however, suggest the use of Critical-Path Project Management (CPPD), Life Cycle Assessment (LCA) or other methodologies, such as mass-balance, assessment of environmental loads, etc.

As shown in Figure 1.15, there are a number of common elements linking ISO 9001:2000 with ISO 14001 and safety management systems such as BS 8800 and OHSAS 18001:1999.

 Note: Although BS 8800 has not yet obtained international (i.e. ISOP) status, it is generally accepted as defining the minimum requirements required to

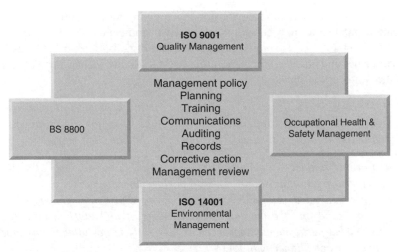

Figure 1.15 Relationship between management systems

control Occupational Health & Safety (OHS) risks, improve its performance and assist in complying with safety legislation.

1.8.3 ISO 9004:2000

Quality Management Systems – Guidelines for performance improvement *(superseding ISO 9004–1:1994 'Quality Management and Quality System Elements – Guidelines').*

ISO 9004:2000 provides guidance on QMSs, including the processes that are required for continual improvement and, ultimately, customer satisfaction. The guidance should be viewed as generic and with the overall aim of being applicable to all organisations, regardless of the type, size and the product provided.

The standard is focused towards providing '*benefits for all interested parties through sustained customer satisfaction*'. ISO 9004:2000 also includes the requirements of ISO 9001:2000 in text boxes inserted in appropriate places (which means perhaps that organisations only need to purchase ISO 9004:2000 and not both standards – how strange of ISO to miss this: funny old world!).

ISO 9004:2000 now includes an annex giving guidance on 'self-assessment' to enable an organisation to check the status of their QMS. This will prove very useful for organisations who are considering applying for ISO 9001:2000 certification, but are unsure what additional quality documentation will be required.

ISO 9004:2000 is also aimed at improving an organisation's overall quality performance and provides a stepping stone to Total Quality Management (TQM). In the words of the standard:

'ISO 9004:2000 is designed to go beyond quality management requirements and provide organisations with guidelines for performance improvement through sustained customer satisfaction. In doing so it:

- *provides guidance to management on the application and use of a QMS to improve an organisation's overall performance;*
- *is recommended as a guide for organisations whose management wishes to move beyond the minimum requirements of ISO 9001 in pursuit of increased performance improvement ISO 9004 is not intended as guidance for compliance with ISO 9001;*
- *defines the minimum QMS requirements needed to achieve customer satisfaction by meeting specified product requirements;*
- *can be also be used by an organisation to demonstrate its capability to meet customer requirements'.*

 Note: This international standard is **not** a guideline for implementing ISO 9001 and is **not** intended for certification, regulatory or contractual use.

For completeness, a new standard has been written to assist auditing systems against ISO 9001:2000; this is ISO 19011:2002 (see below).

 Note: All of the other standards and documents within the ISO 9000:1994 family that were submitted for formal review by ISO member bodies during the committee stages are gradually being withdrawn.

1.8.4 ISO 19011

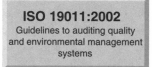

ISO 19011:2002
Guidelines to auditing quality
and environmental management
systems

Guidelines on auditing quality and environmental management systems
(superseding ISO 10011–1:1990 'Guidelines for Auditing Quality Systems – Auditing', ISO 10011–2:1991 'Guidelines for Auditing Quality Systems – Qualification criteria for quality system auditors', ISO 10011–3:1991 'Guidelines for Auditing Quality Systems – Management of audit programmes', as well as ISO 14010:1996 'Guidelines for Environmental Auditing – General principles', ISO 14011:1996 'Guidelines for Environmental Auditing – Audit

procedures – Auditing of environmental management systems' and ISO 14012:1996 'Guidelines for Environmental Auditing – Qualification criteria for environmental auditors').

The ISO 9000 and ISO 14000 series of standards highlight (and emphasise) the importance of using audits as a management tool for monitoring and verifying the effective implementation of an organisation's quality and/or environmental policy.

To assist in this activity, ISO 19011:2002 has been produced so that it provides guidance on the management of audit programmes, the conduct of internal or external audits of quality and/or environmental management systems, as well as the competence and evaluation of auditors. It is intended to apply to a broad range of potential users, including auditors, organisations implementing quality and/or environmental management systems, organisations needing to conduct audits of quality and/or environmental management systems for contractual reasons and organisations involved in auditor certification or training, in certification and/or registration of management systems.

The standard provides guidance on managing and conducting quality and environmental management system audits and is applicable to all organisations who need to complete internal or external audits against the requirements of ISO 9000 and ISO 14000 or to manage an audit programme.

1.8.5 What other standards are based on ISO 9001:2000?

During its lifetime, the 1994 version of ISO 9000 was frequently used as the generic template for other industry management system standards. The problem with using ISO 9001:1994, however, was that because it was a requirements-based quality management system (primarily designed for manufacturers) it was not entirely suitable for all industries. As a result, these other industries found that they had to leave out some of the requirements of this standard whilst, at the same time, include additional topics that were specific to their own particular industry.

By the end of the 1990s there were a growing number of these 'ISO 9000 equivalent standards' and standards for telecommunications (TL 9000), the automotive industry (QS 9000) and medical devices (ISOs 13485 and 13488:1966) were widely used. To simplify matters, it was agreed that part of ISO TC-176's work in upgrading the 1994 standard would, therefore, be to take these 'sons of 9000' into consideration and try to produce one standard that would cover virtually all industries – not just one for the manufacturers of a product.

Currently, although there are still a number of these other industry standards available, they are all gradually being rewritten around the requirements and recommendations of ISO 9001:2000 and the following is a selection of some of the most important ones.

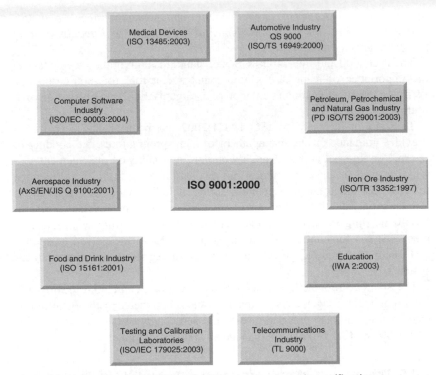

Figure 1.16 Associated ISO 9001:2000 standards and specifications

Telecommunications industry

TL 9000 (*Quality management standard for the telecommunication sector*) is a set of quality system requirements for the telecommunications industry which were originally developed by the QuEST Forum (Quality Excellence for Suppliers of Telecommunications Leadership) and was first published in November 1999. It has now been updated to conform to ISO 9001:2000.

The purpose of TL 9000 is to provide a quality management system for the design, development, production, delivery, installation and maintenance of telecommunication products and services, using ISO 9000 as the base with certain specific additions. It applies to all suppliers of telecommunications hardware, software and services and – as it is totally compatible with existing ISO 9000 protocols – registration to TL 9000 reduces the need to meet other telecommunication quality management standards.

The three registration options (or any combination of these three) being offered are:

TL 9000 – H (Hardware quality system requirements and metrics);
TL 9000 – S (Software quality system requirements and metrics);
TL 9000 – V (Services quality system requirements and metrics).

Further information about the QuEST Forum is available from their website (www.questforum.org) or from the American Society for Quality at www.asq.or.

Automotive industry

QS-9000 (*Quality System Requirements QS-9000*) is a common supplier quality standard for the Daimler Chrysler Corporation, Ford Motor Company and General Motors Corporation. It is based on the 1994 edition of ISO 9001, but contains additional requirements that are particular to the automotive industry.

QS-9000 applies to all suppliers of production materials, production and service parts, heat treating, painting and plating and other finishing services for the 'Big Three' and its requirements are divided into three sections, as follows:

- Section 1: Common requirements – the exact text of ISO 9001 with the addition of automotive/heavy trucking requirements;
- Section 2: Additional requirements – requirements beyond the scope of ISO 9001, common to all three manufacturers;
- Section 3: Customer specific sections – requirements unique to Ford, General Motors or Chrysler.

Being specific to the automotive industry, additional documentation is required for the QS 9000 programme and consists of:

- QS-9000 Quality System Requirements;
- Advanced Product Quality Planning and Control Plan (APQP);
- Failure Mode and Effects Analysis (FMEA);
- Measurement Systems Analysis;
- Fundamental SPC;
- Production Part Approval Process (PPAP) manual and the
- Quality System Assessment (QSA) manual.

When ISO 9001:2000 was released it was realised that this standard with its process-oriented approach more closely met the requirements of the automotive industry and so a working party was set up to amend QS 9000. This resulted in the publication of ISO/TS 16949:2002 (*Quality management systems – Particular requirements for the application of ISO 9001:2000 for automotive production and relevant service part organisations*) which, in conjunction with ISO 9001:2000, now defines the quality management system requirements for the design and development, production and, when relevant, installation and service of automotive-related products.

ISO/TS 16949:2002 was released in March 2002 and provides suppliers to vehicle manufacturers with a QMS that is recognised by all of the IATF (International Automotive Task Force). The Big Three (as part of IATF) have agreed to adopt ISO/TS 16949:2002 as the minimum qualifying standard for suppliers to vehicle manufacturers and as from 14 December 2006 the current

QS-9000 standard (which includes text from the old ISO 9000:1994) will cease to exist.

More information on ISO/TS 16949:2002 is available from the following websites:

- IATF Oversight Organization at www.iaob.org;
- Automotive Industry Action Group at www.aiag.org (which also contains information on qualified registrars);
- Chrysler Group suppliers hg3@daimierchrysier.com;
- Ford Motor suppliers rhopkins@ford.com;
- General Motors 103114.2516@compuserve.com.

Medical devices

ISO 13485:2003 (*Medical devices – Quality management systems – Requirements for regulatory purposes*) is intended for the medical device industry, regardless of the type and/or size of the organisation. The standard specifies the requirements for a quality management system and is aimed at ensuring that all medical devices manufactured and/or provided by an organisation continue to meet customer and regulatory requirements applicable to those medical devices.

As patient safety is involved, **all** of the requirements of ISO 13485:2003 are mandatory and so this standard differs from ISO 9001:2000 by including some additional requirements that are intended only for medical devices and, at the same time, excluding some ISO 9001:2000's requirements that are inappropriate. One major change is that rather than targeting customer satisfaction – as the new ISO 9001 does – ISO 13485 targets customer requirements. Because of these exclusions, an organisation that is registered to ISO 13485:2003 **cannot** also claim conformity to ISO 9001:2000 unless their QMS also covers the excluded ISO 9001:2000 requirements.

For further details about ISO 13485:2003 contact one of the following: the Medical Device Manufacturers' Association mdmainfo@medicaldevices.org, Medicines and Healthcare Products Regulatory Agency (MHRA) info@mhra.gsi.gov.uk or the Food and Drug Administration, www.fda.gov.

Testing and calibration laboratories

ISO/IEC 17025:2000 (*General requirements for the competence of testing and calibration laboratories*) was produced as a result of EN 45001 and ISO/IEC Guide 25 and contains requirements for all test and calibration laboratories wishing to demonstrate that they are technically competent and operate an acceptable quality system.

The standard is applicable to all laboratories (regardless of size) and laboratories meeting this standard are certified as being able to produce test and calibration results which are mutually acceptable between countries. The standard has two main requirement clauses, Clause 4 (which specifies the management requirements) and Clause 5 which specifies the technical requirements.

Clause 4 has been written around the 1994 version of ISO 9000 and emphasises the need for:

- a quality manual (containing quality policy statement, supporting procedures and a formalised document control system – so very much the same as ISO 9001:2000);
- procedures for the review of requests, tenders and contracts;
- purchase control (including subcontractor management);
- corrective and preventive action (including control of non-conforming product and cause analysis);
- control of records (particularly technical records);
- regular internal and management audits.

Clause 5 is specifically aimed at testing and calibration laboratories and covers additional items such as:

- competence of personnel performing the tests and calibrations;
- laboratory facilities (accommodation, infrastructure and environmental conditions);
- test and calibration methods (plus method evaluation);
- control of data (in particular computer software);
- control of equipment (records, maintenance plan, transportation, etc.);
- measurement traceability (calibration of test equipment, reference standards);
- sampling plan;
- reporting the results of testing and calibrations (test reports, calibration certificates and test reports).

This standard is currently being updated to comply with the basic management system requirements of ISO 9001:2000.

Petroleum, petrochemical and natural gas industries

PD ISO/TS 29001: 2003 (*Petroleum, petrochemical and natural gas industries – Sector specific quality management systems – Requirements for product and service supply organisations*) is another new technical specification that has recently been developed by ISO as a quality management system for these particular industries.

As with all QMSs, the aim is for continual improvement and this specification is no different except, in this particular case, continual improvement is focused on:

- defect prevention;
- reduction of variation and waste in the supply chain;
- reduction of variation and waste from service providers.

The requirements specified in PD ISO/TS 29001:2003 are supplementary to ISO 9001:2000 and have been developed separately to ensure that the requirements for the design, development, production, installation and service of products are clear and auditable. The standard also helps to guarantee a global consistency and improved assurance in the quality of goods and services supplied from providers – the failure of which could have severe ramifications for the companies and industries involved.

Further details concerning this technical specification are available from the Association for Petroleum and Explosives Administration (APEA) via admin@apea.org.uk.

Aerospace

AS/EN/JIS 9100 (*Quality Management Systems – Aerospace – Requirements*) is an international aerospace standard for quality assurance in design, development, production, installation and servicing. ASQ 9100 certification can be obtained by companies specialising in design and manufacture of equipment, aircraft accessory supply, airport and airline operations, spares supply and maintenance, flight operations or cargo handling. An increasing number of major aerospace contractors (e.g. Boeing, Rolls Royce Allison, GEAE, NASA and Honeywell, etc.) are now encouraging suppliers to use ASQ 9100, which is boosting ('propelling' one might even say!) its use throughout the industry.

For further details about the requirements of AS 9100, try the American Society for Quality (ASQ) website at www.asq.org.

Computer software

ISO/IEC 90003:2004 (*Software engineering – Guidelines for the application of ISO 9001:2000 to computer software*) provides guidance for organisations using ISO 9001:2000 to purchase, supply, develop, operate and maintain computer software and related support services. It is suitable for all software that is:

- part of a commercial contract with another organisation;
- a product available for a market sector;
- used to support the processes of an organisation;
- embedded in a hardware product; or
- related to software services.

ISO/IEC 90003:2004 itself is independent of the technology, lifecycle models, development processes, sequence of activities and business structure used by an organisation. It does not add to or otherwise change the requirements of ISO 9001:2000 and the guidelines provided are not intended to be used as assessment criteria in quality management system registration/certification.

Food and drink industry

ISO 15161:2001 (*Guidelines on the application of ISO 9001:2000 for the food and drink industry*) is aimed at organisations involved in all aspects of this industry sector, including sourcing, processing and packaging food and drink products.

The standard provides guidelines for the food and drink industry for implementing a QMS based on ISO 9001:2000 and provides information on the possible interactions between ISO 9000 and the Hazard Analysis and Critical Control Point (HACCP) system for food safety requirements.

This International Standard is not intended for certification, regulatory or contractual use.

Education

IWA 2:2003 (*Quality management systems – Guidelines for the application of ISO 9001:2000 in education*).

International Workshop Agreement IWA 2:2003 provides guidelines for the application of ISO 9001:2000 in educational organisations providing educational products. These guidelines do not add to, change or modify the requirements of ISO 9001:2000 and are not intended for use in contracts for compliance assessments or for certification.

Each clause of ISO 9001:2000 is included before the corresponding text of IWA 2:2003. The whole text of ISO 9004:2000 is also included to provide a complete vision of the continual performance improvement of organisations.

Iron ore industry

ISO/TR 13352:1997 (*Guidelines for interpretation of ISO 9000 series for application within the iron ore industry*) was written around the old procedural-based 1994 version of ISO 9000 with certain additions that were specific for the mining and quarrying (iron ore) industry.

It is currently being updated to comply with the basic management system requirements of ISO 9001:2000.

TickIT

TickIT procedures relate directly to the requirements set out in ISO 9001:2000 and similar to this standard, certification is conducted by an independent third party certification body using specialist auditors trained by the International Register of Certificated Auditors (IRCA) with the support of the British Computer Society. A successful audit by a TickIT-accredited certification body results in the award of a certificate of compliance to ISO 9001:2000, endorsed with a TickIT logo.

TickIT is supported by the UK and Swedish software industries with the aim of stimulating software system developers to think about:

- what quality really is in the context of the processes of software development;
- how quality may be achieved;
- how quality management systems may be continuously improved.
  through the following objectives:
  - to improve market confidence in a third party QMS certification through software sector accredited certification bodies,
  - to improve professional practice amongst software sector QMS auditors,
  - to publish authoritative guidance material (i.e. *The TickIT Guide*) for use by all stakeholders.

TickIT, therefore, provides software developers with an accredited quality certification scheme that meets the special needs of the industry, enjoys the confidence of professional staff and commands respect from purchasers and suppliers. It applies to all types of information system suppliers (software houses and in-house developers) which involve software development processes. TickIT disciplines are also relevant to the development of embedded software.

Within the UK, TickIT is recognised by all Government departments and major purchasers and it is compatible with European requirements for accredited quality system certification. Worldwide, over 1400 TickIT certificates have now been issued and currently 50% of all new certificates are being granted to organisations outside the United Kingdom.

For more information about this scheme, contact the TickIT Office at BSI (Floor 8E), 389 Chiswick High Road, London W4 4AL, Tel. +44(0) 20 8996 7427, Fax. +44(0) 20 8996 7429, e-mail **tickit@bsi-global.com**.

2

Background notes for auditors

One of the requirements of ISO 9001:2000 (Section 8.2.2) is that:

> 'The organisation shall conduct internal audits at planned intervals to determine whether the quality management system:
>
> a. conforms to the requirements of the ISO 9001:2000 standard and to the quality management system requirements established by the organisation and,
> b. is effectively implemented and maintained.'

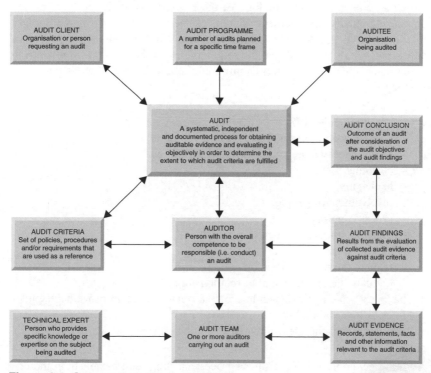

Figure 2.1 Concepts relating to quality

In order to meet and satisfy this requirement, organisations must continually review their Quality Management System (QMS):

- to ensure its continuing suitability and success;
- to reveal defects, danger spots or irregularities;
- to suggest possible improvements;
- to eliminate wastage or loss;
- to check the effectiveness of management at all levels;
- to be sure that managerial objectives and methods are effective and are capable of achieving the desired result.

Above all, organisations must be prepared to face up to an audit of their quality processes and procedures from potential customers and prove to them that their QMS fully meets the recommendations, requirements and specifications of ISO 9001:2000 and their promises made regarding product and/or service quality.

Whilst the previous 1994 editions of ISO 9000 were primarily concerned with manufacturers, ISO 9001:2000 being a process-oriented requirements standard is equally applicable to service industries and manufacturing plants. With the publication of the new ISO 9000 series, therefore, auditors, whether external or internal, will have to demonstrate their competence not only on the structure, content and terminology of the revised standards, but also on the underlying quality management principles. The revised standards will require that auditors be able to understand the organisation's activities and processes and appropriately audit against the requirements of the standard in relation to the organisation's objectives. As a minimum, auditors must demonstrate competency in:

- the requirements of ISO 9001:2000;
- the concepts and terminology of ISO 9000:2000;
- the eight quality management principles, namely:
  - customer focus,
  - leadership,
  - involvement of people,
  - process approach,
  - system approach to management,
  - continual improvement,
  - factual approach to decision making, and
  - mutually beneficial supplier relationships;
- having a general understanding of the performance improvement guidelines of ISO 9004:2000;
- familiarity with the latest draft of the auditing guidance standard (ISO 19011).

Auditing generally follows a linear process starting with establishing the criteria against which you are auditing and leading to a report concluding whether

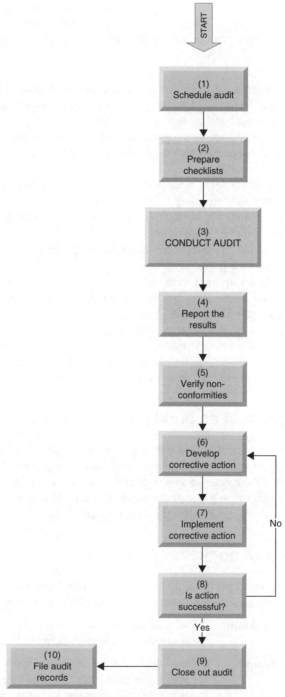

Figure 2.2 A generic audit process

the criteria is being met. Should the audit find problems with the performance of a process, then you will implement corrective action aimed at preventing recurrence. A simple process map of the internal audit procedure is shown in Figure 2.2.

1. An audit programme is agreed (see associated text later in this chapter) which should be aimed at auditing areas of concern more frequently than those parts of the business that are performing well.
2. Using the organisation's management system requirements as a yardstick, checklists are prepared which the auditor can use as an aide mémoire when completing his audit.
3. All management system processes are checked to see that they are appropriate and that they are being followed correctly.
4. Results of the audit are summarised in a report which will document both non-conformities and good practices.
5. If non-conformities have been found, an investigation is completed to determine why the process is failing.
6. A plan is drawn up to prevent recurrence of non-conformances (in some cases this may mean redrafting an existing management system process).
7. Process improvements are put in place.
8. An evaluation of the implemented corrective action is completed and adjustments (if necessary) made.
9. Once all corrective actions have been completed the audit may be closed out.
10. A complete documented record of the audit is retained for future reference.

2.1 Purpose of an audit

The primary purpose of an audit is to enable organisations to evaluate their process management systems, determine deficiencies, and generate cost effective and efficient solutions. An audit is performed to check practice against procedure, and to thoroughly document any differences. It is used to measure an organisation's ability '*to do what it says it is going to do*'.

2.2 Types of audit

There are several types of audit that can be completed under the general umbrella of '*audits measuring conformance with ISO 9001:2000*' such as:

Quality System Audits An overall measurement of an organisation's capability to meet the requirements of ISO 9001:2000.

Management Audits Checks carried out to see if a business's strategic plan reflects its business objectives and more specifically it has met the requirements of the intended market.

Process Audits	Focuses specifically on single processes to verify if they are capable of delivering the outputs expected of them.
Procedural Audits	Verification that documented practices are sufficient to ensure the implementation of approved policies and are capable of controlling the organisation's operations.
System Audits	Carried out to ensure a business management system is sufficiently comprehensive to control all of the activities within that business. Generally, this type of audit would look for gaps in the management system that may result in them not achieving their business objectives.
Product/Service Audits	Verification that an organisation's plans and proposals for supplying a product or service will ensure that that product or service fully meets specified requirements.

2.3 Audit categories

Whilst the common aim of all audits is to establish that an organisation's documented policies, processes and procedures, when implemented, are fit for their purpose and satisfy the needs of those who require them, the actual type of audit will depend on whether it is a First, Second or Third Party Audit. These are the three main types of audit associated with ISO 9001:2000 and are used as follows:

First Party	Audits of an organisation, or parts of an organisation, by personnel employed by that organisation. These audits are usually referred to as Internal Audits where (as the name suggests) members of a business look inwards at their own processes. This is the least effective form of auditing, as generally the auditors will find it difficult to criticise their own work.
Second Party	Audits carried out by customers upon their suppliers and are completed by an organisation independent of the organisation being audited. These audits are usually referred to as External Audits or Vendor Audits.

 Note: As all organisations are '*suppliers*' of one sort or another this can also, in some cases, be an audit by an external customer, of that organisation's premises and products.

Third Party	Audits carried out by personnel that are employees of neither the customer nor the supplier. They are usually employees of certification bodies or registrars such as BSI, TÜV and

Yardley, etc. These are also External Audits and are sometimes referred to as Certification Audits, Compliance Audits or Quality System Assessments.

 Note: What is the difference between validation and verification? There is often confusion between a product being 'validated' and a product that has been 'verified'. As shown in Figure 2.3, validation has to do with the subject matter being the right subject (i.e. product meets the initial product requirement) as opposed to 'verification' which has to do with the subject being right (i.e. the design output meets the requirements of the design input). For example, a product may have been verified as compliant with a particular specification but is not validated for this application.

Figure 2.3 Verification versus validation

2.4 First party (internal) audit

The type and content of any first party internal quality audit will vary according to the size and activities of the organisation. Its purpose is to:

- identify potential danger spots;
- eliminate wastage;
- verify that corrective action has been successfully achieved;
- provide a comparison between what the QMS or Quality Plan stipulates should be done and what is actually being done;
- confirm that everything is OK;
- identify non-compliance with previously issued instructions;
- identify deficiencies within the QMS;
- recommend any corrective actions that can be achieved to improve the system.

To meet these aims, the auditor must prepare an audit plan to determine whether the QMS is effectively achieving its stated quality objectives. It should be established as soon as possible and the procedures with which to carry out these audits should always be documented and available.

 Note: To be effective, an internal audit should always include members of the organisation's quality control staff, provided that they are **NOT** responsible for the quality of that particular product.

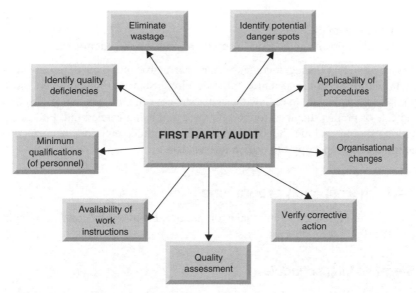

Figure 2.4 First party (internal) audit

The selection of the department to be audited should always be completed on a random basis and normally these internal audits will be scheduled every three months or so.

Ideally, the audit should be pre-planned so that it covers all aspects of quality control within one calendar year and the audit plan should:

- cover the specific areas and activities that are to be audited;
- stipulate the reasons why an internal audit is being completed (e.g. organisational changes, reported deficiencies, survey or routine check);

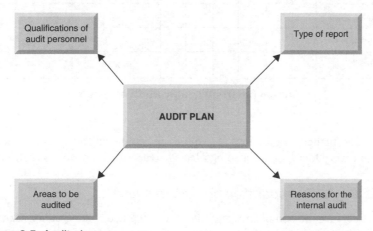

Figure 2.5 Audit plan

- stipulate the minimum qualifications of the personnel who are to conduct or assist with the audit;
- describe how the audit report should be finalised and submitted.

It is essential that management take timely corrective action on all deficiencies found during an internal audit. In some circumstances this can even mean going as far as having to review the statistical control methods that are used to indicate or predict the need for corrective action being carried out. Follow-up actions should include the verification of the implementation of corrective action and the reporting of verification results.

2.4.1 Internal audit programme

As shown in Figure 2.6 an internal audit programme normally consists of eight separate (but interrelated) steps:

Step 1 – Audit schedule

Internal quality audits are usually planned and initiated by the Quality Manager in relation to the status and importance of the various activities of a section and/or deliverable. For large organisations, it would be quite normal for all departments and sections to be subject to at least three **complete** quality audits every year as shown in the example below.

FUNCTION/ DEPARTMENT	JAN	FEB	MAR	APR	MAY	JUN	JULY	AUG	SEPT	OCT	NOV	DEC
Administration and finance	x				x				x			
Drawing office		x				x				x		
Workshops			x				x				x	
Stores				x				x				x

Annual (internal) quality audit schedule

 Note: For smaller organisations (e.g. those only employing a handful of people) an audit every four months or so of selected areas would probably be sufficient.

Step 2 – Audit preparation and organisation

Depending on the complexity and the size of the audit, the Quality Manager may perform the audit himself, or (when sections are too large, or when activities

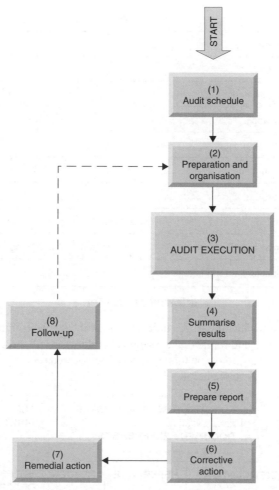

Figure 2.6 Internal audit programme

from other sections are involved) he can assign a lead auditor and a team of auditors to complete the task.

The Quality Manager (or lead auditor) is then responsible for organising an agenda which will include the:

- scope and objectives of the audit;
- persons having direct responsibilities for the procedure(s) to be audited;
- reference documents;
- name of lead auditor and name(s) of assigned auditor(s);
- date when audit is to be concluded.

Audit Reference No.:	File No.: ....
Purpose of audit:	
Scope of audit:	
Lead auditor assigned:	
Location(s) of audit:	
Unit or area to be audited:	
Reference documents:	
Team members:	
Date of audit:	Anticipated duration of audit: ....
Time of opening meeting:	Anticipated time of closing meeting: ......
Facilities requested:	

Internal audit plan

Following a review of earlier audit reports on the same section or the same subject, the lead auditor and the assigned auditor(s) will prepare an audit checklist containing all of the topics/items to be covered together with an audit programme (see example below).

AUDIT CHECKLIST	FUNCTION/PROCESS AUDITED: .... DOCUMENT REFERENCES:			AUDIT NO.: .... AUDIT DATE: ....
ITEM NO.	AUDIT QUESTIONS	REFERENCE	RESULT	NOTES/ OBSERVATIONS
	PREPARED BY:	PAGE .... OF		DATE PREPARED: ....

Audit checklist

TIMETABLE	TEAM A	TEAM B	AUDITEE PARTICIPATION
0900–0930	Opening meeting		Senior Management and Department Heads
0930–1030	Managing Director Quality Policy Management Review	Laboratory 1	Technical Director
1030–1100	Review of: Document Control Non-conformity	Laboratory 2	Department Heads
1100–1200	Purchasing	Laboratory 2	Department Heads
1200	Lunch		
1330–1500	Purchasing	Laboratory 2 (cont.)	Department Heads
1500–1600	Personnel Training	Electrical Test House	Department Heads
1600–1700	Commercial/Sales	Calibration Service	Department Heads

Audit programme

Step 3 – Audit execution

An initial meeting between the auditor(s), the auditee(s) and the Quality Manager is held during which:

- a brief summary of the methods and procedures that will be used to conduct the audit is given;
- the method of communication between auditor(s) and auditee(s) is agreed; and
- the audit programme confirmed.

In accordance with ISO 9001:2000 (Section 8.2.2) all organisations are required to have a documented procedure for conducting internal quality audits. Normally this procedure will distinguish between two kinds of internal quality audits, namely a 'standards audit' and a 'procedures audit'.

 Note: The standards audit evaluates how well the ISO standard is being applied, whilst the procedures audit evaluates how effective the organisation's quality procedures, policies, plans and instructions are.

Using the standards audit the auditor will begin collecting evidence of compliance by interviewing auditee personnel, reading documents, reviewing manuals, checking records, examining data, observing activities and studying working conditions. As the evidence is collected the auditor will answer each audit question and record his observations as either:

YES   *means that this activity is in compliance with the standard*

NO   *means this activity is not in compliance*

Not applicable *means that this question is not applicable in this activity's situation*

Once the auditor has completed the audit questionnaire, he will make a list of all the non-conformities (i.e. the 'NOs') and summarise his evidence.

Similarly, using the procedures audit, each applicable quality procedure, policy, plan and work instruction will be looked at from the point of view of *Is it documented? Is it being followed? Is it effective?* On the basis of evidence collected, the auditor will record his observation as:

YES *means that this activity is in compliance*

NO *means that this activity is not in compliance*

Auditors will record all their observations on the Audit Observation Sheet (see example below) and all non-compliances will then be listed on a 'non-compliance worksheet' which will eventually form part of the final audit report.

Section or project to be audited:		
Reason for audit:		
Audit No.:		Date:
Auditor:		Sheet ... of ...

Serial No.	Observation/supporting evidence Action required	Yes/No

Circulation:		
Attached sheets:		

Signed:		Name:		Date:	

Audit observation sheet

Step 4 – Summarise audit results

Auditors will then meet to discuss all of their observations (particularly any non-compliances that they may have found) with the Quality Manager.

 Note: All observations of non-conformity **must** be formally acknowledged by the manager responsible for the activity being audited.

A closing meeting of auditor(s), auditee(s) and Quality Manager will then be held during which:

- audit observations will be clarified;
- the critical significance of observations will be presented;
- conclusions drawn about compliance will be presented;
- system effectiveness in achieving the quality objectives will be presented;
- corrective actions will be agreed;
- the date for completion of the audit report will be agreed.

 Note: Minutes of **all** relevant meetings, decisions and agreements must be attached to the audit report.

Step 5 – Prepare audit report

The lead auditor now needs to prepare an audit report using an Audit Report Form similar to the one shown below.

Section or project audited:			
Reason for audit:			
Audit No.:		Date:	
Auditor:		Sheet ... of ...	
Audit area(s):			
Reference document(s):			
Summary:			
Audit observation sheet number	Observation number	Comments	Corrective action requirement
Prepared:	Name:	Date:	
Agreed:	Name:	Date:	
Circulation:		Attached sheets:	

Audit report form

The report must be signed by all members of the audit team, plus the Quality Manager, and copies sent to auditee(s) and company management as required.

The audit report will list all non-conformities discovered, observations made and discuss any conclusions drawn. It will also detail (in the summary) recommendations that should be implemented in order to correct or prevent non-conformities occurring and to make improvements.

Step 6 – Corrective action

After the closing meeting, the lead auditor will prepare a Corrective Action Request (similar to the example below) for each agreed corrective action.

Note: Corrective Action Requests should always state who is responsible for carrying out the corrective action and the timescale for its completion.

Section or project audited:				
Reason for audit:				
Audit No.:		Audit date:		
Auditor(s):		Auditee(s):		
Audit area(s):				
Reference document(s):				
Non-conformance details:				
Signed: (Auditor)		Name:	Date:	
Agreed corrective action:				
Signed: (Auditee)		Name:	Date:	
Agreed time limit:				
Signed: (Actionee)		Name:	Date:	
Progress			Signed:	Date:

Corrective action request

Note: One sheet should be used for **each agreed** corrective action.

Step 7 – Take remedial action

The section/department that has been audited is then responsible for ensuring that the agreed corrective actions are implemented and that any observations, comments and recommendations made by the audit team have been taken into account.

Step 8 – Follow-up

Finally, the lead auditor is then responsible for ensuring that corrective action has been carried out and for notifying the Quality Manager of the status and/or completion of corrective actions.

2.5 External audit

2.5.1 The old audit process

The checklist for an audit to ISO 9001:1994 was traditionally completed by element (vertically); only a few auditors addressed fully the linkages and the relationships between elements. After completion of the audit, the organisation would then be subject to ongoing maintenance audits (focused on continued conformance to the planned arrangements that were agreed during the audit process outlined above), normally at a six- or twelve-month frequency.

Figure 2.7 External audit

All organisations are eventual 'suppliers' of their product or service and in order to stay in business they will have to provide proof that they can continue to provide a quality product/service. This is actually a 'measurement of their quality control' and usually takes the form of a supplier's evaluation, surveillance and/or external audit.

 Note: Although the supplier may have been able to convince the purchaser that their QMS is effective, it is in the interests of the purchaser to conduct their own evaluation (i.e. audit) of the supplier. This is usually done on an irregular basis. The supplier must, of course, agree to the principle of purchaser evaluations being carried out and it is usual to find this as a separate clause in the contract.

External audits are audits carried out by an organisation independent of the organisation being audited, 'independence' being taken as there is no financial association other than by a contract. The audits are carried out by personnel that are neither employees of the customer nor the supplier and are usually belonging to certification bodies or registrars such as BSI, TÜV and Yardley, etc.

The purpose of both these audits is to ensure that:

- the organisation's QMS is being correctly and effectively implemented and that a corresponding compliance with the ISO 9001:2000 quality standard is maintained;
- any relevant legislation and standards are being adhered to;
- the system and procedures in operation are still effective and remain accurate for the working practices used;
- the data and information feedback from internal audits, complaints, compliments or routine work is considered at senior management level so that adjustments to the systems can be made;
- potential danger spots are identified, wastage eliminated and corrective action successfully achieved.

If the organisation is a manufacturer as opposed to being a service provider, then they will have to adhere to the relevant national and international quality management standards requiring manufacturers and suppliers to establish and maintain a fully documented method for the inspection of their system for quality control. Procedures for classifying lots, cataloguing characteristics, selecting samples and rules for acceptance and/or rejection criteria, together with procedures for segregating and screening rejected lots, need to be identified and developed.

Normally these audits are fairly simple, but (particularly when the material, product or service being purchased is complex) the purchaser will need to have a reasonably objective method of evaluating and measuring the efficiency of the quality control at the supplier's premises. The auditor needs to be certain that the system established by the supplier complies with laid down standards and is, above all, effective. This method is known as the 'supplier evaluation'.

2.5.2 External audit programme

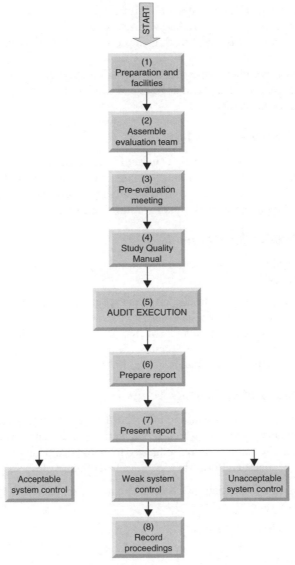

Figure 2.8 External audit programme

Step 1 – Preparation and facilities

Part of the initial contract between a supplier (particularly those who actually manufacture a product) and a purchaser will normally stipulate that the supplier provides access, accommodation and facilities to the purchaser's inspectors.

These facilities will depend upon the level of surveillance, but could require the supplier to provide:

- suitable office and administrative facilities;
- adequate work space for product verification;
- access to those areas where work is in progress or to those which affect the work;
- help in documenting, inspecting and releasing products and services;
- the use of inspection and test devices and availability of personnel to operate them are necessary.

Step 2 – Assemble evaluation team

The evaluation team will normally consist of a Lead Auditor assisted by two or more inspectors from the purchaser's organisation. These inspectors must be thoroughly skilled in the requirements of quality assurance and are normally drawn from the purchaser's own quality control section.

Step 3 – Pre-evaluation meeting

Before the evaluation team visits the supplier's premises, they must first be given the chance to:

- meet the supplier's staff to discuss the procedures being used;
- identify the areas that will be tested;
- decide which representative(s) of the supplier's organisation will be required to accompany the evaluation team during their inspection;
- agree dates and outline timetables, etc.

Step 4 – Study of the Quality Manual

Prior to commencing an evaluation, the Lead Auditor must be given a copy of the supplier's Quality Manual which he will scrutinise not only for its accuracy and clarity but also for its position compared to national and international standards and to see that it conforms to the relevant sections of ISO 9001:2000.

 Note: An essential part of an ISO 9001:2000 quality management system is its relationship to:

- customer requirements;
- customer perceptions;
- organisation's business goals.

Step 5 – Audit execution

Having completed the pre-evaluation, the evaluation team will now go to the supplier's premises to fully scrutinise every aspect of the supplier's QMS. If the supplier is a manufacturer, then the evaluation team will pay particular attention to the supplier's design office, purchasing department, storekeeping, manufacturing, assembly and test facilities to see that the work carried out complies with the procedures and promises made in their Quality Manual.

Preparing for the on-site audit activities

The three main actions that must be completed prior to actually starting the audit are:

- to thoroughly plan and agree all on-site audit activities;
- to allocate audit team work assignments;
- to prepare work documents (e.g. audit report forms).

 Note: Identified exclusions will be a key input to scope definition and subsequent audit planning.

Owing to ISO 9001:2000's process-oriented approach, this part of the audit will now have to be completed in a different manner to previous 1994 audits and without any 'official template' to follow, the actual layout and content of quality documentation will vary from organisation to organisation. In some cases there may be a distinct lack of documents (after all, a Quality Manual can, now, consist of just a few pages or fill two or three filing cabinets depending on the organisation) and so any document review will have to reflect this and concentrate on trying to understand the important customer and business issues. Auditors can react in different ways to this changed need and whilst some may want to complete the document review on site, others may require all quality management system documents (manual, procedures, flowcharts, working documents, etc.) be submitted for review, prior to the site audit.

On-site audit activities

There are six separate activities to an on-site audit:

- the opening meeting;
- collecting and verifying information;
- identifying audit findings;
- communication during the audit;
- preparation for closing meeting;
- the closing meeting.

For an auditor, much more emphasis now needs to be placed upon the policy requirements and objectives and how these have been covered in the organisation's QMS. Whilst the old style tick-in-the-box checklist will now **not** provide an effective audit, checklists and questionnaires still serve a useful purpose – if used correctly.

Chapter 3 provides a series of example checklists so as to provide an indication of the areas of an organisation's QMS that could be looked at and possibly further investigated during internal, external and/or third party audits or to confirm that an organisation's QMS fully covers the requirements (i.e. clauses) of ISO 9001:2000.

 Note: Auditors can select the most relevant ones to include in their own checklist supplemented by each specific case that they have to deal with. The experienced auditor will be able to extend this checklist using earlier experience coupled with experts in this field.

As the focus of an ISO 9001:2000 audit has been significantly changed, an appropriate change must also occur to the audit methodology used. The emphasis now will be very much on 'walking-the-walk' to see if the stated objectives have been achieved. Did the system improve? Is the organisation's stated policy being achieved? In particular, auditors will now have to ensure that exclusions are identified during the initial audit stage and that justification of any exclusion is appropriate.

Step 6 – Prepare report

The lead auditor now needs to prepare an audit report using an Audit Report Form similar to the one shown below:

Section or project audited:			
Reason for audit:			
Audit No.:		Date:	
Auditor:		Sheet ... of ...	
Audit area(s):			
Reference document(s):			
Summary:			
Audit observation sheet number	Observation number	Comments	Corrective action requirement
Prepared:	Name:		Date:
Agreed:	Name:		Date:
Circulation:		Attached sheets:	

Audit report form

The report must be signed by all members of the audit team, plus the Quality Manager, and copies sent to auditee(s) and company management as required.

Step 7 – Present report

At the end of this evaluation, a meeting will be arranged between the evaluation team and the organisation's management to discuss their findings and to be sure that there are not any misunderstandings, etc. The eventual evaluation report will then be formally presented at a meeting with the management and the result of this meeting could be one of the following:

Acceptable system control   This means that the evaluation has shown that the supplier has a satisfactory QMS, there are no deficiencies and the supplier has been able to give an assurance of quality. When this happens, there should be no reason why the purchaser should feel it necessary to demand any radical changes to the supplier's system.

Weak system control   This covers the situation where the evaluation team find several significant weaknesses in the supplier's system.

 Note: If this happens, the supplier will have to take steps to overcome these failures and improve their QMS. Having done this, the supplier can then ask for another evaluation to be carried out to confirm that their quality now meets the required standards.

Unacceptable system control   This is when the evaluation team find that the number of deficiencies – or the lack of quality discipline at the supplier's premises – mean that the supplier will have to make radical changes to improve their overall QMS before they are anything like acceptable to the potential purchaser.

 Note: When the supplier has completed the necessary changes, they will then require a second evaluation to see that their improvements are satisfactory.

Step 8 – Record proceedings

Having been inspected, it is important that the records of this inspection are safely filed away in case they may be required to reinforce some point at a later stage or to provide statistical data for the analysis of a supplier's performance. This is sometimes referred to as Vendor Rating.

2.5.3 Ongoing supplier surveillance visits

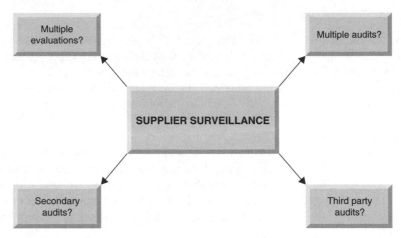

Figure 2.9 Ongoing supplier evaluations and audits

Although an organisation may well have successfully passed their initial evaluation and the purchaser may well be satisfied that the supplier is capable of providing an assurance of quality, it cannot be assumed that the supplier will be able to retain, or even capable of retaining, this status forever. Many things can happen to change this situation such as staff moving through promotion or natural wastage, changes in the product design that may or have been necessary, or perhaps a new man-management philosophy.

For this reason it is quite possible that the purchaser might want to make irregular surveillance visits of the supplier's premises to further examine a particular aspect of their QMS. These surveillance or audit visits by the purchaser will be run on exactly the same lines as the supplier evaluation and are aimed at providing the purchaser with a confidence in the supplier and an assurance that they are capable of still providing the purchaser with the quality of service, goods and/or products that they require.

 Note: The aim of these audit visits should be that all the important aspects of the quality control system are checked, in rotation.

Multiple evaluations and audits

It is possible that some suppliers might well be providing the same product to several different customers and it could just happen that all of these customers ask to have an audit – at the same time. This obviously cannot be allowed to happen as the supplier would forever have people visiting the organisation which would be disturbing, not only the labour force, but also the production line. Purchasers can avoid this problem by agreeing to accept a secondary audit.

Secondary audits

If a purchaser indicates that they want to carry out an audit, the supplier can offer to provide the details of another customer's audit or the result of a third party's evaluation that has recently been carried out at their premises. If this does not quite cover the problem area sufficiently, then the supplier could offer to check in more detail the appropriate points raised by the purchaser.

Maintenance audit

The focus of maintenance audits will change from planned arrangements to achievement and management of defined objectives. The system will be reviewed for continual improvement, and enhancement of customer satisfaction.

2.6 Third party certification audits

ISO 9001:2000 certificates are available to those organisations who see the need for formal recognition that they are working in conformance with the requirements and recommendations of ISO 9001:2000.

Certificates are awarded by Inspection Bodies (also known as Certification Bodies and/or Registrars) who have, themselves, been assessed as being competent by an official Assessment Body – but be warned, **not** all companies who profess to being able to award ISO 9001:2000 certificates are accredited!

Within the UK, the Directory of Accredited Inspection Bodies shows which organisations have been accredited by the United Kingdom Accreditation Service (UKAS) and also the field and range of inspections for which they are accredited.

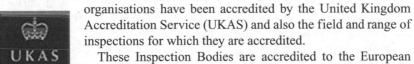

These Inspection Bodies are accredited to the European Standard EN 45004 – *General Criteria for the Operation of Various Types of Bodies Performing Inspection* and are authorised to issue accredited inspection reports/certificates for work covered by their scope of accreditation. Such reports/certificates will carry the national mark for inspection bodies.

For more information regarding accreditation and UKAS's services, use one of the contact numbers below:

UKAS points of contact

	Telephone	Fax	e-mail
UKAS information and helpdesk			
	020 8917 8556	020 8917 8499	rdj@ukas.com
	020 8917 8555	020 8917 8499	ikc@ukas.com

Administration enquiries

Publication sales	020 8917 8454	020 8917 8500	eab@ukas.com
Certification bodies	020 8917 8417/8	020 8917 8499	jeh@ukas.com
Inspection bodies	020 8917 8420	020 8917 8499	av@ukas.com
Laboratories	020 8917 8415	020 8917 8500	eab@ukas.com

Within the USA, the American National Standards Institute (ANSI) accredits Certification Bodies and they can be contacted at:

1819 L Street, NW
US-Washington, DC 20036
Tel: +1 212 642 49 00
Fax: +1 212 398 00 23
E-mail: info@ansi.org
Web: http://www.ansi.org

What is the difference between being certified and being registered?

Actually there is no difference! In some countries organisations will say that they are 'certified', in others they will say that they are 'registered' – but it means the same thing.

What is the difference between being certified and being compliant?

When an organisation claims that they are ISO 9000 certified or registered, they mean that a Notified Body (that is, an independent registrar) has audited their QMS, certified that it meets the requirements of ISO 9001:2000, given them a written assurance that ISO's quality management system standard has been met and registered their organisation as having been certified.

On the other hand, when an organisation says that they are ISO 9000 'compliant', they usually mean that they have met ISO's quality system requirements but have **not** been formally certified by an independent registrar. In effect, they are self-certified and whilst this is perfectly acceptable for many organisations, especially the smaller ones, an official certificate issued by an independent registrar does tend to carry more weight in the marketplace.

Note: As ISO 9001:2000 is a process standard (and not a product standard), when a company says that they are certified or compliant, they are **not** saying that their products and/or services meet the ISO 9000 requirements.

What is the difference between being certified and being accredited?

Inspection Bodies (also known as Certification Bodies and/or Registrars) audit and certify organisations who wish to become ISO 9000 registered. Accreditation

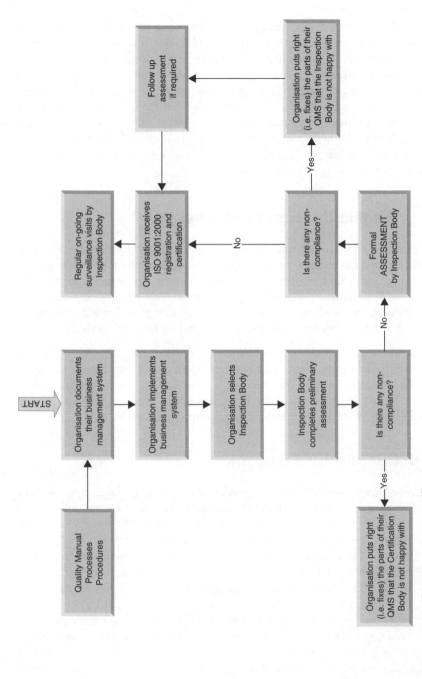

Figure 2.10 Typical route to certification

Bodies like UKAS (United Kingdom Accreditation Service) and the American National Standards Institute (ANSI), on the other hand, evaluate and accredit the Inspection Bodies.

In effect accreditation bodies audit the auditors and certify that the Inspection Bodies are competent and authorised to issue ISO 9001:2000 certificates in specified business sectors. A typical certification route is shown in Figure 2.10.

The amount of time required to attain certification is dependent upon a number of variables including the size of the company, the complexity of its business processes, the resources available to develop the QMS, etc. Experience shows that for most small and medium enterprises allowing one year is not unreasonable. However, some larger companies have been known to attain certification in considerably less time, but this is usually down to the employment of a dedicated quality development team.

2.7 What is the cost of certification?

The cost of certification can vary significantly as Certification Bodies have different pricing structures. Some will charge for each and every visit, assessment and follow-up surveillance inspections. Others may be happy to settle for a one-off fixed payment to take the organisation through the certification process, followed by an annual renewal fee. When considering a suitable Certification Body it would be best to obtain a number of quotes to establish the best offer.

 Note: Certification Bodies do not generally provide a consultancy service so it is desirable to use an independent consultant to ease the way through the certification process. You could of course do it yourself, but there are pitfalls that an experienced consultant would help you over (and potentially save you money by avoiding unnecessary repeat visits from the Certification Body).

2.8 Conformity assessment

In these days of international markets and cross-border trading, many national regulations require that a product or deliverable is first tested for compliance with an internationally agreed specification for safety, environmental and/or quality conformance before they can be released to the market.

This sort of testing is referred to as 'conformity assessment' and in its simplest form means that a product, material, service, system (or in some cases) people have been measured against the specifications of a relevant standard – which, in most cases, will be an internationally agreed standard.

Although some conformity assessment can be completed using internal facilities, when a product has health and/or environmental implications, national legislation will probably stipulate that testing is carried out by an independent registrar, Notified Body or specialist organisation, in other words, by a third party.

Design

Manufacture of product
or implementation of service

Acceptance

In-service

End of life

Figure 2.11 Quality assurance lifecycle

There exist many testing laboratories and certification bodies which offer independent conformity assessment services performed either as a commercial venture, or under mandate to their national government.

 Note: For details of availability in your area try the DTI website www.dti.gov.uk or perhaps one of the search engines (e.g. www.google.com).

2.9 Quality assurance during a product's or service's lifecycle

The life of a manufactured product or implemented service can be split into five stages as shown in Figure 2.11.

Figure 2.12 Quality assurance measurements

As quality assurance affects the product throughout its lifecycle, it is important that quality assurance procedures are introduced for design, manufacturing and acceptance stages, as well as in service utilisation.

2.9.1 Design stage

'Quality must be designed into a product before manufacture or assembly' (ISO 9004:2000).

Throughout the design stage of a service or product, the quality of that design must be regularly checked. Quality procedures have to be planned, written and implemented to predict and evaluate the fundamental and intrinsic reliability of the proposed design.

It doesn't matter whether the responsibility for the design of a product rests purely with the supplier, the purchaser, or is a joint function. It is essential that the designer is fully aware of the exact requirements of the project and has sound background knowledge of the relevant standards, information and procedures that will have to be adopted during the design stages.

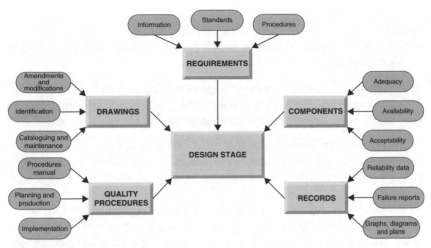

Figure 2.13 Design stage

This is extremely important, because the actions of the design office not only influence the maintenance of quality during manufacture and/or supply, but also play a major part in setting the quality level of the eventual product or service. From the point of view of a supplied product, if there is no quality control in a manufacturer's drawing office, then there is little chance of there ever being any on the shop floor. When the engineers are trying to manufacture something (or a technician is attempting to assemble a system or module) to a set of drawings that have countless mistakes on them, what chance is there of them ever being able to produce an acceptable item!

These problems, although not specifically stipulated in ISO 9001:2000 should nevertheless be addressed. The design office (or team) should produce some sort of Procedures Manual, which lists and describes the routine processes, procedures and instructions that are required to turn a concept into a set of functional product or service drawings.

For all suppliers, these procedures will cover such activities as:

- the numbering of drawings and documents (i.e. document control);
- authorisation to issue amendments and modifications to documents and drawings;
- how to control changes to documents and drawings;
- the method of withdrawing obsolete documents and drawings;
- the identification, cataloguing and maintenance of documents and drawings.

For product manufacturers the design office (in addition to these procedures, etc.) will also:

- have to provide a complete listing of all the relevant components and their availability, acceptability and adequacy;

- be aware of all the advances in both materials and equipment that are currently available on today's market which are relevant to the product;
- assist in the analysis of failures, swiftly produce solutions and forestall costly work stoppages.

 Note: One of the main problems to overcome is the ease with which the design office can make an arbitrary selection, but then find that the size and tolerance is completely inappropriate for the manufacturing or assembly process.

In order that the statistical significance of a particular failure can be assessed and correct retroactive action taken, it is essential that the design team also has access to all the records, failure reports and other data as soon as it is available.

The storage, maintenance and analysis of reliability data will require the design team to follow the progress of the product throughout its productive lifecycle, its many in-service and/or maintenance cycles and to take due note of customers' comments. The compilation and retention of this reliability data is not only very important, but also essential to the reliability of the product and/or service.

Nowadays, of course, most large design offices are computerised and use processors to store their records on discs so that these records can be continually updated and amended. This information (data) can then be used with standard software such as Computer Aided Design (CAD) programs and computer aided design facilities to produce lists, graphs and drawings. The possibilities are almost endless but there are associated problems such as security against virus attack and computer crashes.

 Note: See Chapter 3, Section 3.7.1 (p. 204), for a typical example of an audit check sheet for the design stage.

2.9.2 Manufacturing stage

Manufacture of product or implementation of service

'*Manufacturing operations must be carried out under controlled conditions*' (ISO 9004:2000).

During all manufacturing processes (and throughout early in-service life), the product must be subjected to a variety of quality control procedures and checks in order to evaluate the degree of quality.

One of the first things that must be done is to predict the reliability of the product's design. This involves obtaining sufficient statistical data so as to be able to estimate the actual reliability of the design before a product is manufactured.

All the appropriate engineering data has to be carefully examined, particularly the reliability ratings of recommended parts and components. The

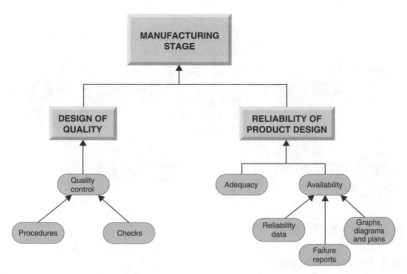

Figure 2.14 Manufacturing stage

designer then extrapolates and interpolates this data and uses probability methods to examine the reliability of a proposed design.

Note 1: Design deficiencies such as assembly errors, operator learning, motivational or fatigue factors, latent defects and improper part selection are frequently uncovered during this process.

Note 2: See Chapter 3, Section 3.7.2 (p. 207), for a typical example of an audit check sheet for the manufacturing stage.

2.9.3 Acceptance stage

'*The quality of a product must be proved before being accepted*' (ISO 9004:2000).

During the acceptance stage, the product or service will be subjected to a series of tests designed to confirm that the workmanship of the product/service fully meets the levels of quality required, or stipulated by the user and that the product/service performs the required function correctly.

Acceptance

In the case of a manufactured product, it will range from environmental tests of individual components to field testing complete systems. Three mathematical expressions are commonly used to measure reliability and each of these expressions can be applied to a part, component assembly or an entire system. They are, probability function (PF), failure rate (FR) and mean time between failures (MTBF).

Note: See Chapter 3, Section 3.7.3 (p. 208), for a typical example of an audit check sheet for the acceptance stage.

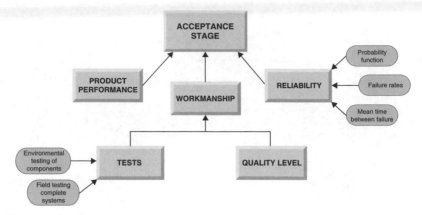

Figure 2.15 Acceptance stage

2.9.4 In-service stage

In-service

'*Evaluation of product performance during typical operating conditions and feedback of information gained through field use – improves product capability*' (ISO 9004:2000).

During the in-service stage the purchaser is, of course, principally concerned with system and equipment reliability.

Although reliability is based on the product system's generic design (and can be easily proved by statistics) its practical reliability is often far less design dependent. This difference can be due to poor documentation, faulty operating procedures, operating the system beyond its design

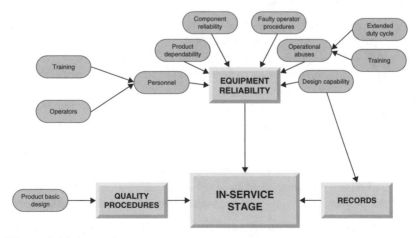

Figure 2.16 In-service stage

capability or operational abuses (e.g. personal – extended duty cycles – neglected maintenance – training etc.). Each of these hazards will have a detrimental effect on the product/service.

For manufactured products, the problems associated with poorly trained, poorly supported, or poorly motivated maintenance personnel with respect to reliability and dependability require careful assessment and quantification.

Note: According to recent studies completed by the British Institute of Management, the maintenance technician (or engineer) still remains the primary cause of reliability degradations during the in-service stage.

The most important factor that affects the overall reliability of a modern product, nevertheless, is the increased number of individual components that are required in that product. Since most system failures are actually caused by the failure of a single component, the reliability of each individual component must be considerably better than the overall system reliability.

Information obtained from in-service use and field failures are enormously useful (always assuming that they are entirely accurate, of course!) in evaluating a product's performance during typical operating conditions. But the main reason for accumulating failure reports from the field is to try to improve the product. This can be achieved by analysing the reports, finding out what caused the failure and taking steps to prevent it from recurring in the future.

Because of this requirement, quality standards for the maintenance, repair and inspection of in-service products have had to be laid down in engineering standards, handbooks and local operating manuals (written for specific items and equipment). These publications are used by maintenance engineers and should always include the most recent amendments. It is **essential** that quality assurance personnel also use the same procedures for their inspections.

Note: See Chapter 3, Section 3.7.3 (p. 209), for a typical example of an audit check sheet for the acceptance stage.

2.9.5 Supplier's responsibilities

The supplier's prime responsibility must always be to ensure that anything **and everything** leaving their organisation whether it is a document, product or service conforms to the specific requirements of the purchaser – particularly with regard to quality.

In this respect, the supplier is responsible for ensuring that:

● all managerial staff, from the most junior to the most senior, firmly believe in the importance of quality control and quality assurance and understand how to implement them;

● managerial staff create an atmosphere in which quality assurance rules are obeyed and not simply avoided just because they are inconvenient, time consuming, laborious or just too boring to bother with;

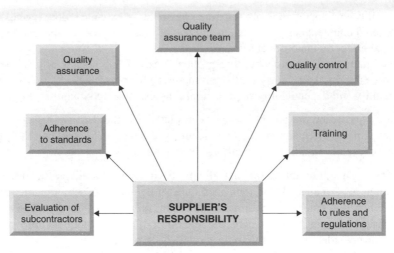

Figure 2.17 Supplier's responsibilities

- there is an accepted training scheme to ensure that all members of the firm are regularly brought up to date with the ongoing and the latest requirements of quality assurance;
- there is a quality assurance team available to oversee and make sure that quality control and quality assurance are carried out at all times and **at all levels**, within their premises.

Lack of quality control and quality assurance can cause a supplier providing manufactured products to:

- replace scrapped material or have to rework unsatisfactory material;
- reinspect and reprocess material returned as unsatisfactory by the purchaser;
- lose money by having to send staff to the purchaser's premises to sort out their complaints of unsatisfactory labour;
- lose money through a major quality failure halting production;
- lose money through field repairs, replacements and other work having to be carried out under warranty;
- lose money by having to carry out investigations into claims of unsatisfactory work;
- lose money by having to investigate alternative methods of producing an article without quality failures;
- lose their image or reputation;
- lose market potential;
- have to acknowledge complaints, claims, liabilities and be subject to waste of human and financial resources;

But most of all …

- lose customers!

2.9.6 Purchaser's responsibilities

Quite a number of problems associated with service or product quality are usually the fault of the purchaser! Obviously, the purchaser can only expect to get what he ordered. It is, therefore, extremely important that the actual order is not only correct, but also provides the supplier or manufacturer with all the relevant (and accurate) information required completing the task.

In the case of a manufactured product, this can be achieved by providing a drawing, which contains all the relevant details such as:

- type of material to be used;
- the materials grade or condition;
- the specifications that are to be followed;
- all the relevant dimensional data, sizes, tolerances etc.
- reference to one of the accepted standards.

 Note: Where possible, the graphic order/drawing should be to scale.

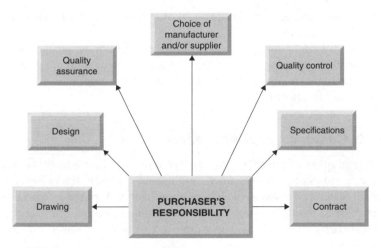

Figure 2.18 Purchaser's responsibilities

In the case of a service provider, the supplier must have the service specification fully defined, documented and agreed before work is commenced.

By not insisting that the supplier abides by a set of recognised quality standards, the purchaser can be involved in:

- delays in being able to use the product or service and the possibility of the purchaser losing orders because of it;

- possible increases in their organisation, operation, maintenance downtime and repair costs;
- dissatisfaction with goods and services;
- health and safety aspects (now a mandatory requirement of ISO 9001:2000);
- lack of confidence in the supplier.

2.10 The effect of ISO 9001:2000's new requirements

In addition to the requirements replicated from the previous 20-element ISO 9001:1994 standard, auditors now have to address the following.

2.10.1 Customer focus

Organisations under ISO 9001:2000 have to have in place a system for determining customer needs and expectations including:

- requirements not specified by the customer but necessary for intended service or product use;
- obligations related to the product and/or service, as well as regulatory and legal requirements;
- a system for monitoring customer satisfaction and/or dissatisfaction;
- a system for ensuring that customer needs and expectations are determined, converted into requirements, and fulfilled with the overall aim of achieving customer satisfaction.

2.10.2 Customer communication

The organisation will need to have in place a process for customer communications relating to: inquiries, order handling, or contracts (including amendments); customer feedback (including complaints). A process also needs to be established by the organisation for monitoring customer satisfaction and/ or dissatisfaction as one of the measurements of quality management system performance.

2.10.3 Training

Evidence that training has been provided is not enough! An evaluation of the **effectiveness** of training is now also required. Another requirement for top management is that the requirements of the organisation's QMS and adherence to the organisation's QMS processes needs to be effectively communicated among all tiers and functions of the organisation.

2.10.4 Legal and regulatory compliance

Increased emphasis has now been placed on the role of top management to develop and improve the system, integrate legal and regulatory requirements, and establish measurable objectives at appropriate levels of the organisation.

2.10.5 QMS development and improvement

To satisfy the requirements of ISO 9001:2000, top management must now provide evidence of its commitment to the development and improvement of their QMS. This evidence must include a procedure that lays emphasis on the importance of meeting customer needs, as well as regulatory and legal requirements.

The organisation will also need to show how it plans and manages the processes necessary for the continuous improvement of the quality management system through the use of the quality policies, objectives, audit results, data analyses, corrective and preventive actions, and management review.

2.10.6 Product conformity

From a manufacturer's point of view, the requirement for an organization to identify, provide and maintain the facilities it needs to achieve conformity of product (including: workspace and associated facilities; equipment, hardware and software; and supporting services) has now been expanded to include the identification and management of the work environment and, in particular, the need to consider the human and physical factors required to achieve conformity of product.

2.10.7 Measurement and continual improvement

Measurement and monitoring activities are a new requirement. Organisations must determine the requirements and uses of 'applicable methodologies,' including statistical techniques.

To achieve this requirement, the organisation must establish a process for collecting and analysing appropriate data to determine the suitability and effectiveness of the quality management system, to identify potential improvements and to data to provide information on customer satisfaction and/or dissatisfaction and conformance to customer requirements.

2.10.8 Quality Management System requirements

'A Quality Management System is a system to establish a quality policy and quality objectives and to achieve these objectives' (ISO 9000:2000).

It is an organisational structure of responsibilities, activities, resources and events that together provide procedures and methods of implementation to ensure the capability of an organisation to meet quality requirements.

Within ISO 9001:2000, there is now greater emphasis on the structure of a process-orientated QMS.

 Note: The following section (which was part of a previous publication by the author) is included here as a reminder for auditors.

2.11 Basic requirements of a Quality Management System

To be successful, an organisation must:

- be able to offer products and/or services that satisfy a customer's expectations;
- agree with the relevant standards and specifications of a contract;
- be available at competitive prices;

and

- supply at a cost that will still bring a profit to that organisation.

They must, above all, provide a quality product and/or service that will promote further procurement and recommendations and they must be able to prove to their potential purchasers that they are capable of continually providing a quality

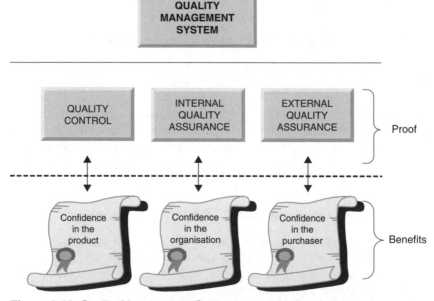

Figure 2.19 Quality Management System – organisational structure

product/service. To satisfy these requirements an organisation's QMS has to encompass all the different levels of quality control that are required during the various stages of design, manufacture, supply, incorporation/installation and acceptance of a product and/or service and be capable of guaranteeing quality acceptance.

These requirements are covered by national, European and international standards. However, although these standards may vary slightly from country to country, they are very similar and cover the following topics:

- organisational structure;
- measurement of quality assurance;
- the contract;
- design control;
- purchasing and procurement;
- production control;
- product testing;
- handling, storage, packaging and delivery;
- after-sales service.

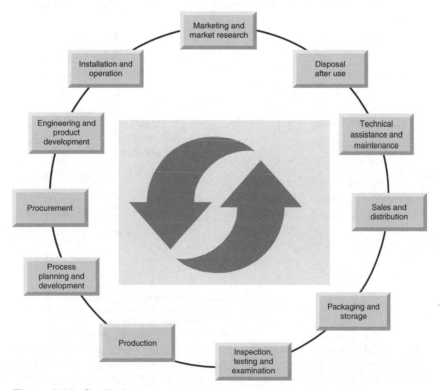

Figure 2.20 Quality loop

2.11.1 Quality Management System principles

The first thing that ISO 9001:2000 requires is for an organisation to set up and fully document their position with regard to quality assurance. These documents comprise the organisation's QMS and describe the organisation's capability for supplying goods and services that will comply with laid down quality standards. It contains a general description of the organisation's attitude to quality assurance and specific details about the quality assurance and quality control within that organisation.

To be successful an organisation must be able to prove that they are capable of producing the component, product or service to the customer's complete satisfaction so that it conforms exactly to the purchaser's specific requirements and that it is always of the desired quality. An organisation's QMS is, therefore, the organisational structure of responsibilities, procedures, processes and resources for carrying out quality management and as such must be planned and developed in order to be capable of maintaining a consistent level of quality control.

The QMS must be structured to the organisation's own particular type of business and should consider all functions such as customer liaison, designing, purchasing, subcontracting, manufacturing, training, installation, updating of

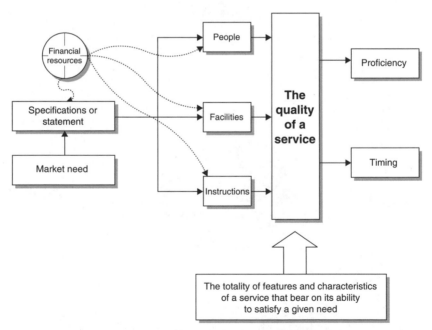

Figure 2.21 Some of the determinants and measurements of the quality of a service. (This is an extract from BS 4778:1979 which has been reproduced with the kind permission of BSI. The 1979 edition has been superseded but these figures are included here since they illustrate the concept.)

quality control techniques and the accumulation of quality records. In most organisations this sort of information will normally be found in the organisation's Quality Manual.

The type of QMS chosen will, of course, vary from organisation to organisation depending upon its size and capability. There are no set rules as to exactly how these documents should be written. However, they should – as a minimum requirement – be capable of showing the potential customer exactly how the manufacturer or supplier is equipped to achieve and maintain the highest level of quality throughout the various stages of design, production, installation and servicing.

As an example, some of the determinants and measures of the quality of a service are shown in Figure 2.21 whilst those affecting the quality of a product are shown in Figure 2.22.

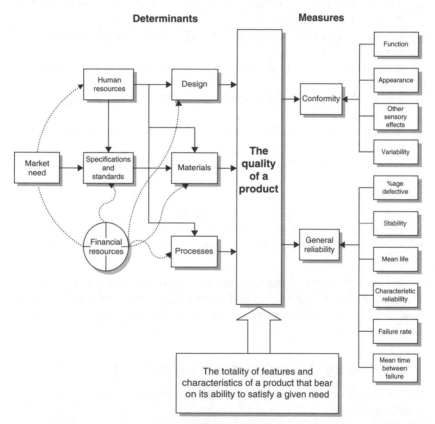

Figure 2.22 Some of the determinants and measurements of the quality of a product. (This is an extract from BS 4778:1979 which has been reproduced with the kind permission of BSI. The 1979 edition has been superseded but these figures are included here since they illustrate the concept.)

2.11.2 Quality Management System approach

Customers require products and/or services that continually meet their needs and expectations and in order to be profitable, an organisation must be able to offer them so that it can continually achieve customer satisfaction and satisfy its customers' requirements. As well as providing a framework for providing customer satisfaction, a QMS also provides confidence (to the organisation and to its customers) that the organisation is capable of providing products and services that consistently fulfil requirements. This is achieved by:

- determining the needs and expectations of the customer;
- establishing the quality policy and quality objectives of the organisation;
- determining the processes and responsibilities necessary to attain the quality objectives;
- establishing measures for the effectiveness of each process towards attaining the quality objectives;
- applying the measures to determine the current effectiveness of each process;
- determining means of preventing non-conformities and eliminating their causes;
- looking for opportunities to improve the effectiveness and efficiency of processes;
- determining and prioritising those improvements which can provide optimum results;
- planning the strategies, processes and resources to deliver the identified improvements;
- implementing the plan;
- monitoring the effects of the improvements;
- assessing the results against the expected outcomes;
- reviewing the improvement activities to determine appropriate follow-up actions.

Note: Any organisation that adopts the above approach will create confidence in the capability of its processes and the reliability of its products. It will also provide a basis for continual improvement and can lead to increased customer satisfaction.

2.11.3 Quality Management System reliability

For an organisation to derive any real benefit from a QMS, everyone in the organisation must:

- fully appreciate that quality assurance is absolutely essential to their future;
- know how they can assist in achieving quality;
- be stimulated and encouraged so to do.

In addition, their organisation's QMS must be fully documented and it must be capable of providing an adequate and uninterrupted control over all internal and external activities that affect the quality of a service or product. This QMS must emphasise all preventive actions that are required to avoid problems recurring and working systems will have to be developed, issued and maintained.

These regulations and requirements will normally be found in the organisation's Quality Manual.

2.11.4 Quality Management System structure

An organisation's QMS defines the policy, organisation, and responsibilities for the management of quality within that organisation. It ensures that all activities comply with an agreed set of rules, regulations and guidelines and that the end product (i.e. the deliverable) conforms to the customer's (i.e. the user's) contractual requirements.

A QMS can only be effective if it is fully documented, understood and followed by all. Within the ISO 9001:2000 Quality Model, there are four levels of documentation, and these are structured as shown in Figure 2.23.

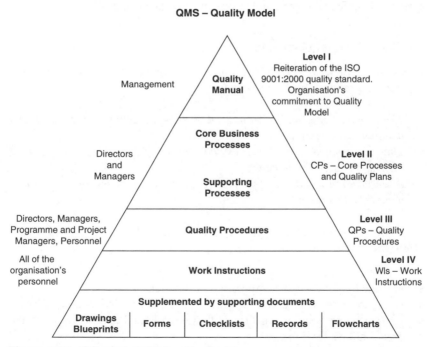

Figure 2.23 ISO 9001:2000 Quality Model

Table 2.1 QMS documentation

Level 1	Quality Manual	The main policy document that establishes the QMS and how it meets the requirements of ISO 9001:2000.
Level 2	Processes	The Core Business Process plus Supporting Processes that describe the activities required to implement the QMS and to meet the policy requirements made in the Quality Manual.
Level 3	Quality Procedures	A description of the method by which quality system activities are managed.
Level 4	Work Instructions	A description of how a specific task is carried out.

2.11.4.1 Quality Manual

This is the main policy document that establishes the QMS and how it meets the requirements of ISO 9001:2000. It provides general information on the system (i.e. objectives, goals, roles, organisation and responsibilities).

ISO 9001:2000 requirements

Clause 4.2.2 of ISO 9001:2000 requires the organisation '*to establish and maintain a quality manual that includes:*

- *The scope of the quality management system, including details of and justification for any exclusions;*
- *The documented procedures established for the quality management system, or reference to them;*
- *A description of the interaction between the process of the quality management system.*'

An organisation's Quality Manual is the formal record of that firm's QMS. It:

- is a rule book by which an organisation functions;
- is a source of information from which the client may derive confidence;
- provides consistent information, both internally and externally, about the organisation's QMS;

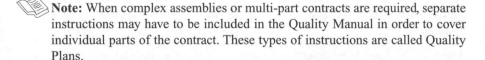

Figure 2.24 Quality Manual

- is a means of defining the responsibilities and interrelated activities of every member of the organisation;
- is a vehicle for auditing, reviewing and evaluating the organisation's QMS.

To be effective:

- the Quality Manual will have to include a firm statement of the organisation's policy towards quality control;
- it must contain details of their quality assurance section, its structure and organisation, together with a description of their responsibilities;
- it must indicate quality assurance training programmes etc.

The Quality Manual will describe how the organisation:

- documents and records inspections;
- how their goods inwards facility operates;
- how they monitor quality.

Note: When complex assemblies or multi-part contracts are required, separate instructions may have to be included in the Quality Manual in order to cover individual parts of the contract. These types of instructions are called Quality Plans.

The Quality Manual will also identify the organisation's business-critical processes and their associated Quality Procedures (QPs) and Work Instructions (WIs). The Quality Manual will also provide examples of the various forms and documentation used by the manufacturer – such as production control forms, inspection sheets and documents used to purchase components from subcontractors.

 Note: For a complete description and guidance on how to develop a Quality Manual, the reader is referred to ISO 10013.

2.11.4.2 Processes

Processes describe the activities required to implement the QMS and to meet the policy requirements made in the Quality Manual. Core Business Processes describe the end-to-end activities involved in project management and are supplemented by a number of supporting processes.

2.11.4.3 Quality procedures

QPs are formal documents that describe the method by which the Core Business and supporting processes are managed.

They describe how the policy objectives of the Quality Manual can be met in practice and how these processes are controlled. They contain the basic documentation used for planning and controlling all activities that impact on quality.

There are two types of procedure, namely:

- system level procedures that are used to detail the activities required to implement the QMS;
- procedures that describe the sequence of processes necessary to ensure the conformity of a product or service.

ISO 9001:2000 requirement

In section 4.2.2 of ISO 9001:2000, the standard requires the organisation to:

establish and maintain a quality manual that includes the documented procedures established for the quality management system.

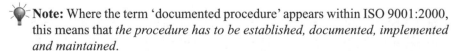**Note:** Where the term 'documented procedure' appears within ISO 9001:2000, this means that *the procedure has to be established, documented, implemented and maintained.*

There is no restriction about how many of these documented procedures an organisation should have to cover company-specific requirements. ISO

9001:2000 does, however, contain a mandatory requirement for formal documented procedures to be produced for:

ISO 9001:2000 section	Intent
1 **Control of documents** (4.2.3)	• Using the wrong version of a design or work instruction can be very costly to a business. Consequently, a process must be developed that ensures you only use the correct version of a document. • These documents must be: – Approved prior to use, – Catalogued to record the current issue in use, – Periodically reviewed to ensure they are still suitable.
2 **Control of quality records** (4.2.4)	• Records are the tangible proof that your management system is being operated correctly. • Records must be kept for a specified period of time, in good condition and readily retrievable. • An organisation's procedure shall detail: – What records are required, – Where they are stored and in what medium, – How they can be retrieved, – Their retention period and method of subsequent disposal.
3 **Internal audits** (8.2.2)	• Internal auditing is an extremely important aspect of ISO 9001:2000 and is intended to prove whether an organisation is doing what they have stated within their management manual. • The written procedure shall identify responsibilities and ensure that non-conformities are actioned without undue delay. • The organisation will also need to provide an audit programme to support the procedure, which will specify the frequency and extent of audits.
4 **Control of non-conforming products** (8.3)	• Defective or damaged products must not be used or delivered to a customer. • An organisation's written procedure must ensure that these non-conforming products are dealt with in one of three ways: – Defect rectification – once a defect is removed, the product must be rechecked against the original specification,

(continued)

ISO 9001:2000 section	Intent
	– Use under concession – a substandard product 'may' be used subject to it being formally authorised (usually with the customer's consent), – Prevention of use – usually achieved through quarantine and subsequent controlled disposal (or destruction).
5 Corrective actions (8.5.2)	● Nothing works perfectly all the time, so when things do go wrong the organisation will need to establish why and find ways to prevent recurrence. ● Once corrective action has been implemented the organisation will also need to review the action to see if it has been effective. ● An organisation's written procedure will, therefore, include the identification, investigation, rectification and verification of corrective action.
6 Preventive actions (8.5.3)	● Preventive action involves predicting the causes of potential failures (non-conformities) before they occur. Clearly preventing a non-conformance is cheaper than rectification after the event. ● There are numerous methods that can be applied but risk assessment is more desirable than a crystal ball! ● As with corrective actions the organisation must record the results of actions taken and review the effect of preventive action.

By implication, documented procedures should also be included for:

1. Customer communications (7.2.3) (which states '*The organisation shall determine and implement effective arrangements for communication with customers*').
2. Purchasing process (7.4.1) (which states '*Criteria for selection, evaluation and re-evaluation shall be established*').

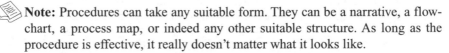 **Note:** Procedures can take any suitable form. They can be a narrative, a flow-chart, a process map, or indeed any other suitable structure. As long as the procedure is effective, it really doesn't matter what it looks like.

Whilst these are the only *written* procedures the standard demands, an organisation is at liberty to set down, in words, as many procedures as they feel appropriate to amplify the detail shown on process maps.

2.11.4.4 Work Instructions

WIs describe in detail how individual tasks and activities are to be carried out, e.g. what is to be done, by whom and when it has to be completed.

2.11.5 Quality Plan

The accepted definition (as provided in ISO 9000:2000) of a Quality Plan is that it is '*a document specifying the QMS elements and the resources to be applied in a specific case*'. In setting out the specific quality practices, resources and sequence of activities relevant to a particular product, project or contract, a Quality Plan, therefore, ensures that specific requirements for quality are appropriately planned and addressed. It should state its purpose, to what it applies its quality objectives (in measurable terms), specific exclusions and, of course, its period of validity.

Quality Plans describe how the QMS is applied to a specific product or contract. They may be used to demonstrate how the quality requirements of a particular contract will be met, and to monitor and assess adherence to those requirements. While a Quality Plan usually refers to the appropriate parts of the Quality Manual, it can be used in conjunction with a QMS or as a stand-alone document.

Figure 2.25 Quality Plan

Note: Quality Plans provide a collated summary of the requirements for a specific activity. They include less information than the organisation's QMS but,
with all the detail brought together, the requirement for performance should be
more readily understandable and the risk of non-conformance and misinterpret-
ation of intentions should be reduced.

Quality assurance for the manufacture of complex assemblies can be very
difficult to stipulate in a contract especially if the most important inspections
have to be left until the assembly is almost complete – and by which time many
of the subassemblies and components will have become almost inaccessible! In
these cases it is essential for the organisation's Quality Manager to develop and
produce a Quality Plan that details all the important information that has to be
provided to the shop floor management.

The Quality Plan will cover all of the quality practices and resources that are
going to be used, the sequence of events relevant to that product, the specific
allocation of responsibilities, methods, QPs and WIs, together with the details
of the testing, inspection, examination and audit programme stages. The
Quality Plan should, nevertheless, be flexible and written in such a way that it
is possible to modify its content to reflect changing circumstances.

The main requirement of a Quality Plan, however, is to provide the customer
(and the workforce) with clear, concise instructions and guidance as well as the
appropriate inspection methods and procedures; the results of inspections
(including rejections) and details of any concessions issued for rework or
repair. All these must be clearly recorded and available for a purchaser's future
(possible) examination.

A well-thought-out Quality Plan will divide the project, service, product or
assembly work into stages, show what type of inspection has to be completed at
the beginning, during, or end of each stage and indicate how these details should
be recorded on the final document. The Quality Plan should be planned and
developed in conjunction with design, development, manufacturing, subcontract
and installation work and ensure that all functions have been fully catered for.

One of the main objectives of quality planning is to identify any special or
unusual requirements, processes, techniques including those requirements that
are unusual by reason of newness, unfamiliarity, lack of experience and/or
absence of precedents. As ISO 9004:2000 points out, if the contract specifies
that Quality Plans are required, then these Quality Plans should fully cover the
following areas and ensure that:

- design, contract, development, manufacturing and installation activities are
  well documented and adequate;
- all controls, processes, inspection equipment, fixtures, tooling, manpower
  resources and skills that an organisation must have to achieve the required
  quality, have been identified, recorded and the necessary action taken to
  obtain any additional components, documentation etc. that is required;
- quality control, inspection and testing techniques (including the development of new instrumentation) have been updated;

- any new measurement technique (or any measurement involving a measurement capability that exceeds the known state of the art) that is required to inspect the product, has been identified and action taken to develop that capability;
- standards of acceptability for all features and requirements (including those which contain a subjective element) have been clearly recorded;
- compatibility of design, manufacturing process, installation, inspection procedures and applicable documentation have been assured well before production begins;
- as each special requirement is identified, the means for testing and being able to prove successfully that the product or service is capable of successfully complying with the requirements has be considered.

 Note: In certain cases (e.g. new techniques), existing inspection practices may be inadequate and new ones will have to be developed.

The integration of special or unusual requirements into the QMS must be carefully investigated, planned and documented.

A Quality Plan is effectively a subset of the actual Quality Manual. The layout of the Quality Plan is very similar to that of the Quality Manual and refers (other than system-specific QPs and WIs) normally to the QPs and Work Instructions contained in that Quality Manual.

The following briefly describes how each of the main requirements of ISO 9001:2000 is covered in a Quality Plan.

2.11.5.1 Management responsibility

The Quality Plan should show who is responsible for:

- ensuring activities are planned, implemented, controlled and monitored;
- communicating requirements and resolving problems;
- reviewing audit results;
- authorising exemption requests;
- implementing corrective action requests.

Where the necessary documentation already exists under the present QMS, the Quality Plan need only refer to a specific situation or specification.

Document and data control

Document and data control should refer to:

- what is provided and how it is controlled;
- how related documents will be identified;
- how and by whom access to the documents can be obtained;
- how and by whom the original documents are reviewed and approved.

Figure 2.26 Management responsibility

Process control

Process control may include:

- the procedures/instructions;
- process steps;
- methods to monitor and control processes;
- service/product characteristics.

The plan could also include details of:

- reference criteria for workmanship;
- special and qualified processes;
- tools, techniques and methods to be used.

Contract review

Contract review should cover:

- when, how and by whom the review is made;
- how the results are to be documented;
- how conflicting instructions or ambiguities are resolved.

Design control

Design control should indicate:

- when, how and by whom the design process, validation and verification of the design output is carried out, controlled and documented;

- any customer involvement;
- applicable codes of practice, standards, specifications and regulatory requirements.

Purchasing

Under the heading of purchasing the following should be indicated:

- the important products to be purchased;
- the source and requirements relating to them;
- the method, evaluation, selection and control of subcontractors;
- the need for a subcontractor's Quality Plan in order to satisfy the regulatory requirements applicable to purchase products/services.

Customer supplied product

Customer supplied products should refer to:

- how they are identified and controlled;
- how they are verified as meeting specified requirements;
- how non-conformance is dealt with.

Product identification and traceability

If traceability is a requirement then the plan should:

- define its scope and extent (including how services/products are identified);
- indicate how contractual and regulatory authority traceability requirements are identified and incorporated into working documents;
- indicate how records are to be generated, controlled and distributed.

Inspection and testing

Inspection and testing should indicate:

- any inspection and test plan;
- how the subcontractor's product shall be verified;
- the location of inspection and test points;
- procedures and acceptance criteria;
- witness verification points (customers as well as regulatory);
- where, when and how the customer requires third parties to perform:
  - type tests;
  - witness testing;
  - service/product verification;
  - material, service/product, process or personnel certification.

Inspection, measuring and test equipment

Inspection, measuring and test equipment should:

- refer to the identity of the equipment;
- refer to the method of calibration;

- indicate and record calibration status and usage of the equipment;
- indicate specific requirements for the identification of inspection and test status.

Non-conforming service/product

Under the heading of nonconforming service/product, an indication should be given:

- of how such a service/product is identified and segregated;
- the degree or type of rework allowed;
- the circumstances under which the supplier can request concessions.

Details should also be provided with respect to:

- corrective and preventive action;
- handling, storage, packaging, preservation and delivery.

Other considerations

Quality Plans should:

- indicate key quality records (i.e. what they are, how long they should be kept, where and by whom;
- suggest how legal or regulatory requirements are to be satisfied;
- specify the form in which records should be kept (e.g. paper, microfilm or disc);
- define liability, storage, retrievability, disposition and confidentiality requirements;
- include the nature and extent of quality audits to be undertaken;
- indicate how the audit results are to used to correct and prevent recurrence of deficiencies;
- show how the training of staff in new or revised operating methods is to be completed.

Where servicing is a specified requirement, suppliers should state their intentions to assure conformance to applicable servicing requirements, such as:

- regulatory and legislative requirements;
- industry codes and practices;
- service level agreements;
- training of customer personnel;
- availability of initial and ongoing support during the agreed time period;
- statistical techniques, where relevant.

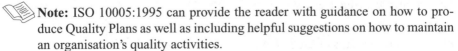 **Note:** ISO 10005:1995 can provide the reader with guidance on how to produce Quality Plans as well as including helpful suggestions on how to maintain an organisation's quality activities.

2.11.6 Quality records

Quality records provide objective evidence of activities performed or results achieved.

Records of QMS inspections and tests concerning the design, testing, survey, audit and review of a product or service are the evidence that a supplier is capable of and is indeed meeting the quality requirements of the customer.

Records such as QMS audit reports, calibration of test and measuring equipment, inspections, tests, approvals, concessions, etc., ensure that an organisation is capable of proving the effectiveness of their QMS.

Records, therefore, are important parts of quality management and the QMS will have to identify exactly what type of record is to be made, at what stage of the production process they should be made and who should make them etc. To be of any real value it is essential that these records are covered by clear, concise instructions and procedures. Above all, the storage of records should be systematic and capable of being easily and quickly accessed.

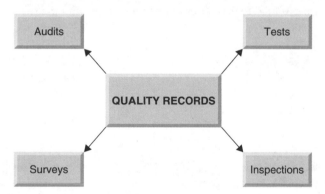

Figure 2.27 Quality records

Having agreed and decided on the necessity for records, the next step is to:

- establish methods for making changes, modifications, revisions and additions to these records;
- establish methods for accounting for the documents;
- show their retention time;
- lay down methods for the disposal of those that are superseded or become out of date;
- show how they should be stored.

These procedures would be written up as QPs and will normally form part of the Quality Manual. WIs should also be available to show how important it is to keep records of defects, diagnosis of their causes and details of the corrective action that was carried out together with the success or failure of this corrective action.

If this information is stored in a computer, then it is essential that the integrity of that system **must** also be satisfactorily assured.

The retention of records is an aspect that is far too often overlooked by organisations. Records are very important, not only from a historical point of view, but also as a means to settling disputes about bad workmanship, identifying faults and settling production problems whether this be internally, by the supplier, or externally, by the organisation.

2.12 Quality organisational structure

2.12.1 Management

The main requirement of the organisation's management is that they establish, define and document their organisation's policy, objectives and commitments to quality. This document must include details of the organisation's Quality Management System (QMS) and the aims, policies, organisation and procedures that are essential to demonstrate that they agree with the requirements of ISO 9001:2000.

Figure 2.28 Quality organisational requirements

Having established their overall position, the management will then have to:

- develop, control, co-ordinate, supervise and monitor their corporate quality policy and ensure that this policy is understood and maintained throughout the organisation;
- ensure that the organisation's QMS always meets the requirements of the national, European or international standard that that particular organisation has chosen to work to and where this fails to happen, see that corrective actions are carried out;
- define objectives such as fitness for use;
- ensure that the performance, safety and reliability of a product or service is correct and make sure that the costs associated with these objectives are kept to a reasonable figure.

Note: Organisations having difficulty in establishing their own particular level of managerial responsibility with regard to organisation quality assurance should obtain a copies of BS 6143:1992 'Guide to the economics of quality' Parts 1 and 2. These standards are available from the BSI and are a user-friendly guide to:

- the costs for continuous improvement and Total Quality Management (TQM) (Part 1);
- the costs of defect prevention and a study of the various activities and losses due to internal or external failures (Part 2).

2.12.2 The Quality Manager

Quality assurance is concerned with a consistency of quality and an agreed level of quality. To achieve these aims the organisation must be firmly committed to the fundamental principle of consistently supplying the right quality product. Equally, a purchaser must be committed to the fundamental principle of only accepting the right quality product.

Thus, a commitment within all levels of an organisation (manufacturer, supplier or purchaser) to the basic principles of quality assurance and quality control is required. It is, therefore, essential that the management representative, who is completely independent of all other responsibilities, deals solely with quality matters. This person is called the 'Quality Manager'.

The Quality Manager will answer directly to the Managing Director and will be responsible for all matters regarding the quality of the end product together with the activities of **all** sections within the organisation's premises.

In small organisations this requirement might even be part of the General Manager's duties, but regardless of who it may be, it is essential that this person must be someone who is completely independent of any manufacturing or user function and has a thorough working knowledge of the requirements and recommendations of ISO 9001:2000.

In addition, owing to the importance of quality assurance, it is essential that the Quality Manager is fully qualified (both technically and administratively) and can quickly exert (show) his position and authority.

The Quality Manager's job is usually a very busy one (even in a small organisation!), and the Quality Manager's responsibilities are spread over a wide area which covers all of the organisation's operations.

2.12.2.1 General functional description

The Quality Manager is responsible for ensuring that the organisation's QMS is defined, implemented, audited and monitored in order to ensure that the organisation's deliverables comply with both the customer's quality and safety standards together with the requirements of ISO 9001:2000.

2.12.2.2 Tasks

The Quality Manager reports directly to the general manager and his tasks will include:

- ensuring the consistency of the organisation's QMS;
- ensuring compliance of the organisation's QMS with ISO 9001:2000;
- maintenance and effectiveness of the organisation's QMS;
- ensuring that the quality message is transmitted to and understood by everyone.

2.12.2.3 Responsibilities

- The Quality Manager is responsible for:
- ensuring that the Quality Manual and individual Quality Plans are kept up to date;
- assisting and advising with the preparation of organisation procedures;
- producing, reviewing and updating the organisation QMS;
- ensuring compliance with the organisation QMS by means of frequent audits;
- maintaining organisation quality records;
- producing, auditing and maintaining division, section and project Quality Plans;
- identifying potential/current problem areas within the organisation's life-cycle through analysis of organisation error reports;
- holding regular division quality audits.

2.12.2.4   Co-ordination

The Quality Manager shall:

- act as the focal point for all organisation quality matters within the organisation;
- co-ordinate and verify all internal procedures and instructions are in accordance with the recommendations of ISO 9001:2000;
- operate the QMS as described in the Quality Manual and ensure that its regulations are observed.

Above all the Quality Manager must always ensure that the customer's interests are protected. Even if this means, at times, that he and his division become very unpopular with the rest of the organisation and sometimes they even have to assume the mantel of organisation 'scapegoat'!

3

ISO 9001:2000 checklists

Since the introduction of ISO 9001:2000 there are certain sections of the industry that see compliance auditing as being no longer 'fashionable' and performance auditing is the only way forward. Compliance auditing is, however, a mandatory requirement under clause 8.2.2 which clearly states that '*The organisation shall conduct internal audits at planned intervals to determine whether the quality management system **conforms** to the planned arrangements **to the requirements of this international standard** and the quality management system requirements established by the organisation.*'

This is amplified in clause 6.4.3 of ISO 19011:2002 ('*Guidelines for quality and/or environmental management systems auditing*') which states:

> *The audit team members should review information relevant to their audit assignment and prepare work documents as necessary for reference and for recording audit proceedings. Such documents may include:*
>
> - *Checklists and audit sampling plans, and*
> - *Forms for recording information, such as supporting evidence, audit findings and records of meetings.*
>
> *The use of checklists and forms should not restrict the extent of audit activities, which can change as a result of information collected during the audit.*

Thus, creating an auditing system will require putting together audit checklists.

Whilst not always required by management system standards, audit checklists (composed of items relating to both compliance with the requirements of the standard and items that check the performance of the organisation's processes) are just one tool available from the 'auditor's toolbox'. Most auditors will find it beneficial to audit from the organisation's quality management system up to the ISO 9001:2000 requirements as shown in Figure 3.1.

Alternatively, a checklist may be used to ensure that all the relevant ISO 9001:2000 requirements have been addressed in the management system.

There are both advantages and disadvantages to using audit checklists. It depends on many factors, including customer needs, time and cost restraints, auditor experience and sector scheme requirements. Auditors should therefore

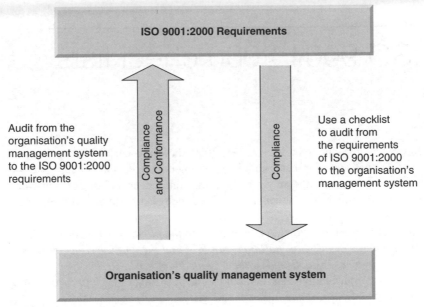

Figure 3.1 Example auditing approach

assess the value of the checklist as an aid in audit process and consider its use as a functional tool.

Advantages of using an audit checklist

Checklists, if developed for a specific audit and used correctly, can:

- act as a sampling plan and time manager;
- be provided to the auditee ahead of the on-site audit;
- be used as an information base for planning future audits;
- ensure a consistent audit approach;
- ensure that adequate evidence is obtained;
- ensure that the audit scope is being followed;
- help an auditor to perform better during the audit process;
- help to ensure that an audit is conducted in a systematic and comprehensive manner;
- provide a means of communication and a place to record data for use for future reference;
- provide a repository for notes collected during the audit process (i.e. audit field notes);
- provide a record that the QMS was examined;

- provide objective evidence that the audit was performed;
- provide structure and continuity to an audit;
- serve as a memory aid.

Disadvantages of using an audit checklist

When audit checklists are not available, or poorly prepared, the following disadvantages can happen and should be taken into consideration:

- an inexperienced auditor may not be able to clearly communicate what he is looking for;
- checklists can be restrictive if used as the auditor's only support mechanism;
- checklists should not be a substitute for audit planning;
- generic checklists, which do not reflect the specific organisational management system, may not add any value and may interfere with the audit;
- poorly prepared checklists can slow down an audit due to duplication and repetition;
- the focus of the checklist may be too narrow in scope to identify specific problem areas.

Note: Checklists can be seen as intimidating to the person(s) being audited!

There now follows a number of sections that have been constructed with the specific aim of assisting auditors to complete internal and external audits. They consist of:

3.1	**ISO 9001:2000 headings**	A complete listing of the sections and subsections making up ISO 9001:2000 requirements together with a brief explanation of their requirements.
3.2	**ISO 9001:2000 – explanation and likely documentation**	A brief explanation of the specific requirements (i.e. the 'shalls') of each element of ISO 9001:2000 together with a description of the likely documentation that an organisation would need to have in place to meet the requirements.
3.3	**ISO 9001:2000 – organisational requirements**	A summary of how an organisation is expected to work in conformance with the requirements and recommendations of ISO 9001:2000.

3.4	**ISO 9001:2000 – management requirements**	Complete details of all the mandatory requirements listed in ISO 9001:2000 for top management (totalling 21) together with those (over 250) for the general management of an organisation.
3.5	**ISO 9001:2000 audit questionnaire**	An indication of areas of an organisation's QMS that could be looked at and possibly further investigated during internal, external and/or third party audits.
3.6	**Additional (general purpose) audit checks**	Lists of some of the most important questions that an external auditor would be likely to ask when assessing an organisation's QMS for conformance to ISO 9001:2000.
3.7	**Stage audit check sheet**	List of the most important questions that an external auditor is likely to ask when evaluating an organisation for their: ● design stage; ● manufacturing stage; ● acceptance stage; ● in-service stage.
3.8	**Complete index for ISO 9001:2000**	A listing of all the main topics and subjects covered in ISO 9001:2000.
3.9	**ISO 9001:2000 crosscheck and correspondence**	The intention of this form is to show how and where the requirements of ISO 9001:2000 have been met in an organisation's quality management system.
3.10	**Audit check sheet**	A list of the most important questions an auditor should ask.
3.11	**Comparison between ISO 9001:2000 and ISO 9001:1994**	A complete list of the sections and subsections making up ISO 9001:2000 requirements cross-referenced to the previous ISO 9001:1994 elements.
3.12	**Counter-comparison between ISO 9001:1994 and ISO 9001:2000**	A complete list of the elements making up ISO 9001:1994 cross-referenced to the sections and subsections of ISO 9001:2000.

3.13	**A selection of audit forms**	A selection of forms used by auditors (File 58).
3.14	**ISO 9001:2000 – elements covered and outstanding**	A checklist used by auditors to confirm that the client's QMS fully covers the requirements (i.e. clauses) of ISO 9001:2000.
3.15	**Acronyms and abbreviations used in quality**	An extensive list of acronyms and abbreviations encountered by auditors.
3.16	**Glossary of terms used in quality**	An extensive list of terms and conditions used in quality management.
3.17	**References**	A guide to the most common publications and references for quality management.

 Note: To save you having to photocopy these checklists, explanations and questionnaires (and/or having to type them all out again), 'unlocked', fully accessible, non-.pdf, soft copies of all these files (plus copies of the generic example Quality Manual, Business Processes and Quality Procedures from the sister publication *ISO 9001:2000 for Small Businesses*, third edn) are available on a CD (for a small additional charge) from the author. He can be contacted at ray@herne.org.uk.

3.1 ISO 9001:2000 – headings

ISO 9001 is the only standard within the 2000 edition to which an organisation can be certified. It includes all the key points from the previous 20 elements of ISO 9001:1994 and integrates them into four major generic business processes, namely:

- **Management responsibility**
  (policy, objectives, planning, responsibilities and system review).
- **Resource management**
  (human resources, training, facilities and work environment).
- **Product realisation**
  (customer focus, design and development, purchasing, production, verification and validation).
- **Measurement, analysis and improvement**
  (internal audit, process/product control and continual improvement).

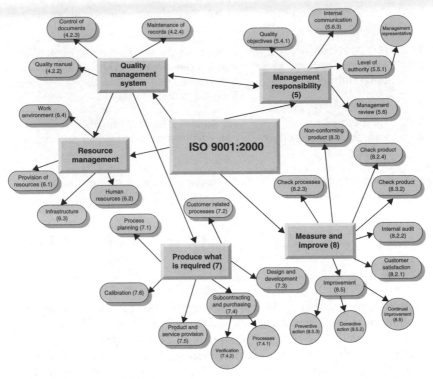

Figure 3.2 ISO 9001:2000

In outline, the structure of the standard is as follows:

1   Scope
This clause provides an overview of the standard.

1.1   General
       A description of what the standard covers and explanation of its primary
       objectives.

1.2   Application
       It is possible that due to the nature of the product that an organisation pro-
       vides (or manufactures) that some of the sub-clauses within Clause 7
       may not be applicable and can be excluded. In all cases, they may be
       excluded, **provided** that the reason(s) why they are not entirely applica-
       ble to that particular organisation are fully documented in the organisa-
       tion's Quality Manual.

2   Normative reference

Details of all the standards that form a **mandatory** input to ISO 9001:2000 are listed here.

3   Terms and definitions

This clause confirms the use of the term 'Organisation' (instead of 'Supplier') in ISO 9001:2000.

4   Quality Management System

Clause 4 of ISO 9001:2000 contains the basic requirements for an organisation to establish, document, implement, maintain and continually improve its Quality Management System (QMS) in accordance with the requirements of this standard.

4.1   General requirements

   The QMS needs to address some basic areas. Organisations need to consider who will have ultimate responsibility for the system, look at what kinds of resources will be needed, agree how to measure the quality of their processes (and their product) and implement actions to ensure that desired results will be achieved.

4.2   Documentation requirements

4.2.1   General

   Organisations need to document – either electronically or on paper – their quality policy, aims and objectives. The types of areas that need to be looked at specifically are procedures, planning, and operations and organisations need to describe what they do to control quality in these particular areas. Organisations will also need to retain quality records that would prove that a procedure has been followed (e.g. inventory control listings, travellers, work orders, signed contracts, etc.). There are no specific requirements regarding the type or size of the documentation. It can vary from one organisation to another depending on its size, its type of activities, and/or the complexity of its processes.

4.2.2   Quality Manual

   The Quality Manual is at the very heart of an organisation's quality management system and should document the organisation's aims, policies and objectives with regard to their business and how they propose doing it. It should describe how procedures interact with organisations' QMS and how they achieve the desired results.

4.2.3   Control of documents

The organisation needs to ensure that all of the documents in their QMS have been appropriately identified, reviewed, authorised, issued and distributed. They need to ensure that old and/or obsolete documents are not being used and (if required for future use) they are stored in a secure location. Organisations also need to make sure that any external documents that they use in their QMS are identified within their system and that access to these documents is controlled and restricted.

4.2.4   Control of records

Organisations need to make sure that the documents that they retain prove that their QMS is doing what they say it should. These documents must be legible and easily retrievable and organisations must have a consistent policy for retaining both active and inactive documents.

5   Management responsibility

Clause 5 covers management commitment, customer satisfaction, quality policy, planning, administration (e.g. the appointment of a management representative) and management review.

5.1   Management commitment

ISO 9001:2000 recognises and requires that an organisation's top management needs to be involved and committed to implementing an effective quality programme and begins by assigning top management with responsibility for:

- overseeing the creation of QMS;
- communicating its requirements with all responsible parties;
- making sure there are adequate resources committed to the operation of the QMS;
- completing a review procedure to make sure the QMS is operating as planned.

5.2   Customer focus

Top management should make sure that the QMS identifies customer requirements in each important area of service or product delivery and that the QMS has a procedure in place for ensuring that customer requirements are fulfilled. The goal of any QMS should be to improve customer satisfaction.

5.3   Quality policy

The organisation's quality policy should identify the main goals of the QMS and explain why the organisation is adopting them. Depending on the organisation (and its type of product or service) this quality policy may just be a very simple statement outlining the goals to be met, or it can be a more detailed document defining the goals, objectives and responsible parties of each area covered by ISO 9001:2000. In order to conform to the standard, a quality policy must ensure that it:

- is appropriate to the organisation's purpose;
- is communicated throughout the organisation;
- is reviewed for suitability;
- strives to improve its effectiveness;
- complies with customer requirements.

5.4 Planning

This clause requires an organisation to list its objectives and show how it intends to achieve these objectives.

5.4.1 Quality objectives

The organisation should ensure measurable and consistent quality objectives are established and communicated throughout their organisation.

5.4.2 Quality management system planning

The organisation should ensure that it addresses and achieves the goals that the organisation has set out in their QMS and strive for continuous improvement and customer satisfaction.

5.5 Responsibility, authority and communication

This clause shows how an organisation should document and administer its QMS.

5.5.1 Responsibility and authority

Effective communication and management can only be achieved if everyone knows what their responsibilities are and whom they report to. To accomplish this goal, it is important that the organisation's QMS identifies responsible parties and describes how much authority they have.

5.5.2 Management representative

The organisation will need to appoint someone who has operational responsibility for the organisation's QMS. This individual (normally referred to as the Quality Manager) is responsible for the following:

- ensuring that the processes required for the organisation's QMS are established, implemented and maintained;
- reporting on the performance of the QMS and improvements needed;
- promoting awareness of customer requirements throughout the organisation.

5.5.3   Internal communication
Organisations will need to set up an effective system of communication between management and employees with respect to implementing the organisation's QMS and will need to allow for feedback from the employees to management.

5.6   Management review
This clause covers how top management reviews the organisation's QMS.

5.6.1   General
To monitor the QMS, top management will have to review certain aspects of the QMS to make sure that the goals are being achieved and to look for ways of improving the QMS. These meetings need to be documented so as to indicate when they took place and what was discussed.

5.6.2   Review input
Regularly scheduled management review meetings should be held. These meetings should address the following areas:

- internal audit results;
- customer feedback;
- the effectiveness of processes and products;
- the status of previously identified problems;
- items identified for follow-up in previous management reviews;
- planned process or product changes that could affect quality;
- recommendations for improvement generated through the operation of the QMS;
- employee feedback;
- outstanding actions from previous management meetings.

5.6.3   Review output
After a management review meeting has been held, follow-up actions should be taken if, as a result of the meeting, top management decided that the effectiveness of the QMS could be improved. These improvements could mean that customer requirements could be better evaluated or better met, and/or that there is a need for additional resources to support the QMS.

6   Resource management
Clause 6 covers the provision of resources, infrastructure, human resources, dissemination of information, work environment and facilities.

6.1   Provision of resources
        The organisation has a responsibility to make sure that resources are
        sufficient to implement and maintain the QMS and that enough
        resources are available to make sure that the goals of continuous
        improvement and meeting customer satisfaction are also met.

6.2   Human resources
        Clause 6.2 covers how human resources to implement and improve the
        QMS are identified.

6.2.1   General
        The organisation must assess the skills and competencies of their
        employees and should consider whether they have the skills and abili-
        ties to perform the tasks that have been assigned to them in the organi-
        sation's QMS.

         Note: Organisations should pay particular attention to prior
        education, training and experience.

6.2.2   Competence, awareness and training
        An organisation has a responsibility to see that their employees have
        sufficient training to be effective in all the tasks that have been assigned
        to them. This can either be accomplished by hiring trained and compe-
        tent personnel or ensuring that they have a plan in place for providing
        training where there may be gaps in needed skills and for bringing new
        needed skills to an organisation's existing workforce. The assessment
        of employees' skills, training plans and actual training provided must
        all be documented.

6.3   Infrastructure
        The infrastructure for a QMS can be described as including the work-
        space, the equipment and the supporting services involved in creating
        the organisation's products or services. The organisation will need to
        determine, provide and maintain the infrastructure needed to achieve
        the planned results.

6.4   Work environment
        The work environment of an organisation needs to enable (and enhance)
        the ability of employees to perform effectively in order to meet quality
        expectations. Elements of a good work environment include the following:

        ● ability of the employee to be creative and become involved;
        ● clean work areas;

- proper safety rules and equipment;
- ergonomically appropriate work areas;
- pollution control;
- ability to interact with others.

7   Product realisation

Clause 7 covers customer-related processes, design and development, purchasing, production and service operation.

7.1   Planning of product realisation

Product realisation deals with the steps and processes that the organisation goes through in order to deliver their finished product or service. This approach must be planned and the important steps and stages must be documented.

7.2   Customer-related processes

The clause covers the identification, review and interaction with customers and customer requirements.

7.2.1   Determination of requirements related to the product

ISO 9001:2000 requires an organisation to assess their product and process requirements.

 Note: These requirements could come from the customer, could be mandated by law or could be generally accepted standards within the organisation's industry.

7.2.2   Review of requirements related to the product

After an organisation has determined what the product or service requirements are, the organisation needs to make sure that they are actually capable of meeting these requirements. The normal sequence to perform this review would be to make sure:

- the requirements are defined;
- the organisation has the ability to meet the requirements;
- process or production changes are reviewed and documented.

7.2.3   Customer communication

Organisations should make sure that their customers have (readily available) sufficient information regarding their product, the status of contract negotiations, handling of orders and how customers (i.e. the customer) can provide feedback to organisations or express any complaints.

7.3   Design and development
Clause 7.3 covers the availability of an organisational process to control design and development stages within an organisation.

7.3.1   Design and development planning
In order to effectively plan the design and development process, organisations need to follow three steps:

*   clearly define the stages involved in the process;
*   identify the responsible parties for each of those stages;
*   review that these responsibilities have been carried out effectively.

7.3.2   Design and development inputs
In order to properly design and develop an effective product or service organisations must consider all relevant factors as well as addressing the marketability of the product or service. Critical areas that an organisation should consider include performance, legal and regulatory requirements together with any other requirements, such as industry, or organisation standard practices.

7.3.3   Design and development outputs
Information included in the output of design and development should include sufficient information to show that the requirements specified in the inputs document are being met by the product as designed and how potential risks have been mitigated. It should also include information on how the product is to be built, including such things as specifications, purchasing, testing, the records and documentation required during manufacturing, training requirements, user and customer information together with any other information needed by the organisation to build and use the product so that it meets the requirements. This process should be documented and approved.

7.3.4   Design and development review
After organisations have determined what the design and development requirements are, they need to review them to make sure that they are capable of meeting these requirements. Employees who have been involved in the process should be used to perform this review and determine that the design and development processes are in fact meeting the requirements, problems are identified and solutions are

proposed. Organisations need to retain records of design and development review.

7.3.5   Design and development verification
Once organisations have planned and reviewed the design and development process, they need to test, or verify, that the final output did in fact meet the requirements. There are a variety of methods that organisations can use to perform these tests and an organisation's particular situation will dictate the best method to use. Organisations must maintain the records of the test results together with any follow-up actions that have, or are going to be, taken.

7.3.6   Design and development validation
After the design outputs have been verified, validation is performed under actual operating conditions. If the product has multiple uses, each use should be validated separately using the validation methods defined in the design output. Whenever possible, the validation of a new product or service should be performed prior to delivery to the customer!

7.3.7   Control of design and development changes
Initial designs are often changed to accommodate custom orders, to try to improve performance, to accommodate a changing input component, or for some other valid reason. The standard requires organisations to identify and document these engineering change requests. Organisations also need to analyse proposed changes prior to implementation and consider what the total impact of the changes may be. Organisations will need to maintain records of these analyses, and any follow-up actions taken.

7.4   Purchasing
Clause 7.4 covers how an organisation should ensure that product specifications are fulfilled and that the finalised product meets the original input requirements.

7.4.1   Purchasing process
Organisations will need to have a controlled process for dealing with their suppliers. An organisation's purchasing group will need to establish criteria for how they evaluate and choose their organisation's vendors. These criteria should be based on the suppliers' ability to meet their organisation's order specifications. Organisations will need to

have procedures for making sure that the purchased product meets their organisation's specifications and must maintain records that show how the purchased product was evaluated and what they did when they discovered problems.

7.4.2   Purchasing information
Purchasing information describes the product to be purchased and can be included on contracts, purchase orders or other documents. Organisations should also describe any particular conditions for the purchasing information to comply with specific requirements in the organisation's QMS.

7.4.3   Verification of purchased product
Organisations will need to put in place inspection procedures, when and where appropriate, to determine that the purchased products and services ordered meet organisations' predetermined specifications. Organisations will need to complete a test (to some degree) in order to ensure that these specifications have been met and the results of these tests will need to be documented.

7.5   Production and service provision
Clause 7.5 covers the availability of a process to cover all the organisation's production and service operations.

7.5.1   Control of production and service provision
Planning and production activities should take place in a controlled environment (i.e. an environment where all of the organisation's employees have access to and instructions on how to do their jobs and have all the equipment necessary to assemble and test the product or deliver the service).

 Note: This controlled environment should exist from the time product requirements are developed to the time the product or service is delivered.

7.5.2   Validation of processes for production and service provision
Validation demonstrates that proper application of the processes can achieve the planned results. When it is not possible to verify the finished good or service through monitoring or measurement, an organisation's QMS should call for validation. Validation is particularly important where deficiencies cannot be identified until the product is in use, or the service is delivered. When validation is appropriate, an

organisation's QMS will need to define the criteria for the following areas involved in the process:

- approval of validation procedures and equipment;
- qualification of personnel;
- backup plan if validation fails.

7.5.3   Identification and traceability
When a product is being tested or measured, at any point in the production cycle, it must be identified. This identification should provide for traceability or the ability to follow the product throughout the production process, both physically and through documentation.

7.5.4   Customer property
Special care must be taken when a customer provides organisations with their property for use, or incorporation into, the product. Organisations will need to identify and protect any customer property provided and maintain records of lost, damaged or unsuitable customer property.

7.5.5   Preservation of product
The standard requires organisations to maintain procedures for the handling, storage, packaging, preservation and delivery of parts and products throughout all processes.

7.6   Control of monitoring and measuring devices
This clause covers the controls that an organisation has in place to ensure that equipment (including software) used for proving conformance to specified requirements is properly maintained.

8   **Measurement, analysis and improvement**
Clause 8 covers internal audits, customer satisfaction, corrective and preventive action, continual improvement and control of non-conformity.

8.1   General
In order to determine that an organisation's QMS is improving, organisations will have to develop some form of monitoring and measurement technique(s) to measure its effectiveness. Once an organisation has developed these techniques, they will need to demonstrate that the QMS is in fact increasing in effectiveness.

8.2   Monitoring and measurement
        Clause 8.2 concerns the analysis of customer satisfaction and the control of products and processes.

8.2.1   Customer satisfaction
        Since one of the goals of an organisation's QMS is to meet customer requirements, organisations will need to determine how they will measure customers' satisfaction against their organisation's product or service.

8.2.2   Internal audit
        Internal audits, in the most basic sense, are double checks performed by an organisation's own personnel to determine that required procedures are being followed. ISO 9001:2000 requires organisations to perform such internal audits on each area covered by their organisation's QMS. All audits must be documented and address the following:

        ● scope (what areas are to be tested and to what degree they will be tested);
        ● methods to be used (such as interview or review of documentation);
        ● who is responsible to perform the audit.

8.2.3   Monitoring and measurement of processes
        ISO 9001:2000 requires organisations to measure that their processes produce desired results. If planned results are not achieved, corrective action must be taken and the effectiveness of the processes must be examined.

8.2.4   Monitoring and measurement of product
        During the production process, organisations will need to monitor and measure the product in order to determine that requirements are met. Organisations will need to document the following:

        ● the product meets acceptance criteria;
        ● the product is reviewed prior to release;
        ● the person who authorised the product to be released to the customer.

8.3   Control of non-conforming product
        Non-conforming product is any product or service that does not measure up to requirements. Non-conforming product can be identified at

any point in the production process (e.g. upon receipt of raw materials, finished goods inspection or anywhere in between) and organisations will need to define and document procedures to control, identify and prevent use of non-conforming products. As far as practicable, organisations will need to control non-conforming products by taking action to eliminate or correct them and must maintain records documenting processes and actions taken.

8.4   Analysis of data
ISO 9001:2000 requires organisations to collect information on the functionality of their QMS and to analyse the information collected in order to evaluate the effectiveness and efficiency of their system. Information collected and analysed should include information related to specific quality objectives (such as ensuring that customer requirements are met, continuously improving their QMS and evaluating the performance of their suppliers).

 Note: Statistics should be used when appropriate to control processes and product characteristics.

8.5   Improvement
Clause 8.5 covers how an organisation controls corrective and preventive actions and how they ensure the continual improvement of their product.

8.5.1   Continual improvement
As added emphasis, the goal of achieving a continuously improving QMS is restated in this particular clause.

8.5.2   Corrective action
Corrective action requests (commonly referred to by the acronym CAR) are controlled documents that reflect the actions taken to fix problems related to an organisation's QMS. These problems can be 'non-conformances' where the QMS does not measure up to the requirements of ISO 9001:2000 or, more commonly, problems that have occurred as the organisation goes about producing its finished goods or services. Effective corrective action must be documented and call for the following:

●   identifying the problem;
●   examining the root cause of the problem;
●   putting a plan in place to prevent recurrence;
●   evaluating the effectiveness of the plan.

8.5.3   Preventive action
The same actions taken in performing corrective actions should also be taken with respect to preventive actions. Effective preventive action calls for the identification of potential problems that are likely to occur and setting in place a process for preventing it from happening to the detriment of the product. Preventive action will include identifying the potential problem, examining the root cause, putting a plan in place to prevent recurrence and evaluating the effectiveness of the plan.

 Note: Naturally, all of the above must be documented.

3.2 ISO 9001:2000 – explanation and likely documentation

The following is a brief explanation of the specific requirements (i.e. the 'shalls') of each element of ISO 9001:2000 together with a description of the likely documentation that an organisation would need to have in place to meet the requirements.

Clause No.	ISO 9001:2000 title	Explanation	Likely documentation
4	Quality Management System		
4.1	General requirements	A definition of the processes necessary to ensure that a product conforms to customer requirements and that they are capable of being implemented, maintained and improved.	• Core Business Processes supplemented by: – Supporting Processes; – QPs; – WIs.
4.2	Documentation requirements		
4.2.1	General	Documented proof of a Quality Management System.	• Quality Manual. • High level policy statement on organisational objectives and quality policy. • Procedures. • Quality records.
4.2.2	Quality Manual	A document which describes an organisation's quality policies, procedures and practices that make up the QMS.	• A Quality Manual containing everything related to quality controls within an organisation.

(continued)

Clause No.	ISO 9001:2000 title	Explanation	Likely documentation
4.2.3	Control of documents	How an organisation's documents are approved, issued, numbered, etc. How revisions are recorded and implemented and obsolete documents removed.	• Document control procedures.
4.2.4	Control of records	What quality records need to be kept to demonstrate conformance with the requirements of an organisation's QMS and how they are identified, stored, protected, etc.	• Record keeping procedures.
5	Management responsibility	Management responsibility and quality requirements.	• Quality Manual.

5.1	Management commitment	A written demonstration of an organisation's commitment to:
		• sustaining and increasing customer satisfaction;
		• establishing quality policies, objectives and planning;
		• establishing a QMS;
		• performing management reviews;
		• ensuring availability of resources;
		• determining the legal and mandatory requirements its products and/or services have to meet;
		• continuous improvement.
			• High level policy statement on organisational objectives and quality policies.
			• A list of Government regulatory, legal and customer-specific requirements.
			• Procedures describing:
			  – resource management;
			  – contract review procedures;
			  – management reviews;
			  – financial business plan(s).

5.2	Customer focus	How an organisation ensures that customer needs, expectations and requirements are determined, fully understood and met.	• Procedures describing:
			  – resource management;
			  – contract review procedures;
			  – management reviews;
			  – financial business plan(s).

5.3	Quality policy	How an organisation approaches quality and the requirements for meeting them, ensuring that: • they are appropriate for both customer and organisation; • there is a commitment to continually meet customer requirements;	• High level managerial statement on an organisation's quality policy containing clear responsibilities, training and resources required for each organisational activity.

Clause No.	ISO 9001:2000 title	Explanation	Likely documentation
		• these commitments are communicated, understood and implemented throughout an organisation; • there is a commitment for continual improvement.	
5.4	Planning	The planning of resources, etc. to meet an organisation's overall business objectives.	• Quality Manual.
5.4.1	Quality objectives	The quality objectives that an organisation expects to achieve within each function and level of the organisation.	• Policy statements defining the objectives of the company and those responsible for achieving the objectives.
5.4.2	Quality Management System planning	The identification and planning of activities and resources required to meet an organisation's quality objectives.	• The processes and procedures used by senior management to define and plan the way that the organisation is run.
5.5	Responsibility, authority and communication	How the organisation has documented its QMS.	• A Quality Manual containing everything related to quality controls within the organisation.
5.5.1	Responsibility and authority	A definition of the roles, responsibilities, lines of authority, reporting and communication relevant to quality.	• Job descriptions and responsibilities. • Organisation charts showing lines of communication.
5.5.2	Management representative	The identification and appointment of a 'Quality Manager' with responsibility for the QMS.	• Job description and responsibilities. • Organisation charts showing lines of communication.
5.5.3	Internal communication	How the requirements of an organisation's QMS are communicated throughout the company.	• Team briefings, organisational meetings, notice boards, in-house journals/magazines, audio-visual and other forms of e-information.

5.6	Management review	How senior management reviews the QMS to ensure its continued suitability, adequacy and effectiveness (in the context of an organisation's strategic planning cycle).	• Procedures concerning:
			  – process, product and/or service audit procedures;
			  – customer feedback;
			  – process and product performance;

(continued)

Clause No.	ISO 9001:2000 title	Explanation	Likely documentation
			– corrective and preventive action; – supplier performance; – record keeping.
5.6.1	General	The requirement for management to establish a process for the periodic review of the QMS.	• Management review and QMS audit procedures.
5.6.2	Review input	The documents and information required for management reviews.	• Results of audits, customer feedback, analysis of process performance and product conformance, corrective and preventive action reports and supplier performance records.
5.6.3	Review output	Result of the review.	• Minutes of the meetings where the overall running of the company is discussed.
6	Resource management	A description of resources with regard to training, induction, responsibilities, working environment, equipment requirements, maintenance, etc.	• Quality Procedures. • Quality Plans. • Work Instructions.
6.1	Provision of resources	How resource needs (i.e. human, materials, equipment, infrastructure) are identified.	• Quality Plans identifying the resources required to complete a particular project or activity.
6.2	Human resources	Identification and assignment of human resources to implement and improve the QMS and comply with contract conditions.	• Quality Procedures. • Quality Plans. • Work Instructions.
6.2.1	General	How an organisation assigns personnel on the basis of competency, qualification, training, skills and experience relevant to specific tasks.	• Job descriptions and responsibilities. • Training records. • Staff evaluations. • Project plans identifying the human resources required to complete the task.
6.2.2	Competence, awareness and training	Documents showing how an organisation selects, trains and assigns personnel to specific tasks.	• System level procedures for: – training; – staff evaluations; – review of work assignments; – staff assessments; – records.

Clause No.	ISO 9001:2000 title	Explanation	Likely documentation
6.3	Infrastructure	How an organisation defines, provides and maintains the infrastructure requirements to ensure product conformity (e.g. infrastructure, plant, hardware, software, tools and equipment, communication facilities, transport and supporting services, etc.).	• Policies, procedures and regulatory documents stating the infrastructure requirements of an organisation and/or their customers. • Financial documents. • Maintenance plans. • Project plans identifying the human resources required to complete the task.
6.4	Work environment	How an organisation defines and implements the human and physical factors of the work environment required to ensure product conformity (health and safety, work methods, ethics and ambient working conditions).	• Environmental procedures. • Project Plans. • Budgetary and legal processes and procedures.
7	Product realisation	The requirements for process control, purchasing, handling and storage, measuring devices, etc.	• Quality Manual and associated Processes, QPs, Quality Plans and WIs.
7.1	Planning of product realisation	The availability of documented plans for all product processes required to realise a product, and the sequences in which they occur.	• Process models (flow-charts) showing the sequence of activities that an organisation goes through to produce a product. • Documented QPs and WIs to ensure that staff work in accordance with requirements. • Records that prove the results of process control. • Quality Plans.
7.2	Customer-related processes	The identification, review and interaction with customer requirements and customers.	• Quality Manual and Quality Plans.
7.2.1	Determination of requirements related to the product	How an organisation determines and implements customer requirements.	• Contract review procedures. • Regulatory and legal product requirements. • Formal contracts.
7.2.2	Review of requirements related to the product	How an organisation reviews product and customer requirements in order to check that they can actually do the job.	• Contract review procedures. • Regulatory and legal product requirements. • Project Plans showing lines of communication with the customer.

(continued)

Clause No.	ISO 9001:2000 title	Explanation	Likely documentation
7.2.3	Customer communication	How an organisation communicates (i.e. liaises) with their customers, keeps them informed, handles their enquiries, complaints and feedback.	• Project Plans showing lines of communication with the customer.
7.3	Design and development	The control of design and development within an organisation.	• Processes and procedures for design and development. • Design Plans.
7.3.1	Design and development planning	How an organisation goes about planning and controlling the design of a product (e.g. design stages, development processes, verification and validation, responsibilities and authorities).	• Design and Development Plans. • Procedures detailing the design process and how designs are verified and validated. • Risk assessment. • Job descriptions and responsibilities.
7.3.2	Design and development inputs	How an organisation identifies the requirements to be met by a product.	• Project Plans (detailing policies, standards and specifications, skill requirements). • Specifications and tolerances. • Regulatory and legal requirements. • Information derived from previous (similar) designs or developments. • Environmental requirements. • Health and safety aspects.
7.3.3	Design and development outputs	How an organisation ensures that the design output meets the design input requirements.	• Drawings, schematics, schedules, system specifications, system descriptions, etc.
7.3.4	Design and development review	How an organisation evaluates their ability to fulfil product requirements, identify problems and complete follow-up actions.	• Procedures detailing how changes are made to designs and how they are approved, recorded and distributed. • Design process review procedures. • Management reviews and audit procedures. • Records.
7.3.5	Design and development verification	How an organisation ensures that product specifications are fulfilled and that the design and development output meets the original input requirements.	• Design process review procedures. • Procedures for periodic reviews. • Records.

Clause No.	ISO 9001:2000 title	Explanation	Likely documentation
7.3.6	Design and development validation	How an organisation ensures that the design is actually capable of doing its intended job.	• Procedures for in-process inspection and testing. • Final inspection and test. • Records.
7.3.7	Control of design and development changes	How changes to a design are approved, together with consideration of how these changes may influence other aspects of the business.	• Procedures detailing how changes are made to designs and how they are approved, recorded and distributed. • Design process review procedures. • Management reviews and audit procedures. • Records.
7.4	Purchasing	How an organisation controls the purchase of materials, products and/or services from suppliers and third parties.	• Documented procedures for purchasing and the evaluation of suppliers.
7.4.1	Purchasing process	The controls that an organisation has in place to ensure purchased products and services are of an acceptable standard.	• Approved list of suppliers. • Supplier evaluations. • Purchasing procedures. • Purchase orders.
7.4.2	Purchasing information	The details provided by an organisation when placing an order with a supplier and the approval process for purchasing documentation.	• Approved list of suppliers. • Supplier evaluations. • Purchasing procedures. • Purchase orders. • Stock control procedures.
7.4.3	Verification of purchased product	The controls that an organisation has in place to ensure that products and services provided by suppliers meet their original requirements.	• Approved list of suppliers. • Supplier evaluations. • Purchasing procedures. • Purchase orders. • Stock control procedures.
7.5	Production and service provision	The availability of a process to cover all production and service operations.	• Documented Processes, Quality Procedures and Work Instructions for production and service operations.
7.5.1	Control of production and service provision	The provision of anything required to control production and service operations.	• Procedures for the provision of everything necessary for staff to carry out their work. • Project plans and resources required to carry out a job.
7.5.2	Validation of production and service provision	How an organisation identifies processes which cannot be verified by subsequent	• Procedures for tasks which cannot subsequently be proved to be acceptable.

(continued)

Clause No.	ISO 9001:2000 title	Explanation	Likely documentation
		monitoring/testing/inspection (including the validation of these processes to demonstrate their effectiveness).	
7.5.3	Identification and traceability	The means by which the status of a product can be identified at all stages of its production/ delivery.	• Procedures for the provision of everything necessary for staff to carry out their work. • Project plans and resources required to carry out a job.
7.5.4	Customer property	How an organisation looks after property provided by a customer, including identification, verification, storage and maintenance.	• Procedure for the control of customer property.
7.5.5	Preservation of product	How an organisation looks after its own products (i.e. identification, handling, packaging, storing and protecting) including authorisation of release to a customer.	• Product approval procedures. • Procedures which ensure the safety and protection of products.
7.6	Control of monitoring and measuring devices	The controls that an organisation has in place to ensure that equipment (including software) used for proving conformance to specified requirements is properly maintained, calibrated and verified.	• Equipment records of maintenance and calibration. • Work Instructions.
8	Measurement, analysis and improvement	The measurement, monitoring, analysis and improvement processes an organisation has in place to ensure that the QMS processes and products conform to requirements.	• Procedures for inspection and measurement.
8.1	General	The definitions of procedures to ensure product conformity and product improvement.	• Procedures for: – product conformity; – product improvement; – statistical process review.
8.2	Monitoring and measurement	The analysis of customer satisfaction and the control of products and processes.	• Procedures for inspection and measurement.
8.2.1	Customer satisfaction	The processes used to establish whether a customer is satisfied with a product.	• Procedures for: – customer feedback; – change control; – customer complaints.
8.2.2	Internal audit	The in-house checks made to determine if the QMS is	• Audit procedure. • Audit schedules.

Clause No.	ISO 9001:2000 title	Explanation	Likely documentation
		functioning properly. That it continues to comply with the requirements of ISO 9001:2000 and to identify possibilities for improvement.	• Audit plans, check sheets and records.
8.2.3	Monitoring and measurement of processes	The methods used to check if processes continue to meet their intended purpose.	• Audit schedules. • Audit plans, check sheets and records. • Approval procedures for product acceptance. • Processes for failure cost analysis, conformity, non-conformity, life cycle approach, self-assessment. • Compliance with environmental and safety policies, laws, regulations and standards. • Procedures for testing and monitoring processes. • Performance and product measurement procedures.
8.2.3	Monitoring and measurement of product	How an organisation measures and monitors that product characteristics meet the customer's specified requirements.	• Audit schedules. • Audit plans, check sheets and records. • Approval procedures for product acceptance. • Processes for failure cost analysis, conformity, non-conformity, life cycle approach, self-assessment. • Compliance with environmental and safety policies, laws, regulations and standards. • Procedures for testing and monitoring processes. • Performance and product measurement procedures. • Supplier approval procedures.
8.3	Control of non-conforming product	The methods used to prevent the use and/or delivery of non-conforming products and to decide what to do with a non-conforming product.	• Documented procedure to identify and control the use and delivery of non-conforming products. • Approval procedures. • Quarantine procedures. • Change control procedure. • Corrective and preventive action procedures. • Audits.

(continued)

Clause No.	ISO 9001:2000 title	Explanation	Likely documentation
8.4	Analysis of data	The methods used to review data that will determine the effectiveness of the QMS (especially with regard to customer satisfaction, conformance to customer requirements and the performance of processes and products).	• Any data or statistics produced as a result of audits, customer satisfaction surveys, complaints, non-conformances, supplier evaluations, etc.
8.5	Improvement	How an organisation controls corrective and preventive actions and plans for ongoing process and product improvement.	• Documented procedures for: – corrective action; – preventive action; – product/process improvement; – customer complaints/ feedback. • Non-conformity reports. • Management reviews. • Staff suggestions scheme.
8.5.1	Continual improvement	How an organisation goes about continually improving its QMS.	• Procedures, minutes of meetings (especially where improvement to the organisation's business is discussed). • Management reviews.
8.5.2	Corrective action	What an organisation does to identify and put right non-conformities.	• Process for eliminating causes of non-conformity. • Documented complaints. • Complaints procedure. • Staff suggestions scheme.
8.5.3	Preventive action	Random check of products, services and/or client satisfaction aimed at identifying a potential issue before it becomes a problem in need of corrective action.	• Process for the prevention of non-conformity. • Documented complaints. • Complaints procedure. • Staff suggestions scheme.

3.3 ISO 9001:2000 – organisational requirements

The following is a summary of how an organisation is expected to work in conformance with the requirements and recommendations of ISO 9001:2000.

 Note: **Bold text** denotes a mandatory procedure.

Section of ISO 9001:2000	Title of section	Intent of clauses
4	Quality Management System	

4.1	General requirements	• An organisation is required to have a business management system which has been developed and implemented in the course of:
		  – identifying the processes used to carry out the organisation's business;
		  – determining the sequence of these processes;
		  – establishing ways to ensure that the processes are carried out correctly;
		  – ensuring that organisations have adequate and appropriate resources;
		  – showing that organisations monitor and improve their system.

4.2	Documentation requirements	

4.2.1	General	• The following documentation must be included in the management system:
		  – quality policy and quality objectives;
		  – a Quality Manual;
		  – the documented procedures required by the standard (see bold text for mandatory procedures);
		  – the records required by the standard to prove that the organisation has met its requirements.

4.2.2	Quality Manual	• The organisation must have an up-to-date Quality Manual, which addresses the following:
		  – the scope of their management system;
		  – those parts of the standard that do not apply to their organisation (including justifications);
		
		    Note: ONLY those requirements in Section 7 can be excluded.
		
		  – the documented procedures that are required by ISO 9000 (see bold text);
		  – a description of how their organisation's business processes interact.

4.2.3	**Control of documents** **Note:** This is a mandatory requirement for all organisations.	• A process **MUST** be in place to ensure that only correct versions of documents are in use. • Documents must be reviewed and approved prior to use. • The organisation should also have a record of what documents exist and which version is the correct one. • The organisation must periodically review their documents for ongoing fitness for purpose.
4.2.4	**Control of records** **Note:** This is a mandatory requirement for all organisations.	• The organisation **MUST** keep records to prove that they are operating their management system correctly. • Records **MUST** be kept for a predetermined period, in good condition and be readily retrievable. • The procedure **MUST** state storage requirements.

(continued)

Section of ISO 9001:2000	Title of section	Intent of clauses
5	Management responsibility	
5.1	Management commitment	• The organisation shall: – define the commitment of their senior management to the development and improvement of the system; – have a Quality Policy; – define quality objectives; – conduct management reviews; – ensure that sufficient resources are available.
5.2	Customer focus	• Senior management shall define their commitment to determining, meeting and enhancing customer satisfaction.
5.3	Quality Policy	• The organisation must have a Quality Policy that: – is applicable to their products/services; – provides the focus of their quality system; – is the very top document of the management system; **Note:** Unless the organisation also has a mission statement. – includes the necessity for establishing and reviewing quality objectives.
5.4	Planning	
5.4.1	Quality objectives	• The organisation must make sure that they have defined organisational objectives for quality – using measurable terms. • These objectives must align with their organisation's quality policy.
5.4.2	Quality Management System planning	• The organisation must ensure that they have planned and identified organisational objectives for their quality management system. • When changes are made to their organisation's system, the organisation must also ensure that the integrity of the system is maintained such that their system continues to meet the requirements of ISO 9001:2000.
5.5	Responsibility, authority and communication	
5.5.1	Responsibility and authority	• The organisation must define and communicate the roles and responsibilities of the key functions within the organisation, so that all personnel understand who does what.
5.5.2	Management representative	• Senior management must nominate a person responsible for: – ensuring that the quality management processes are installed; – reporting performance of the management system; – promoting awareness of customer requirements. **Note:** This person must be a member of the organisation's management.

Section of ISO 9001:2000	Title of section	Intent of clauses
5.5.3	Internal communication	• The organisation must ensure that adequate communication is put in place (between the various levels of staff) to facilitate a two-way dialogue on the effectiveness of the management system.
5.6	Management review	
5.6.1	General	• The organisation must review the function of the quality system to ensure that it is current and effective. **Note:** This review must also embrace opportunities for improvement.
5.6.2	Review input	• The inputs for the management review must include: – audit results; – customer feedback; – process and product performance/conformity; – status of preventive/corrective actions; – follow-up actions from previous management reviews; – changes that could affect the management system; – recommendations for improvement.
5.6.3	Review output	• The outcome of the management review shall include actions and decisions on: – improvement of the effectiveness of the management system; – improvement of the product (or service); – resources requirements (i.e. what resources the organisation will require to achieve these improvements).
6	Resource management	
6.1	Provision of resources	• The organisation must provide adequate resources to: – implement, maintain and improve the management system; – enhance customer satisfaction.
6.2	Human resources	
6.2.1	General	• The organisation must ensure that they have competent, trained and experienced staff.
6.2.2	Competence, awareness and training	• The organisation must: – define the skills required to perform tasks which affect product quality; – provide training;

(continued)

Section of ISO 9001:2000	Title of section	Intent of clauses
		– evaluate the effectiveness of the training; – ensure personnel are aware of the importance of their tasks; – keep records of the training and experience.
6.3	Infrastructure	• The organisation must provide facilities (in the form of buildings, workspace, tools and equipment, supporting services, etc.) that will ensure that their product/service conforms to their customers' requirements.
6.4	Work environment	• The organisation must determine and manage the environmental factors required to achieve product/service conformity.
7	Product realisation	
7.1	Planning of product realisation	• The organisation must: – determine the quality objectives and requirements for their products; – ensure that they plan all of the processes required to provide their products/services; – plan the required inspection/testing (i.e. verification and validation) activities; – identify what records must be retained in order to provide evidence that the product conforms to requirements.
7.2	Customer-related processes	
7.2.1	Determination of requirements related to the product	• The organisation must establish and (if required) clarify what their customer expects their organisation to deliver and any obligations that arise from it (such as statutory requirements to be met, etc.).
7.2.2	Review of requirements related to the product	• Product requirements must be defined and reviewed prior to committing to supply. • The organisation will need to ensure contract issues are resolved and that they have the necessary resources to deliver. Note: The review shall be recorded. • Where a customer does not provide written requirements the organisation shall confirm their own interpretation of their own needs prior to acceptance of the order. • The organisation must define how changes in requirements are recorded and how the information is circulated around the relevant sections of their organisation.

Section of ISO 9001:2000	Title of section	Intent of clauses
7.2.3	Customer communication	• The organisation must identify lines of communication between the customer and their organisation with regard to product information, enquiries and contract amendments and feedback (including complaints, etc.).
7.3	Design and development	
7.3.1	Design and development planning	• The organisation shall determine the various design and development processes required together with any review, verification and validation stages. **Note:** Responsibilities and authorities shall also be defined.
7.3.2	Design and development inputs	• Design inputs shall be defined (i.e. the information needed to design or develop the product or service). • The organisation's inputs will include any relevant functional requirements, standards, legal requirements (e.g. mandatory safety requirements, packaging disposal/recycling requirements, CE marking requirements, etc.) and, where pertinent, previous designs should also be considered. **Note:** Design inputs must be reviewed for adequacy, be complete, clear and not conflict with each other.
7.3.3	Design and development outputs	• Design (and development) outputs, such as drawings, reports, etc. shall be produced such that they can be checked for compliance against design inputs. • Outputs shall also provide information for purchasing, product acceptance criteria and characteristics that are essential for its safe and proper use.

7.3.4	Design and development review	• Design activities must be reviewed at appropriate stages to evaluate whether they will meet requirements (these reviews can include modelling, prototype tests, beta testing, etc.).
		• The review shall:
		  – include the identification and recording of any problems and follow-up actions;
		  – identify at what stages these reviews will occur.
		
		Note: Records must be kept.

7.3.5	Design and development verification	• Design outputs must be verified to ensure that the design meets the input requirements. • Verification shall be planned and recorded.

(continued)

Section of ISO 9001:2000	Title of section	Intent of clauses
7.3.6	Design and development validation	• The finished product or service shall be validated to check that it is capable of carrying out its intended role. • Validation shall be planned and recorded.
7.3.7	Control of design and development changes	• Design changes must be reviewed and recorded. • The effect of design changes on any sections of the design work already completed must be considered.
7.4	Purchasing	
7.4.1	Purchasing process	• The organisation must ensure that purchased products conform to the requirements originally specified. • The organisation will also ensure that they select (through evaluation) suitable suppliers.
7.4.2	Purchasing information	• Contracts and purchase orders must clearly state what the organisation requires, including if necessary product approval requirements, supplier qualifications and management system requirements. • Purchasing information must be reviewed for adequacy before it is sent to the supplier.
7.4.3	Verification of purchased product	• The organisation is expected to define and implement those inspections needed to satisfy itself that the delivered product meets their specified requirements. Note: This is often referred to as goods inwards inspection.
7.5	Production and service provision	

7.5.1	Control of production and service provision	• Processes that are needed to deliver the organisation's product or service need to be controlled.
		• These controls (which need to be planned and implemented) include:
		  – information that describes the characteristics of the product (so that inspections and tests can be conducted);
		  – work instructions to define 'keystroke' operations expected of a member of staff;
		  – providing appropriate equipment;
		  – availability and use of suitable monitoring and measuring devices;
		  – product release and delivery criteria.

7.5.2	Validation of processes for production and service provision	• The organisation needs to ensure that any of their processes that produce items that cannot be tested directly (sometimes referred to as 'hidden processes') are subject to tighter control by:
		  – reviewing and approving such processes;
		  – approving equipment and personnel;

Section of ISO 9001:2000	Title of section	Intent of clauses
		– defining procedures which must be followed when producing the product/service; – defining what records must be retained; – defining revalidation criteria.
7.5.3	Identification and traceability	• Where appropriate, the organisation must identify materials and goods to allow for traceability. **Note:** Obviously not everything needs to be traceable, but consideration should be given to identifying items which could easily be mixed up or confused, or where proof of calibration to national standards is required.
7.5.4	Customer property	• Customers occasionally supply their own products for incorporation into a system. Where this occurs the organisation must identify, verify, protect and safeguard it. **Note:** If the organisation were to break or lose it then this must be reported to the customer and records kept.
7.5.5	Preservation of product	• The organisation must ensure that processes exist to ensure the safe identification, handling, packaging, storage and preservation of all materials and finished products. • These safeguards must also include delivery to the intended destination.
7.6	Control of monitoring and measuring devices	• Monitoring and measuring is vital to check that a product (or service) meets predetermined requirements. Processes need to be established that will prove that organisations have indeed met the intended specification. • The equipment used to carry out monitoring and measuring will need to be calibrated, identified, safeguarded from adjustment and protected from damage. • Where equipment has been found to be out of calibration organisations are required to have a mechanism in place to intercept the affected product (e.g. product recall).
8	Measurement, analysis and improvement	
8.1	General	• The organisation must plan and implement their monitoring, measuring, analysis and improvement activities, in order to: – demonstrate their product conforms to requirements;

(*continued*)

Section of ISO 9001:2000	Title of section	Intent of clauses
		– demonstrate their management system conforms to ISO 9001:2000; – improve their processes/procedures. **Note:** The organisation will need to consider the statistical techniques and other methods needed to achieve this requirement.
8.2	Monitoring and measurement	
8.2.1	Customer satisfaction	• ISO 9001:2000 is customer focused. It is vital therefore that the: – organisation monitors customer satisfaction through preplanned and defined methods; – resulting information is utilised during management review.
8.2.2	Internal audit **Note:** This is a mandatory requirement for all organisations.	• Internal auditing is a mandatory requirement aimed at determining whether the management system conforms to the planned arrangements that the organisation has detailed in Section 7.1 and also to ISO 9001:2000. • The audit programme **MUST** be planned, with frequency and extent being based on the importance of the processes to be audited. • The written procedure **MUST** identify responsibilities and ensure that non-conformities are actioned without undue delay.
8.2.3	Monitoring and measuring of processes	• The organisation is required to have methods in place for ensuring that their processes are suitable and remain so. **Note:** This will also have to include the actions to be taken when a process is not delivering expected results.
8.2.4	Monitoring and measuring of product	• The organisation is required to monitor and measure the product or service at appropriate stages. • Records must be retained that identify the person who released the goods or services at the predetermined hold points. **Note:** A product must not be released until all of the required actions have been conducted.
8.3	Control of non-conforming product	• The organisation **MUST** have a written procedure to ensure that all non-conforming products (i.e. sub-standard, damaged, etc.) are not used or delivered accidentally. • Non-conforming products can be dealt with in any one of three ways: – removal of the defect (in which case it needs to be reverified against the original specification);

Section of ISO 9001:2000	Title of section	Intent of clauses
		− authorising its use under concession; − preventing its use. Note: These actions should be recorded.
8.4	Analysis of data	• The organisation shall collect and analyse sufficient data to demonstrate the effectiveness of their management system. • Data shall include information relating to customer satisfaction, product conformity, process trends and suppliers. • The analysis will identify where improvements can be made.
8.5	Improvement	
8.5.1	Continual improvement	• The organisation is required to continually improve its management system through the results obtained from data analysis, audit results, management review, corrective/preventive actions, etc.
8.5.2	Corrective action Note: This is a mandatory requirement for all organisations.	• Inevitably things will go wrong from time to time and the organisation should identify, record, investigate and remedy them with the intention of preventing them from occurring again. • A written procedure must capture the organisation's intentions. • The organisation must use corrective action to see if it has been effective.
8.5.3	Preventive action Note: This is a mandatory requirement for all organisations.	• Using suitable methodology, the organisation must attempt to predict the causes of potential non-conformities and implement action to prevent them occurring. Note: Risk assessment is more desirable than a crystal ball! • As with corrective actions, the organisation must: − have a procedure; − record the results of actions taken; − review the effect of preventive action.

3.4 ISO 9001:2000 – management responsibilities

Within ISO 9001:2000 there are over 270 separate requirements of management. Some of these are comparatively minor, whilst others are extremely important and are aimed specifically at top management (i.e. managing director and functional heads, etc.) and which require them to:

- fully endorse (and be committed to) the development and implementation of their organisation's quality system;
- develop and establish a quality policy that can be supported by measurable quality objectives;
- plan, develop, implement, improve and modify their quality management system;
- define and communicate organisational responsibilities and authorities;
- appoint a management representative as the quality manager to oversee the quality management system;
- establish (and use) internal communication processes;
- review the quality management system at planned intervals.

There are 21 specific ISO 9001:2000 requirements of top management and these are described in Section 3.4.1 below. The remaining requirements of general management are described in Section 3.4.2.

3.4.1 Top management responsibilities

In accordance with ISO 9001:2000, *top management shall...*

Section of ISO 9001:2000	ISO 9001:2000 requirement	Explanation

5.1	*provide evidence of its commitment to the development and implementation of the quality management system and continually improving its effectiveness,*	Top management shall fully endorse (and be committed to) the development and implementation of their organisation's quality system by:
		
		• **commitment**
		  – supporting quality;
		  – promoting the importance of having a quality system;
		  – defining the scope of their quality system;
		• **development**
		  – identifying the processes that make up their quality system;
		  – describing their quality management processes;
		• **implementation**
		  – managing their quality management system;
		  – managing process performance;
		• **continual improvement**
		  – monitoring process performance (through management reviews);
		  – improving process performance;
		  – improving their quality management system;
		• **evidence**
		  – developing documents that reflect what their organisation does;
		  – developing documents to implement their quality system.

Section of ISO 9001:2000	ISO 9001:2000 requirement	Explanation
5.1.a (see also 5.2)	*communicate to the organisation the importance of meeting customer as well as statutory and regulatory requirements,*	Top management shall define their commitment to meeting customer, statutory and regulatory requirements by: • setting organisational quality objectives; • identifying (and promoting the need to meet) customer requirements; • enhancing customer satisfaction; • promoting the need to meet regulatory requirements; • promoting the need to meet statutory requirements; • encouraging personnel to meet quality system requirements.
5.1.b (see also 5.3)	*establish the quality policy,*	Top management shall define their organisation's quality policy which: • serves their organisation's purpose; • emphasises the need to meet requirements; • facilitates the development of quality objectives; • makes a commitment to continuous improvement.
5.1.c (see also 5.4.1)	*ensure that quality objectives are established,*	Top management shall set organisational quality objectives which: • promote the importance of quality; • promote the need to meet customer, regulatory and statutory requirements; • provide quality resources to implement their quality management system; • encourage personnel to meet quality system requirements.
5.1.d (see also 5.6.1)	*conduct management reviews,*	Top management shall perform quality management reviews to: • evaluate the performance of their quality system; • evaluate whether their quality system should be improved.
5.1.e	*ensure the availability of resources,*	Top management shall provide quality resources to: • implement their quality system; • improve the quality system.
5.2	*ensure that customer requirements are determined and are met with the aim of enhancing customer satisfaction,* **Note:** *See also Clauses 7.2.1 and 8.2.1.*	Top management shall enhance customer satisfaction by: • identifying and documenting customer requirements; • meeting customers' requirements.

(*continued*)

Section of ISO 9001:2000	ISO 9001:2000 requirement	Explanation
5.3.a	*ensure that the quality policy is appropriate to the purpose of the organisation,*	Top management shall define a quality policy that: • serves their organisation's purpose; • emphasises the need to meet requirements; • assists the development of quality objectives; • makes a commitment to continuous improvement.
5.3.b	*ensure that the quality policy includes a commitment to comply with requirements and continually improve the effectiveness of the quality management system,*	Top management shall define a quality policy that: • emphasises the need to meet customer, statutory and regulatory requirements; • makes a commitment to continuous improvement.
5.3.c	*ensure that the quality policy provides a framework for establishing and reviewing quality objectives,*	Top management shall define a quality policy that: • serves their organisation's purpose; • is capable of developing quality objectives.
5.3.d	*ensure that the quality policy is communicated and understood within the organisation,*	Top management shall publish their quality policy.
5.3.e	*ensure that the quality policy is reviewed for continuing suitability,*	Top management shall define (and document) a management review process.
5.4.1	*ensure that quality objectives, including those needed to meet requirements for product (see 7.1.a), are established at relevant functions and levels within the organisation, (The quality objectives shall be measurable, and consistent with the quality policy.)*	Top management shall set measurable quality objectives: • for functional areas; • for organisational levels; • that make product realisation possible; • that support the quality policy.
5.4.2.a	*ensure that the planning of the quality management system is carried out in order to meet the requirements given in 4.1 as well as the quality objectives,*	Top management shall identify (and plan) quality system processes that: • describe their quality management system; • implement their quality management system; • manage performance; • monitor performance; • improve performance.
5.4.2.b	*ensure that the integrity of the quality management system is maintained*	**Top management shall define and document a process to:** • approve documents before they are distributed;

Section of ISO 9001:2000	ISO 9001:2000 requirement	Explanation
	when changes to the quality management system are planned and implemented,	• provide the correct version of documents at points of use; • review and reapprove documents whenever they are updated; • specify the current revision status of the documents; • monitor documents that come from external sources; • prevent the accidental use of obsolete documents; • preserve the relevance (i.e. usability) of quality documents; • control and use records to prove that requirements have been met.
5.5.1	*ensure that responsibilities and authorities are defined and communicated within the organisation,*	Top management shall define (and communicate) the organisation's roles, responsibilities, and lines of authority relevant to quality.
5.5.2	*appoint a member of management who, irrespective of other responsibilities, shall have responsibility and authority that includes:* *(a) ensuring that processes needed for the quality management system are established, implemented and maintained,* *(b) reporting to top management on the performance of the quality management system and any need for improvement,* *(c) ensuring the promotion of awareness of customer requirements throughout the organisation,* (**Note:** *The responsibility of a management representative can include liaison with external parties on matters relating to the quality management system.*)	**Appoint a management representative as the quality manager to:** • oversee the performance of their quality management system; • report on the status of their quality management system; • support the improvement of their quality management system.
5.5.3	*ensure that appropriate communication processes are established within the organisation …*	**Top management shall ensure that internal communication processes are established.**

(continued)

Section of ISO 9001:2000	ISO 9001:2000 requirement	Explanation
5.5.3 (*continued*)	*... and that communication takes place regarding the effectiveness of the quality management system,*	Top management shall ensure that communication occurs throughout the organisation.
5.6	*review the organisation's quality management system, at planned intervals, to ensure its continuing suitability, adequacy and effectiveness,*	Top management shall evaluate the performance of the quality system.
5.6.1	*review the organisation's quality management system, at planned intervals, to ensure its continuing suitability, adequacy and effectiveness. This review shall include assessing opportunities for improvement and the need for changes to the quality management system, including the quality policy and quality objectives.*	Top management shall evaluate whether the quality system should (and can) be improved.

3.4.2 General management requirements

The following ISO 9001:2000 requirements are shown in the text of the standard as ... *the organisation shall* ... and are intended for the general management of an organisation's quality system.

Note: In most organisations, these requirements will be allocated to specific managers. For example, Clause 4 would normally be the responsibility of the quality manager.

Systemic requirements

Section	ISO 9001:2000 title	Requirement	Explanation
4	Quality management system requirement	Assist in the establishment of a quality system	
4.1	General requirements	Assist in the development of a quality management system	• improve the quality management system; • identify and describe the processes that make up the quality system;

Section	ISO 9001:2000 title	Requirement	Explanation
			• manage process performance; • monitor process performance; • improve process performance.
4.2	Documentation requirements	Assist in documenting the quality system	
4.2.1	General	Assist in the development of quality system documents	• develop documents that reflect what their organisation does; • develop documents to implement their quality system.
4.2.2	Quality Manual	Assist in the preparation of a quality system manual	• define the scope of their part of the quality management system; • describe how the processes interact; • document the procedures.
4.2.3	Control of documents	Assist in the control of quality system documents	• approve documents before they are distributed; • provide the correct version of documents at points of use; • review and reapprove documents whenever they are updated; • specify the current revision status of documents; • monitor documents that come from external sources; • prevent the accidental use of obsolete documents; • preserve the usability of their quality documents.
4.2.4	Control of records	Assist in the maintenance of quality system records	• use records to prove that requirements have been met; • develop a procedure to control these records; • ensure that all records are relevant and usable.

Management requirements

Section	ISO 9001:2000 title	Requirement	Explanation
5	Management responsibility	Assist in the control of quality throughout the organisation.	
5.1	Management commitment	Assist in the support of quality	• promote the importance of quality; • promote the need to meet customer requirements; • promote the need to meet regulatory requirements; • promote the need to meet statutory requirements;

(continued)

Section	ISO 9001:2000 title	Requirement	Explanation
			• support the development of a quality system; • provide quality resources; • implement the quality management system; • encourage personnel to meet quality system requirements; • perform quality management reviews; • aim to continually improve the quality management system.
5.2	Customer focus	Help provide customer satisfaction	• identify customer requirements; • meet their customers' requirements; • enhance customer satisfaction.
5.3	Quality policy	Assist in the establishment of a quality policy	• manage the organisation's quality policy; • communicate this quality policy to their part of the organisation; • review the quality policy to ensure that it is still suitable.
5.4	Planning	Assist in all aspects of quality planning	
5.4.1	Quality objectives	Assist in the setting of quality objectives	• ensure that objectives are set for all functional areas; • ensure that objectives are set at organisational levels; • ensure that objectives facilitate product realisation; • ensure that objectives support the quality policy; • ensure that objectives are measurable.
5.4.2	Quality management system planning	Assist in the planning of the quality management system	• plan the improvement of the quality management system; • plan the modification of their quality management system.
5.5	Responsibility, authority and communication	Assist in the control of the quality system	
5.5.1	Responsibility and authority	Assist in the definition of responsibilities and authorities	• clarify responsibilities and authorities; • communicate responsibilities and authorities.
5.5.2	Management representative	Assist in the appointment of a management representative	• support the improvement of the quality management system.
5.5.3	Internal communication	Assist in the support of internal communications	• ensure that internal communication processes are established; • ensure that communication occurs throughout the organisation.

Section	ISO 9001:2000 title	Requirement	Explanation
5.6	Management review	Perform management reviews	
5.6.1	General	Review quality management system	• evaluate the performance of the quality system; • evaluate whether the quality system should be improved.
5.6.2	Review input	Examine management review inputs	• examine audit results; • examine product conformity data; • examine opportunities to improve; • examine feedback from customers; • examine process performance information; • examine corrective and preventive actions; • examine changes that might affect the management system; • examine previous quality management reviews.
5.6.3	Review output	Generate management review outputs	• generate actions to improve the quality system; • generate actions to improve the products; • generate actions to address resource.

Resource requirements

Section	ISO 9001:2000 title	Requirement	Explanation
6	Resource management	Manage the organisation's resources	
6.1	Provision of resources	Provide quality resources	Identify and provide: • quality resource requirements; • resources needed to support the quality system; • resources needed to improve customer satisfaction.
6.2	Human resources	Provide quality personnel	
6.2.1	General	Use competent personnel	Ensure that their personnel have: • the right experience; • the right education; • the right training; • the right skills.

(*continued*)

Section	ISO 9001:2000 title	Requirement	Explanation
6.2.2	Competence, awareness and training	Support competence	• define acceptable levels of competence; • identify training and awareness needs; • deliver training and awareness programmes; • evaluate effectiveness of training and awareness; • maintain a record of competence.
6.3	Infrastructure	Provide quality infrastructure	Identify, provide and maintain all: • infrastructure needs; • building needs; • workspace needs; • hardware needs; • software needs; • utility needs; • equipment needs; • support service needs.
6.4	Work environment	Provide quality environment	Identify and manage: • needed work environment; • factors needed to ensure products meet requirements.

Realisation requirements

Section	ISO 9001:2000 title	Requirement	Explanation
7	Product realisation	Control the design and implementation of the quality system	

7.1	Planning and realisation	Control realisation planning	• plan product realisation processes;
			• define product quality objectives and requirements;
			• identify product realisation needs and requirements;
			• develop product realisation:
			  – processes;
			  – documents;
			  – record keeping systems;
			• develop methods to control quality during product realisation.

7.2	Customer-related processes	Control customer processes	
7.2.1	Determination of requirements related to product	Identify customers' product requirements	Identify the requirements that: • customers want them to meet; • are dictated by the product's use; • are imposed by external agencies; • their organisation wishes to meet.

Section	ISO 9001:2000 title	Requirement	Explanation
7.2.2	Review of requirements related to product	Review customers' product requirements	• review requirements before orders are accepted from customers; • maintain a record of all product requirement reviews; • control changes in product requirements.
7.2.3	Customer communication	Communicate with their customers	• develop and implement a process to control communications with customers.
7.3	Design and development	Control product development	
7.3.1	Design and development planning	Plan design and development	• define product design and development stages; • clarify design and development responsibilities and authorities; • manage interactions between design and development groups; • update and/or modify design and development plans as changes occur.
7.3.2	Design and development inputs	Define design and development inputs	• specify product design and development inputs; • record product design and development input definitions; • review product design and development input definitions.
7.3.3	Design and development outputs	Generate design and development outputs	• create product design and development outputs; • approve design and development outputs prior to release; • use design and development outputs to control product quality.
7.3.4	Design and development review	Carry out design and development reviews	• perform product design and development reviews; • record product design and development reviews.
7.3.5	Design and development verification	Perform design and development verifications	• carry out product design and development verifications; • record product design and development verifications.
7.3.6	Design and development validation	Conduct design and development validations	• perform product design and development validations; • record product design and development validations.
7.3.7	Control of design and development changes	Manage design and development changes	• identify, record and review changes in product design and development;

(continued)

Section	ISO 9001:2000 title	Requirement	Explanation
			• verify changes in product design and development; • validate changes in product design and development; • approve changes before they are implemented.
7.4	Purchasing	Control purchasing function	
7.4.1	Purchasing process	Control purchasing process	• ensure that all purchased products meet requirements; • ensure that suppliers meet requirements.
7.4.2	Purchasing information	Document product purchases	• describe the products being purchased; • specify the requirements that must be met.
7.4.3	Verification of purchased product	Verify purchased products	• verify purchased products at their own premises; • verify purchased products at suppliers' premises (when required).
7.5	Production and service operations	Control operational activities	
7.5.1	Control of production and service provision	Control production and service provision	Control production and service: • processes; • information; • instructions; • equipment; • measurements; • activities.
7.5.2	Validation of processes for production and service provision	Validate production and service provision	Prove that: • special processes can produce planned outputs; • process personnel can produce planned results; • process equipment can produce planned results.
7.5.3	Identification and traceability	Identify and track their products	• establish the identity of their products (when appropriate); • maintain the identity of their products (when appropriate); • identify the status of their products (when appropriate); • record the identity of their products (when required).
7.5.4	Customer property	Protect property supplied by customers	• identify property supplied by customers;

Section	ISO 9001:2000 title	Requirement	Explanation
			• verify property supplied by customers; • safeguard property supplied by customers.
7.5.5	Preservation of product	Preserve their products and components	• preserve products and components during internal processing; • preserve products and components during final delivery.
7.6	Control of measuring and monitoring devices	Control monitoring devices	• identify monitoring and measuring needs; • identify the monitoring and measuring that should be done; • select monitoring and measuring devices; • select devices that meet monitoring and measuring needs; • calibrate monitoring and measuring devices: – perform calibrations; – record calibrations; • protect monitoring and measuring devices: – from unauthorised adjustment; – from damage or deterioration; • validate monitoring and measuring software; • validate monitoring and measuring software before you use it; • revalidate monitoring and measuring software when necessary.

Remedial requirements

Section	ISO 9001:2000 title	Requirement	Explanation
8	Measurement, analysis and improvement	Manage the process for continual improvement	
8.1	General	Perform remedial processes	• plan remedial processes; • plan how remedial processes will be used to assure conformity; • plan how remedial processes will be used to improve the system; • implement remedial processes; • use remedial processes to demonstrate conformance; • use remedial processes to improve quality management system.

(*continued*)

Section	ISO 9001:2000 title	Requirement	Explanation
8.2	Monitoring and measurement	Monitor and measure quality	
8.2.1	Customer satisfaction	Monitor and measure customer satisfaction	• identify ways to monitor and measure customer satisfaction; • monitor and measure customer satisfaction; • use customer satisfaction information.
8.2.2	Internal audit	Plan and perform regular internal audits	• set up and plan an internal audit programme; • develop an internal audit procedure; • plan internal audit projects; • perform regular internal audits; • solve problems discovered during audits; • verify that problems have been solved.
8.2.3	Monitoring and measurement of processes	Monitor and measure quality processes	• use suitable methods to monitor and measure processes; • take action when processes fail to achieve planned results.
8.2.4	Monitoring and measurement of product	Monitor and measure product characteristics	• verify that product characteristics are being met; • keep a record of product monitoring and measuring activities.
8.3	Control of non-conforming product	Control non-conforming products	• develop a procedure to control non-conforming products; • define how non-conforming products should be identified and handled; • identify and control non-conforming products; • eliminate or correct product non-conformities; • prevent the delivery or use of non-conforming products; • avoid the inappropriate use of non-conforming products; • re-verify non-conforming products that were corrected; • prove that corrected products now meet requirements; • control non-conforming products after delivery or use; • maintain records of non-conforming products describing their non-conformity; • describe the actions taken to deal with non-conformities.

Section	ISO 9001:2000 title	Requirement	Explanation

8.4	Analysis of data	Analyse quality information	• define quality management information requirements;
			• define the information required to:
			  − evaluate the quality system;
			  − improve the quality system;
			• collect quality management system data;
			• monitor and measure the:
			  − suitability of the quality system;
			  − effectiveness of the quality system;
			• provide information about:
			  − customers;
			  − suppliers;
			  − products;
			  − processes.

8.5	Improvement	Make quality improvements	
8.5.1	Continual improvement	Improve quality management system	• use audits to generate improvements; • use quality data to generate improvements; • use the quality policy to generate improvements; • use the quality objectives to generate improvements; • use management reviews to generate improvements; • use corrective actions to generate improvements; • use preventive actions to generate improvements.
8.5.2	Corrective action	Correct actual non-conformities	• review non-conformities; • figure out what causes these non-conformities; • evaluate whether corrective action is required; • develop corrective actions to prevent recurrence; • take corrective actions when they are necessary; • record the results that corrective actions achieve; • examine the effectiveness of corrective actions.
8.5.3	Preventive action	Prevent potential non-conformities	• detect potential non-conformities; • identify the causes of potential non-conformities;

(*continued*)

Section	ISO 9001:2000 title	Requirement	Explanation
			• study the effects of potential non-conformities; • evaluate whether you need to take preventive action; • develop preventive actions to eliminate causes; • take preventive actions when necessary; • record the results that preventive actions achieve; • examine the effectiveness of preventive actions.

3.5 ISO 9001:2000 – audit questionnaire

The following is an indication of areas of an organisation's QMS that could be looked at and possibly further investigated during internal, external and/or third party audits.

 Note: This questionnaire is not intended to act as a complete check sheet for auditing a management system for compliance with ISO 9001:2000 (or associated management system), merely as an indication of areas of an organisation's QMS that could be looked at and possibly further investigated during internal, external and/or third party audits.

3.5.1 Section 4 – Quality Management System

4.1 General requirements

1. How did you establish your QMS?
2. How did you identify the processes required for your management systems?
3. How did you determine the sequence and interaction of these processes?
4. How do you ensure the effective operation and control of these processes?
5. Does your QMS include processes for management activities, provision of resources, product realisation and measurement?
6. How do you ensure continual improvement and effectiveness of your QMS?
7. How do you ensure availability of resources and information required to support these processes?
8. How do you monitor, measure and analyse these processes?
9. When an outsourced process affects product conformity, how do you ensure control over such processes and where is this documented in the QMS?
10. How do you ensure that these processes meet the requirements of ISO 9001:2000?

4.2 Documentation requirements

4.2.1 General

1. Does your system documentation include:
   - documented statements regarding quality policy and quality objectives?
   - a quality manual?
   - all of the documented procedures required by ISO 9001:2000?
   - all of the documents required to ensure effective planning, operation and control of your processes?
   - a process for maintaining records?
2. Are all of these documented procedures fully established, documented, implemented and maintained?

4.2.2 Quality Manual

1. Is your Quality Manual fully established, implemented and maintained?
2. Does your Quality Manual include:
   - the scope of the QMS?
   - details of and justification for any exclusions? (see 1.2)
   - details (or reference to) all your documented procedures?
   - describe the interaction between the QMS processes?

4.2.3 Control of documents

1. How do you ensure that all QMS documents are controlled?
2. Have you an established (documented) procedure that defines the controls needed?
3. Is there a separate procedure for controlling records? (see 4.2.4)
4. How do you approve documents for adequacy prior to issue?
5. How do ensure that documents are periodically reviewed?
6. How do you ensure that documents are periodically updated and (where necessary) reapproved?
7. How are document changes identified?
8. How is the current revision status of documents identified?
9. How do you ensure that only the relevant versions of applicable documents are available at points of use?
10. How do you ensure that documents remain legible?
11. How do you ensure that documents are readily identifiable?
12. How are documents from an external origin identified?
13. How do you control the distribution of documents of external origin?
14. How do you prevent the unintended use of obsolete documents?
15. If obsolete documents have been retained for any purpose, how are they identified?

4.2.4 Control of records

1. What records have been established to provide evidence of conformity to QMS requirements?
2. What records have been established to provide evidence of effective operation of the QMS?
3. Have you an established and documented procedure to define the controls needed for the identification, storage, protection, retrieval, retention time and disposition of quality records?
4. How do you ensure that records shall remain legible, readily identifiable and retrievable?
5. What controls have you in place to ensure that all these records are maintained?

3.5.2 Section 5 – Management responsibility

5.1 Management commitment

1. What evidence does top management provide to show its commitment to the development and implementation of the QMS?
2. What evidence does top management provide to show their commitment to continually improving the effectiveness of its QMS?
3. How does top management ensure that the organisation is aware of the importance of meeting customer requirements?
4. How does top management ensure that the organisation is aware of the importance of meeting statutory and regulatory requirements?
5. What evidence can top management provide that it has of establishing a quality policy?
6. What evidence can top management provide that quality objectives are established?
7. What evidence can top management provide that they conduct management reviews?
8. What evidence can top management provide that the availability of resources is established and maintained?

5.2 Customer focus

1. How do you ensure customer requirements are determined and fulfilled?
2. How do you ensure customer satisfaction is identified and maintained?

5.3 Quality policy

1. What is your (i.e. top management's) quality policy?
2. How do you ensure that the quality policy is appropriate to the purpose of the organisation?

3. How does your quality policy provide a commitment to comply with requirements?
4. How does your quality policy provide a commitment to continually improve the QMS's effectiveness?
5. How does your quality policy provide a framework for establishing and reviewing quality objectives?
6. How do you ensure that your quality policy is communicated and understood within the organisation?
7. How is your quality policy reviewed for continuing suitability?

5.4 Planning

5.4.1 Quality objectives

1. How do you ensure that quality objectives are established within the organisation?
2. How do you ensure that quality objectives are measurable and consistent with the quality policy?

5.4.2 QMS planning

1. How do you ensure that the QMS planning meets the requirements given in Section 4.1, as well as the quality objectives?
2. How do you ensure that the integrity of the QMS is maintained when planned changes are made (and implemented) to the system?

5.5 Responsibility, authority and communication

5.5.1 Responsibility and authority

1. Where are the organisation's responsibilities and authorities defined?

5.5.2 Management representative

1. Who has been appointed as the management's representative responsible for establishing, implementing and maintaining the QMS?
2. What are the management representative's duties?
3. How does the management representative ensure that the QMS processes are established, implemented and maintained?
4. How and when does the management representative report to top management on the performance of the QMS?
5. How (and to whom) does the management representative report to when there are needs for improvement?
6. How does the management representative ensure that customer requirements are recognised throughout the organisation?
7. When does the management representative liaise with external parties on matters relating to the QMS?

5.5.3 Internal communication

1. What communication processes have been established within the organisation to promote awareness of QMS policies and requirements?
2. How do you communicate the effectiveness of the QMS?

5.6 Management review

5.6.1 General

1. How do you ensure the continuing suitability, adequacy and effectiveness of your QMS?
2. Are top management reviews of the QMS carried out? If so, when?
3. What is the prime aim of these management reviews?
4. As a result of these reviews, what opportunities for improvement and changes to the management system have been identified?
5. As a result of these reviews, what changes to the organisation's quality policies and objectives have been made?
6. What records from management reviews are maintained? (see 4.2.4)

5.6.2 Review input

1. What information is used as inputs to management reviews?

5.6.3 Review output

1. What are the outputs from management reviews?

3.5.3 Section 6 – Resource management

6.1 Provision of resources

1. How do you determine and provide the resources required to implement and maintain the QMS?
2. How do you determine and provide the resources required to continually improve the effectiveness of the QMS?
3. How do you ensure that the resources available continually improve the effectiveness of the QMS and enhance customer satisfaction by meeting customer requirements?

6.2 Human resources

6.2.1 General

1. How do you ensure that personnel performing work affecting product quality are competent on the basis of appropriate education, training, skills and experience?

2. What records are maintained of personnel education, training, skills and experience?

6.2.2 Competence, awareness and training

1. How do you determine the necessary competence for personnel performing work affecting product quality?
2. How do you ensure that adequate training (or other actions) is taken to satisfy these needs?
3. How do you evaluate the effectiveness of the actions taken to develop personnel competence?
4. How do you ensure that personnel are aware of the relevance and importance of their activities and how they contribute to the achievement of the quality objectives?
5. What records are maintained of personnel education, training, skills and experience?

6.3 Infrastructure

1. How do you determine, provide and maintain the infrastructure needed to achieve conformity to product requirements? For example:
   - buildings, workspace and associated utilities?
   - process equipment, both hardware and software?
   - supporting services such as transport or communication?

6.4 Work environment

1. How do you determine and manage the work environment needed to achieve conformity to product requirement?

3.5.4 Section 7 – Product realisation

7.1 Planning and product realisation

1. How do you plan and develop the processes needed for product realisation?
2. How do you ensure that the planning of product realisation is consistent with the requirements of the other processes of the QMS?
3. How do you determine whether the quality objectives and requirements for the product are appropriate?
4. How do you determine the need to establish processes, documents and provide resources specific to the product?
5. How do you determine whether the quality objectives and requirements for the product are appropriate?
6. How do you determine the amount of verification, validation, monitoring, inspection and test activities (specific to the product and the criteria for product acceptance) that is required?

7. How do you determine what records are needed to provide evidence that the realisation processes and resulting product meet requirements?
8. What is the output from these planning activities?
9. Which QMS document specifies the product realisation processes?
10. Is a quality plan used?

7.2 Customer-related processes

7.2.1 Determination of requirements related to the product

1. How do you determine requirements specified by the customer, including requirements for delivery and post-delivery activities?
2. How do you determine requirements not stated by the customer but necessary for specified or intended use?
3. How do you determine what are the statutory and regulatory requirements related to the product?
4. How do you determine if there are any additional requirements relevant to the product?

7.2.2 Review of requirements related to the product

1. How do you review the requirements related to the product?
2. Is this review conducted prior to giving a commitment to supply a product to the customer (e.g. submission of tenders, acceptance of contracts or orders, acceptance of changes to contracts or orders)?
3. How do you ensure that the product requirements are defined?
4. How do you ensure that any contract and/or order requirements differing from those previously expressed are resolved?
5. How do you ensure that your organisation has the ability to meet the defined requirements?
6. What records of the results of this product requirements review (and actions arising from the review) are maintained?
7. What happens if a customer does not provide a documented statement of requirement?
8. How do you confirm customer requirements before acceptance?
9. What happens if the product requirements are changed?
10. If product requirements have changed, how do you ensure that the relevant documents are amended and that relevant personnel are made aware of the changed requirements?
11. How do you handle Internet sales?

7.2.3 Customer communication

1. How do you communicate product information to customers?
2. How do you handle customer enquiries?

3. How do you process contracts and/or order handling?
4. How do you handle amendments to customer products and/or product information?
5. How do you deal with customer feedback?
6. Have you a procedure for handling customer complaints?

7.3 Design and development

7.3.1 Design and development planning

1. How do you plan and control the design and development of a product?
2. How do you determine the necessary stages of the design and development of a product?
3. How (and when) do you review, verify and validate the design and development stage?
4. How do you ensure that design and development planning results in a clear assignment of responsibility?
5. How do you ensure that the planning output is updated as the design and development progresses?

7.3.2 Design and development inputs

1. How do you determine the inputs relating to product requirements?
2. How do you maintain records of these inputs?
3. How do you ensure that the design and development inputs:
   - are functional and meet performance requirements?
   - are applicable to statutory and regulatory requirements?
   - include (where applicable) information derived from previous similar designs?
   - include other requirements essential for design and development?
4. How do you review the design and development inputs for adequacy?
5. How do you ensure that requirements are complete, unambiguous and do not conflict with each other?

7.3.3 Design and development outputs

1. How do you ensure that the outputs of design and development are provided in a form that enables verification against the design and development input?
2. How do you ensure that these are approved prior to release?
3. How do you ensure that the design and development outputs meet the input requirements for design and development?
4. How do you ensure that the design and development outputs provide the appropriate amount of information for purchasing, production and service provision?

5. How do you ensure that the design and development outputs contain (or reference) product acceptance criteria?
6. How do you ensure that the design and development outputs specify the characteristics of the product that are essential for its safe and proper use?

7.3.4 Design and development review

1. How do you ensure that systematic reviews of design and development are performed at suitable stages?
2. How do you ensure that systematic reviews of design and development are performed in accordance with planned arrangements?
3. How do you evaluate these reviews and ensure that the:
   - design and development meets requirements?
   - problems are identified?
   - necessary actions are proposed?
4. How do you ensure that participants in these reviews include representatives of all the functions concerned with the design and development stage(s) being reviewed?
5. How do you keep records of the results of these reviews?
6. How do you implement the actions recorded from these reviews?

7.3.5 Design and development verification

1. How do you ensure that design and development verification is performed in accordance with planned arrangements?
2. How do you ensure that the design and development outputs have met the design and development input requirements?
3. How are the records of the results of the verification and any necessary actions maintained?

7.3.6 Design and development validation

1. How do you ensure that design and development validation is performed in accordance with planned arrangements?
2. How do you ensure that the resulting product is capable of meeting the requirements for the specified application or intended use?
3. How do you ensure that (wherever practicable) validation is completed prior to the delivery or implementation of the product?
4. What records are maintained of design and development validation together with (where applicable) follow-up actions?

7.3.7 Control of design and development changes

1. How do you identify design and development changes?
2. How are the records of design and development changed?

3. How do you ensure that design and development changes are:
   - reviewed?
   - verified?
   - validated?
   - approved before implementation?
4. How do you evaluate the effect of the changes on constituent parts and delivered product?
5. What records are maintained following a review of changes?
6. How are any necessary actions resulting from this review implemented and recorded?

7.4 Purchasing

7.4.1 Purchasing process

1. How do you ensure that the purchased product conforms to specified purchase requirements?
2. How do you control the suppliers and the purchased product?
3. How do you evaluate and select suppliers?
4. What criteria have been established for selection, evaluation and re-evaluation of suppliers?
5. What records are maintained following the evaluation of suppliers?
6. How are any necessary actions resulting from this review of suppliers implemented and recorded?

7.4.2 Purchasing information

1. How do you ensure that the purchasing information accurately describes the product to be purchased?
2. How do you ensure that the purchasing information includes (where appropriate) the:
   - requirements for approval of product, procedures, processes and equipment?
   - requirements for the qualification of personnel?
   - quality management system requirements?
3. How do you ensure that the specified purchase requirements are accurately communicated to the supplier?

7.4.3 Verification of purchased product

1. How do you ensure that the purchased product meets specified purchase requirements?
2. Do you perform verification at the supplier's premises? If so:
   - how do you communicate to the supplier your intended verification arrangements and method of product release?
   - is this information included in the purchasing information?

7.5 Production and service provision

7.5.1 Control of production and service provision

1. How do you ensure that production and service provision is carried out under controlled conditions?
2. How do you ensure the availability of information describing the characteristics of the product?
3. How do you ensure the availability of any necessary work instructions?
4. How do you ensure that only suitable equipment is used?
5. How do you ensure the availability (and correct use) of monitoring and measuring devices is maintained?
6. How do you ensure that monitoring and measurement provisions are correctly implemented?
7. What release activities are in place for the control of production and service provision?
8. What delivery activities are in place for the control of production and service provision?
9. What post-delivery activities are in place for the control of production and service provision?

7.5.2 Validation of processes for production and service provision

1. How do you validate any processes for production and service provision where the resulting output cannot be verified by subsequent monitoring or measurement?
2. How do you validate processes where deficiencies become apparent only after the product is in use or the service has been delivered?
3. How do you ensure that these processes achieve planned results?
4. What arrangements have been established for these processes?
5. Do these arrangements include (as applicable):
   - defined criteria for review and approval of the processes?
   - approval of equipment and qualification of personnel?
   - use of specific methods and procedures?
   - requirements for records?
   - revalidation?

7.5.3 Identification and traceability

1. How do you identify the product throughout product realisation?
2. How do you identify the product status with respect to monitoring and measurement requirements?
3. Where traceability of the product is a requirement, how do you control and record its unique identification?

7.5.4 Customer property

1. How do you ensure proper care of all customer property while it is under your organisation's control?
2. How do you identify, verify, protect and safeguard customer property provided for use or incorporation into the product?
3. What procedures have you for handling any customer property that is lost, damaged or otherwise found to be unsuitable for use?
4. What procedures do you follow for reporting such losses and damages, etc. to the customer and records maintained? (see 4.2.4).
5. What happens if the customer property includes intellectual property?

7.5.5 Preservation of product

1. How do you ensure that the conformity of product is preserved during internal processing and delivery to the intended destination?
2. What procedures are available to ensure that preservation includes the product's identification, handling, packaging and protection?
3. How do you ensure that the constituent parts of a product are preserved during internal processing and/or delivery?

7.6 Control of monitoring and measuring devices

1. How do you determine the monitoring and measurement to be undertaken?
2. How do you ensure that the monitoring and measuring devices provide evidence of conformity of product requirements?
3. What processes are established to ensure that monitoring and measurement can be carried out in a manner that is consistent with the monitoring and measurement requirements of ISO 9001:2000?
4. How do you ensure that measuring equipment is calibrated and verified at specified intervals (or prior to use) against measurements traceable to international or national measurement standards?
5. What records do you maintain where no such standards exist?
6. How do you ensure that measuring equipment is adjusted and/or readjusted as necessary?
7. How is the calibration status of measuring equipment identified?
8. How is measuring equipment safeguarded from adjustments that would otherwise invalidate the measurement result?
9. How is measuring equipment protected from damage and deterioration during handling, maintenance and storage?
10. How do you assess and record the validity of the previous measuring results when the equipment is found not to conform to requirements?
11. What action do you take when the validity of the previous measuring results is found not to conform to requirements?

12. What records of calibration and verification are maintained?
13. How (and when) do you ensure that computer software (used in the monitoring and measurement of specified requirements) is confirmed?

3.5.5 Section 8 – Measurement, analysis and improvement

8.1 General

1. How do you plan and implement the monitoring, measurement, analysis and improvement processes?
2. How do you demonstrate conformity of the product?
3. How do you ensure conformity of the QMS?
4. How do you continually improve the effectiveness of the QMS?
5. How do you determine the applicable methods (including statistical techniques) and the extent of their use?

8.2 Monitoring and measurement

1. What procedures have you available to ensure customer satisfaction?
2. What procedures have you available to control internal audits?
3. What procedures have you available to ensure effective measurement and monitoring of product and processes?

8.2.1 Customer satisfaction

1. How do you monitor information relating to customer perception as to whether the organisation has fulfilled customer requirements?
2. What methods do you use for obtaining and using this information?

8.2.2 Internal audit

1. Do you have a formal documented procedure for conducting internal audits?
2. When do you conduct internal audits?
3. What is the aim of these audits?
4. How do you ensure that the QMS:
   - conforms to your planned arrangements as described in 7.1?
   - conforms to the requirements of ISO 9001:2000?
   - conforms to the system requirements that you have established?
   - is effectively implemented and maintained?
5. How do you plan your audit?
6. Does this planning take into consideration:
   - the status and importance of the processes and areas to be audited?
   - the results of previous audits?
7. How do you select the auditors to conduct these audits?
8. How do you ensure that they are impartial?

9. How do you ensure that they do not audit their own work?
10. How are the results of internal audits reported?
11. What records do you keep from internal audits?
12. How do you make certain that the management responsible for the area being audited:
    - ensures that actions are taken without undue delay?
    - eliminates detected non-conformities and their causes?
13. Do follow-up activities include the verification of the actions taken?
14. How are the verification results reported?
15. Are you aware of the requirements and guidance of ISO 10011-1, ISO 10011-2 and ISO 10011-3?

8.2.3 Monitoring and measurement of processes

1. How do you monitor and measure the QMS processes?
2. How do you ensure these processes guarantee conformity of the product?
3. How do you ensure that the methods used demonstrate the ability of the processes to achieve planned results?
4. When planned results are not achieved, what corrective action do you take?

8.2.4 Monitoring and measurement of product

1. How do you monitor and measure the characteristics of the product?
2. When do you complete this monitoring and measurement of product?
3. How do you ensure that those product requirements are fulfilled?
4. What evidence do you have that the acceptance criteria are maintained?
5. Who is responsible for authorising release of product?
6. Do appropriate records show this responsibility?
7. How do you ensure that that product release and service delivery does not proceed until all the planned arrangements have been satisfactorily completed?
8. Can the customer (and/or relevant authority) vary these requirements?

8.3 Control of a non-conforming product

1. Do you have a formal documented procedure for a non-conforming product?
2. How do you ensure that a product which does not conform to product requirements is identified and controlled to prevent its unintended use or delivery?
3. Are there any controls and related responsibilities and authorities for dealing with a non-conforming product?
4. How do you ensure that a detected non-conformity is eliminated?
5. Are there any circumstances when you would authorise the use of a non-conforming product?
6. Do you ever release a non-conforming product under a concession rule?

7. Who authorises these concessions?
8. Do you keep records of all non-conformities and any subsequent actions taken (including concessions obtained)?
9. When a non-conforming product is corrected, is it then subject to reverification to demonstrate conformity to the requirements?
10. What do you do when a non-conforming product is detected after delivery or use?

8.4 Analysis of data

1. How do you ensure the suitability and effectiveness of the QMS?
2. How do you evaluate where continual improvement of the QMS can be made?
3. What data do you use to determine where improvements to the QMS can be made?
4. Does this analysis of data provide information relating to:
   - customer satisfaction? (see 8.2.1)
   - conformance to product requirements? (see 7.2.1)
   - characteristics and trends of processes and products including opportunities for preventive action, and suppliers?

8.5 Improvement

8.5.1 Continual improvement

1. What methods are employed to continually improve the effectiveness of your QMS?
2. How do you ensure that appropriate corrective action is taken to eliminate the cause of non-conformities in order to prevent them recurring?

8.5.2 Corrective action

1. Do you have a documented procedure for corrective action?
2. Does this documented procedure define requirements for:
   - reviewing non-conformities (including customer complaints)?
   - determining the causes of non-conformities?
   - evaluating action to ensure that non-conformities do not recur?
   - determining and implementing action needed?
   - recording of the results of action taken?
   - reviewing corrective action taken?
3. What action do you take to eliminate the cause of non-conformities in order to prevent recurrence?
4. How do you ensure that those corrective actions are appropriate to the effects of the non-conformities encountered?

8.5.3 Preventive action

1. Do you have a documented procedure for preventive action?
2. Does this documented procedure define requirements for:
   - determining potential non-conformities and their causes?
   - evaluating the need for action to prevent their recurrence?
   - determining and implementing action needed?
   - recording results of action taken?
   - reviewing preventive action taken?
3. What action do you take to eliminate the cause of non-conformities in order to prevent recurrence?
4. How do you ensure that those preventive actions are appropriate to the effects of the non-conformities encountered?

3.6 Additional (general purpose) check sheets

The following is a list of some of the most important questions that an external auditor would be likely to ask when assessing an organisation's QMS for conformance to ISO 9001:2000.

3.6.1 Quality management system

Typical auditor's questions (quality management system)	Remarks
Who is responsible for ensuring that the company's Quality Manual meets the requirements of the specified standard for the QMS and does it?	
Do the procedures generated as part of the QMS meet the requirements of the Quality Manual?	
Are written procedures in all areas of the QMS unambiguous, understandable (simple enough so that the intended user has sufficient guidance to assure that quality is maintained) and do they specify methods and criteria?	
How does the documented QMS ensure that a product conforms to specified requirements?	

(*continued*)

Typical auditor's questions (quality management system)	Remarks

How does the QMS identify and ensure that new ideas and techniques that affect quality are verified before being introduced?

How does the QMS ensure that adequate resources are available to attain and maintain the level of quality detailed in the Quality Manual and/or any Quality Plans?

How is the QMS represented in contract and new product developments?

Who is responsible for identifying requirements and risks that are on the frontiers of company or known technology, how are they controlled and how are new procedures generated if required?

3.6.2 Documentation requirements

Typical auditor's questions (documentation requirements)	Remarks

Are written procedures in all areas of the QMS unambiguous, understandable (simple enough so that the intended user has sufficient guidance to assure that quality is maintained) and do they specify methods and criteria?

What procedures describe how the documents defined in quality requirements are controlled?

Do the procedures generated as part of the QMS meet the requirements of the Quality Manual?

Who is responsible for ensuring that quality documentation is available and issued to the relevant work areas in the appropriate form and in time?

Who prepares and updates procedures? Who authorises the issue date?

Typical auditor's questions (documentation requirements)	Remarks

Who reviews and approves the documents for adequacy and are they suitably trained, experienced and equipped to do so?

With whose authority is a quality document approved?

In approving the document, is the approval authority using recorded information on past experience and, if so, what proof is there?

How are changes to the document implemented, recorded and approved, and is the approval authority the same as for the original issue?

How is the use of superseded documentation controlled and is there any confusion as to what the issue is?

When are copies of obsolete documents destroyed and by whom? (Check to ensure that only the authorised issue is available for use.)

How is the original and subsequent versions of the document distributed? Is its receipt acknowledged and should it be?

How does the user of the document know what the current version should be?

Who establishes the correct revision of a document if the current issue is not to be used?

Where are the master documents stored and are there any unauthorised modifications?

Who is responsible for the master document?

Who co-ordinates changes to project documentation, is there only one person responsible and, if not, is the route clearly defined?

(continued)

Typical auditor's questions (documentation requirements)	Remarks

When are changes to the contracted scope of work reviewed and by whom?

How are the changes to the design, which affect the initial requirements, reviewed and what mechanism is there to ensure that these are in the customer's interest?

If the document is derived from a standard format, who is responsible for it and do all the users know how to request a change?

Is the document reissued after every change has been included or, if not, who decides when the document will be reissued and is this time period acceptable to the user of the document?

How are customer requests to change documents reviewed and recorded?

How does the documentation system make sure that the relevant information is available for the Inspector (or relevant authority) for verification when he needs it?

Which procedures define the need to keep records to demonstrate the achievement of quality determined?

Who is responsible for generating quality records and is the method of control adequately defined in instructions?

Does the information on the quality record conform to the requirement as defined in the procedures and, if not, how does it deviate?

Where quality records are required to be compiled by suppliers to demonstrate their achievement of quality, how is this requirement specified and met?

Where are quality records kept, for how long, and is the environment suitable to prevent loss or degradation?

Typical auditor's questions (documentation requirements)	Remarks
How are quality records accessed and is it possible to analyse them in order to identify trends?	
Who defines for how long the quality record should be kept and does this period conflict with any contractual or legal requirements?	
How can it be demonstrated that the retention of quality records shows that the QMS is effective?	
What system is available in order to pass quality records to the customer when required to demonstrate the achievement of quality?	
Who is responsible for disposing of quality records and are they disposed of effectively?	
Has adequate documentation been produced to support the product during its expected life and how is this requirement specified?	

3.6.3 Management commitment

Typical auditor's questions (management commitment)	Remarks
Who is responsible for ensuring that the quality policy is understood and implemented?	
How is the quality policy used to set objectives and who is involved in the decision-making?	
Who determines that the quality policies are compatible with other company objectives?	

3.6.4 Customer focus

Typical auditor's questions (customer focus)	Remarks
Who reviews the contract documents for adequacy and are problem areas resolved?	
Are there procedures for contract review, and are the records readily available and complete?	
How are the differences between the tender and the contract identified and reviewed?	
How are the in-house activities affecting the customer co-ordinated and agreed with the customer, before and during the contract?	
Do the same procedures apply to all contracts and is this evident?	
When are customer-specific standards identified and who controls them and are they available for the use of the designer?	
How are products/documents requiring final approval or certification identified for the company or customer use?	
How are customer requests to change documents reviewed and recorded?	
How are the changes to the design, which affect the initial requirements, reviewed and what mechanism is there to ensure that these are in the customer's interest?	
What methods exist for the customer to specify and carry out his own inspection?	

3.6.5 Quality policy

Typical auditor's questions (quality policy)	Remarks
How is the quality policy used to set objectives and who is involved in the decision-making?	
Who determines that the quality policies are compatible with other company objectives?	
Who is responsible for ensuring that the quality policy is understood and implemented?	
How is the QMS represented in contract and new product developments?	

3.6.6 Planning

Typical auditor's questions (planning)	Remarks
How is the quality policy used to set objectives and who is involved in the decision-making?	
How does the QMS identify and ensure that new ideas and techniques that affect quality are verified before being introduced?	
Who is responsible for identifying requirements and risks that are on the frontiers of company or known technology, how are they controlled and how are new procedures generated if required?	
Who is responsible for clarifying or defining quality standards for the acceptability of product and how are these levels demonstrated?	
How is the compatibility of procedures supporting the QMS established and maintained through revisions?	

(continued)

Typical auditor's questions (planning)	Remarks

How does the QMS exercise continuous and adequate control over areas affecting quality?

Are written procedures in all areas of the QMS unambiguous, understandable (simple enough so that the intended user has sufficient guidance to assure that quality is maintained) and do they specify methods and criteria?

Who has the authority to make decisions on the acceptability of the levels of quality achieved?

When is the need for a Quality Plan identified, who produces it and how are the contents validated?

3.6.7 Responsibility, authority and communication

Typical auditor's questions (responsibility, authority and communication)	Remarks

Who determines that the quality policies are compatible with other company objectives?

Who is the management representative, who has the defined authority to implement quality policies and objectives and has he/she sufficient authority to fulfil this task?

Who is responsible for identifying, reviewing and recommending solutions to minimise or prevent quality-related problems and how is this achieved?

Who is responsible for ensuring that the company's Quality Manual meets the requirements of the specified standard for the QMS and does it?

Typical auditor's questions (responsibility, authority and communication)	Remarks

Who has the authority to make decisions on the acceptability of the levels of quality achieved?

Who is responsible for ensuring that the quality policy is understood and implemented?

Who is responsible for ensuring that quality documentation is available and issued to the relevant work areas in the appropriate form and in time?

Who is responsible for identifying requirements and risks that are on the frontiers of company or known technology, how are they controlled and how are new procedures generated if required?

3.6.8 Management review

Typical auditor's questions (management review)	Remarks

How often is the company quality policy reviewed and revised, by whom, and is he/she suitably placed in the company to do so?

How often and by whom is the QMS reviewed for adequacy and how is its performance quantified and reported?

Who reviews quality objectives to ensure that they are achieved or instigates action in order to implement them?

Is the review process effective and how is action monitored?

Are there records that give evidence of the review process?

3.6.9 Provision of resources

Typical auditor's questions (provision of resources)	Remarks
How does the QMS ensure that adequate resources are available to attain and maintain the level of quality detailed in the Quality Manual and/or any Quality Plans?	

3.6.10 Human resources

Typical auditor's questions (human resources)	Remarks
How does the QMS ensure that adequate resources are available to attain and maintain the level of quality detailed in the Quality Manual and/or any Quality Plans?	
Who sets the qualification and experience requirements for job functions and in which procedure are they defined?	
Where personnel performing job functions do not meet the identified requirements, how are their training needs identified?	
Having identified the need for training, who is responsible for training and who is responsible for ensuring that these needs are met?	
Who is responsible for ensuring that records of qualification and experience are maintained to reflect the current qualifications and experience of personnel?	
How are the training needs of new recruits identified? What training is given on commencement of employment and is it adequate?	
When personnel are redeployed, are they given adequate training in order to perform their new function?	

Typical auditor's questions (human resources)	Remarks
Are all personnel, on a need to know basis, aware of the QMS and are they aware of how to suggest changes to it?	
Are all levels of management aware of the company's policies affecting their functions and specifically what the company's policy with respect to quality is?	
Who is responsible for reviewing records of qualification to ensure that any new training needs are identified?	

3.6.11 Infrastructure

Typical auditor's questions (infrastructure)	Remarks
Who identifies the need for a special manufacturing process and has he adequately defined it?	
What systems are in place for ensuring adequate maintenance of production equipment?	
Who is responsible for ensuring that workmanship standards are adequate to process new or modified products?	
What reference is made to workmanship standards in instructions?	

3.6.12 Work environment

Typical auditor's questions (work environment)	Remarks
What systems are in place for ensuring adequate maintenance of production equipment?	

(continued)

Typical auditor's questions (work environment)	Remarks

Who is responsible for ensuring that workmanship standards are adequate to process new or modified products?

Who identifies the need for a special manufacturing process and has he adequately defined it?

3.6.13 Planning and product realisation

Typical auditor's questions (planning and product realisation)	Remarks

Have procedures been generated to ensure that incoming products are verified before being released for use?

Who inspects or otherwise tests the performance of an incoming product before approving it for use and are they aware of the required acceptance criteria?

How are acceptance criteria specified and is there adequate equipment to ensure that these are met?

How are items, which are not verified, marked?

How are items, which do not need to be verified, identified and if they subsequently fail what mechanism is available to recall them for verification?

How is the past performance of suppliers recorded and is it available for the person taking a decision on the need to validate the incoming product?

What is done with incoming documentation to substantiate that the product meets specified requirements?

How are inspection and test points for work-in-progress identified and who carries out the validation?

Typical auditor's questions (planning and product realisation)	Remarks

Who monitors manufacturing processes to ensure that the equipment is fit for purpose and how is this implemented?

Who is responsible for identifying products that fail to meet their specified requirements and how are these controlled?

What mechanism is there to ensure that all specified tests have been performed and that the results are acceptable?

How are the requirements for final inspection and test specified?

Who verifies that completed products are fit for use?

How are test and inspection records held and are they accessible and do they meet any contractual and legal requirements?

Who is responsible for identifying requirements and risks that are on the frontiers of company or known technology, how are they controlled and how are new procedures generated if required?

When is the need for a Quality Plan identified, who produces it and how are the contents validated?

Are the people assigned to the validation and verification adequately trained and equipped?

When appropriate, do all test and inspection records carry the signature or initials of the person performing the validation?

How does the person carrying out the inspection or test know what documentation he needs and its relevant issue?

Where relevant, have all test and inspection methods been adequately defined?

3.6.14 Customer-related processes

Typical auditor's questions   **Remarks**
(customer-related processes)

Are there procedures for contract review, and
are the records readily available and complete?

Who reviews the contract documents for
adequacy and are problem areas resolved?

Who generates and controls contract-
specific procedures and standards and
does the customer approve them?

How are the activities leading up to a tender
presentation or quotation co-ordinated?

Who generates the tender specification and
are they aware of all pertinent information?

Are order acceptance meetings held and,
if so, who attends them?

How are key project personnel identified
and informed of their role in the contract?

What evidence is there that the project
manager has issued all the necessary
documentation as detailed in his procedures
and was it issued in a timely manner?

How are verbal orders handled?

How are the differences between the tender
and the contract identified and reviewed?

Do the same procedures apply to all
contracts and is this evident?

How is the requirement for design
documentation identified and does this
take into consideration the need for training?

Who receives and reviews documentation
from other departments, the customer,
technical authority (national safety
requirements) affecting the design
requirements and what action is taken if
the information is unclear or ambiguous?

Typical auditor's questions (customer-related processes)	Remarks

When are customer-specific standards identified and who controls them and are they available for the use of the designer?

How are products/documents requiring final approval or certification identified for company or customer use?

How are customer requests to change documents reviewed and recorded?

How are the changes to the design, which affect the initial requirements, reviewed and what mechanism is there to ensure that these are in the customer's interest?

What methods exist for the customer to specify and carry out his own inspection?

3.6.15 Design and development

Typical auditor's questions (design and development)	Remarks

Do procedures exist to control and verify the design activities to ensure the design requirements are specified and met?

What method of design planning is used and does it identify the need for personnel and equipment that are required?

How is the requirement for design documentation identified and does this take into consideration the need for training?

Are there any examples of revised design plans and, if so, why were they modified?

Who receives and reviews documentation from other departments, the customer, technical authority (national safety

(continued)

Typical auditor's questions (design and development)	Remarks

requirements) affecting the design requirements and what action is taken if the information is unclear or ambiguous?

Are conflicts and additions to the initial design specification resolved with the person responsible for generating the requirement and, if so, how are unresolved issues progressed?

How are changes to the design specification and documentation communicated to other departments?

Who is responsible for defining and subsequently updating the distribution list for design documentation?

Is the design specification broken down into smaller units of work and, if so, how are the units related to ensure adequacy when integrated into the whole?

How is the design validated (tested) to ensure that it performs as specified and are these tests traceable to the customer requirements or national standards?

Are the design results reviewed and, if so, are they planned and documented?

If design review meetings are held, who attends them and what evidence is there that a critical review of the results was carried out?

How are unacceptable test results identified and what action is taken to resolve the situation?

Where external test houses are required to perform validation, how are they selected, the test specified and the results formatted?

Are suitably qualified and experienced personnel assigned to the validation of the design?

Typical auditor's questions (design and development)	Remarks

Where do the design change requests originate from, how are they reviewed, and are affected documents quarantined until a decision is taken as to the required action to be taken?

How are approved design changes incorporated into the relevant documentation and are those who need to know informed of the pending changes?

How is the effect of introducing a design change on the product specification assessed to ensure that no degradation of its performance is introduced?

How are superseded design documents identified and removed from other relevant areas?

How are necessary design changes affecting the contract agreed with the customer and, if so, at what point does this happen?

When are customer-specific standards identified and who controls them and are they available for the use of the designer?

Are members of the design function aware of the procedures and standards that they should be using and, if so, how can they identify the correct issue?

Are suitably qualified and experienced staff allocated to the design and verification activities?

How are products/documents requiring final approval or certification identified for the company or customer use?

When was the design documentation as detailed in the procedures produced and has it all been adequately controlled?

(continued)

Typical auditor's questions (design and development)	Remarks
How are completed designs identified and are there any methods of identifying the product status?	
Has adequate documentation been produced to support the product during its expected life and how is this requirement specified?	
Who is responsible for setting design standards and specifications and are all those who need to know aware of these requirements?	
What opportunities are there for designers to assess the requirements and capabilities of the functions that will realise their design and are they aware what they are?	
How are amendments to the purchase orders controlled and authorised and what reference is made to the initial purchase order?	
How are design or specification changes controlled and implemented?	

3.6.16 Purchasing

Typical auditor's questions (purchasing)	Remarks
What procedures cover the purchasing activities?	
How are the acceptance criteria for the product performance defined to ensure that it meets specified requirements?	
How are prospective suppliers assessed with respect to quality and other requirements? What are they?	

Typical auditor's questions (purchasing)	Remarks

Who keeps records of supplier performance and are these records available for purchasing decisions?

What action is taken if a non-approved supplier is selected for an order?

What data is included on the purchase order and does it meet customer and company requirements?

Who reviews the purchase order to ensure that it adequately specifies the product?

Who determines the quality standards to be defined for the order?

Who is responsible for approving the purchase order before release to the supplier and is this value dependent?

When does the requirement to verify products during manufacture get defined on the purchase order?

How are any validation stages notified to the company and who ensures that the relevant testing is performed before progressing with manufacture?

What methods exist for the customer to specify and carry out his own inspection?

How are amendments to the purchase orders controlled and authorised and what reference is made to the initial purchase order?

How are designs or other requirement changes communicated to suppliers and are these instructions clear?

What routes are available for suppliers to resolve queries and what method of progress is used?

3.6.17 Production and service provision

Typical auditor's questions (production and service provision)	Remarks

Who verifies that purchaser (customer) supplied products are fit for the purpose and what method of validation is used and has it been specified?

Who determines whether specific instructions are required for the maintenance of purchaser supplied products during storage and how are the instructions implemented?

Where are products that fail to meet specified requirements stored and how are they identified?

Who prepares specific project instructions for the testing of customer supplied products?

If there are no written instructions for testing, how is the product validated?

How are inspections of stored items recorded and who receives them and reviews them to ensure that unsatisfactory test results are analysed and action taken to resolve the situations?

How are purchaser supplied products stored and are they segregated to identify those that are not fit for use?

Are products reinspected prior to use and, if not, how is the product validated to ensure that it is still satisfactory for use?

Who resolves problems with the customer with respect to products which are unfit or are not available for use? What records are kept?

Have special storage and inspections been specified by the customer and how can you be sure that these are correct and adequate?

Typical auditor's questions (production and service provision)	Remarks

Are products clearly identified at all stages of the process?

How are products in storage identified?

How are visually identical parts with different characteristics identified?

Who determines the need to identify products and are instructions issued to define what the products should be traceable to?

How are the requirements for traceability recorded and are the instructions explicit?

How are the requirements for traceability on a product/batch which may cause the loss of life, serious injury or loss of production determined, who is assigned this responsibility and are they suitably trained and experienced?

How is the batch/product marked to ensure that it is uniquely identified and do all associated documents carry the same reference?

How is traceability assured throughout the life of the product?

When are the production/installation processes that need to be controlled in order to assure the required level of quality identified?

Who is responsible for these processes and can they demonstrate that adequate validation and verification takes place to ensure the correct manufacturer?

Who identifies the need for WIs and are they responsible for updating them to take into account new working practices and techniques?

(continued)

Typical auditor's questions (production and service provision)	Remarks

Where are the WIs filed, are they under control and are the people who are expected to use them aware of them?

Who has been nominated to ensure that the finished product meets its process requirements and does he have detailed acceptance criteria for assessing the work?

Who is responsible for ensuring that workmanship standards are adequate to process new or modified products?

What reference is made to workmanship standards in instructions?

When the end product of a process can neither be verified nor validated at its completion, do procedures exist in order to accept it during work-in-progress and what records are available to prove this?

Who identifies the need for a special manufacturing process and has he adequately defined it?

Who is responsible for discussing special processes with the customer/supplier before an order is accepted or placed?

If the process requires a controlled environment, who has specified its acceptance limits and has it been documented and controlled to these requirements?

Have the people who have been assigned process duties been adequately equipped to perform the task and is there sufficient space to carry out the work?

How is reprocessing controlled, and does it follow the same process or do other WIs apply?

Typical auditor's questions (production and service provision)	Remarks

How can you show that the WIs, build documentation and other manufacturing data are at the correct issue and are there any unauthorised additions?

How are design or specification changes controlled and implemented?

What systems are in place for ensuring adequate maintenance of production equipment?

What method of identification is used to identify the inspection or test status of a product and does it provide adequate information?

Have all the specified inspections/tests been carried out and who has performed them and are they suitably authorised to do so?

Where are test and inspection records stored and are they easily traceable to the product?

Who has the authority to remove a test or inspection indicator?

Have detailed instructions with respect to defining the status been written?

Who is responsible for defining the acceptable test status?

Has provision been made for entering a new status as a result of retesting/ inspecting the product?

What methods of indicating product status are used by suppliers and are they acceptable?

Who identifies the requirements for handling, storage and packaging and how are they specified?

(*continued*)

Typical auditor's questions (production and service provision)	Remarks

Who is responsible for ensuring that the handling, storage and packaging requirements are met and if any validation is required, how is it done?

How can damage due to inappropriate handling or storage be detected and have procedures been written to ensure that periodic reinspection, when required, is carried out to ensure fitness for purpose?

Where a storage area has been set up, do methods of receiving and despatching products exist and are all relevant staff knowledgeable?

How is a product authorised to enter and leave the storage areas?

Does the product maintain its identity at all stages of handling, storage, packing and delivery and is there evidence to support this?

Who specifies packaging standards, are there any specific contract requirements and who is responsible for the final packing?

How are environmental conditions considered when determining requirements to ensure the preservation of quality?

Who defines the path for the processing of the product and do these instructions define all the relevant processes to be followed?

Who is responsible for stores records and do they adequately define the current stockholding?

How are different batches or versions of the same product identified, stored, packed and delivered and is there any scope for confusion?

Typical auditor's questions (production and service provision)	Remarks

Who is responsible for ensuring that servicing meets specified requirements and how is this achieved?

What procedures exist to define the manner of servicing and reporting?

Who is responsible for generating instructions to ensure that the servicing or after sales support is adequately defined and who is responsible for ensuring that this information is in a suitable format?

Who is responsible for providing that adequate back-up is available to ensure that installed and accepted equipment is supported?

How are requests for support on sites handled, and are all queries responded to in a timely manner?

How is feedback from servicing handled and how is this feedback co-ordinated?

3.6.18 Control of monitoring and measuring devices

Typical auditor's questions (control of monitoring and measuring devices)	Remarks

Who determines which measuring or test equipment needs to be calibrated and how are acceptance limits established and documented?

Who decides the period of validity for the calibration and is there any provision for subsequently changing it based on past records?

How is equipment used for indicating rather than measuring identified and has it been calibrated?

(*continued*)

Typical auditor's questions (control of monitoring and measuring devices)	Remarks

How are the measurement requirements specified and, if appropriate, is the type of test equipment specified in instructions?

How is the measurement uncertainty specified and are operators aware of what this should be for the work being carried out?

How is the national standard to which the equipment is to be calibrated specified and, if no suitable standard exists, how is it specified?

Who is responsible for ensuring that new or reclassified equipment is included in a calibration schedule and how is he informed?

What action will be taken if an item sent for calibration fails to meet the specified requirements?

Where appropriate, is it possible to identify the calibration status of inspection equipment used to demonstrate the adequacy of the product?

How is it possible to identify the test or inspection equipment used to demonstrate the adequacy of the product?

How is equipment not needing calibration identified, is it ever used to demonstrate the acceptability of products?

Who is responsible for ensuring that all calibrated equipment is maintained and stored in a suitable environment so as not to invalidate the calibration?

Have any special control conditions been defined for calibrated equipment and should it be used under environmentally controlled conditions?

Typical auditor's questions (control of monitoring and measuring devices)	Remarks

How is the calibrated equipment checked prior to use to ensure that it is fit for the intended purpose?

How are adjustments, which can negate the validity of the calibration results, be set or identified to prevent unauthorised adjustments?

What procedures are in place to control the management and calibration of inspection, measuring and test equipment?

3.6.19 Monitoring and measurement

Typical auditor's questions (monitoring and measurement)	Remarks

Have procedures been generated to ensure that incoming products are verified before being released for use?

Who inspects or otherwise tests the performance of incoming products before approving them for use and are they aware of the required acceptance criteria?

How are acceptance criteria specified and is there adequate equipment to ensure that these are met?

How are items, which are not verified, marked?

How are items, which do not need to be verified, identified and if they subsequently fail, what mechanism is available to recall them for verification?

How is the past performance of suppliers recorded and is it available for the person taking a decision on the need to validate the incoming product?

(continued)

Typical auditor's questions (monitoring and measurement)	Remarks

What is done with incoming documentation to substantiate that the product meets specified requirements?

How are inspection and tests points for work in progress identified and who carries out the validation?

Who monitors manufacturing processes to ensure that the equipment is fit for purpose and how is this implemented?

Who is responsible for identifying products that fail to meet their specified requirements and how are these controlled?

What mechanism is there to ensure that all specified tests have been performed and that the results are acceptable?

How are the requirements for final inspection and test specified?

Who verifies that completed products are fit for use?

How are test and inspection records held and are they accessible and do they meet any contractual and legal requirements?

Are the people assigned to the validation and verification adequately trained and equipped?

When appropriate, do all test and inspection records carry the signature or initials of the person performing the validation?

How does the person carrying out the inspection or test know what documentation he needs and its relevant issue?

Where relevant, have all test and inspection methods been adequately defined?

How effective is the QMS and can this be demonstrated?

Typical auditor's questions (monitoring and measurement)	Remarks

How are audits planned and programmed?

Does the programme cover the whole QMS?

How are the requirements for an audit defined and are these instructions supported by procedures?

Who determines the need for an audit and on what basis do they reach their decision?

What action is taken after an audit?

How are non-conformities found during an audit resolved, and are the relevant managers involved?

How are audit reports controlled and are they circulated to the relevant managers?

How can the QMS identify that timely corrective actions are taken as a result of an audit?

When the corrective action is not effective, who is responsible for resolving the situation?

How are auditors selected and are they suitably trained to carry out an audit?

Are all auditors independent of the activity that they are auditing and how can this be demonstrated?

When carrying out the audit, how are the following assessed: structure, personnel, material, resources and product of the activity, and are they?

How are the results of the audit programme reviewed?

How does the audit programme demonstrate that the QMS is effective?

(*continued*)

Typical auditor's questions (monitoring and measurement)	Remarks
Who is responsible for compiling and distributing a 'close-out report'?	
How, if at all, are the results of previous audits used to structure the audit of the same or similar function?	
Who is responsible for setting the period between audits and are these periods flexed as a result of past performance or inferred non-conformance identified whilst auditing other activities?	
Who determines the need to use statistical methods to determine the level of quality achieved and are the methods directly related to a standard?	
Who is responsible for gathering data for statistical techniques, is the amount of data specified and is this what is collected?	
Who processes the data and are statistics produced in a timely manner, reviewed and analysed so as to provide an indication of the situation?	
How are statistical data and results controlled and is it adequate?	
Who is responsible for reviewing the statistical techniques and the method of data collection?	
Who has documented the methods of statistical techniques being used?	
Who is responsible for ensuring that the statistical techniques in use are suitable?	
What procedures define the manner of application of statistical techniques?	

3.6.20 Control of non-conforming product

Typical auditor's questions (control of non-conforming product)	Remarks

How are products, which do not meet their specified requirement, identified?

What environment is the non-conforming product stored in and is the marking adequate?

What documentation is available to identify where the product fails to meet specified requirements?

Who is responsible for reviewing the documentation in order to recommend a remedial action?

Whilst a decision is being taken, how are other products which may also fail to meet specified requirements, identified and segregated, and are they?

What procedures define the control of a non-conforming product process?

How is remedial action documented and can the product be identified to any such document?

How are non-conforming products, which are reworked, identified and processed and how can you tell?

Where no remedial action is possible and the product must be disposed of, how is this accomplished and is the routine adequate to prevent further use?

If the product is reclassified or accepted as is, how is this documented and is the status of the product obvious?

Are written instructions available as to the required acceptance criteria of the reworked product and how do the revised tests/ inspections get recorded?

(*continued*)

Typical auditor's questions (control of non-conforming product)	Remarks
When non-conformity affects the customer or other suppliers, how are they involved in the decision-making and approval process?	
How do departments carry out an in-depth consideration of major items which fail to meet specified requirements and who decides what is a major item?	
When are records of non-conforming products reviewed to determine any trends and is there any evidence to support this?	
Where do non-conformance reports go for investigation?	
How effective is the corrective action and is it adequate?	

3.6.21 Analysis of data

Typical auditor's questions (analysis of data)	Remarks
Who determines the need to use statistical methods to determine the level of quality achieved and are the methods directly related to a standard?	
Who is responsible for gathering data for statistical techniques, is the amount of data specified and is this what is collected?	
Who processes the data and are statistics produced in a timely manner, reviewed and analysed so as to provide an indication of the situation?	
How are statistical data and results controlled and is it adequate?	
Who is responsible for reviewing the statistical techniques and the method of data collection?	

Typical auditor's questions (analysis of data)	Remarks

Who has documented the methods of statistical techniques being used?

Who is responsible for ensuring that the statistical techniques in use are suitable?

What procedures define the manner of application of statistical techniques?

3.6.22 Improvement

Typical auditor's questions (improvement)	Remarks

How often is the company quality policy reviewed and revised, by whom, and is he/she suitably placed in the company to do so?

How often and by whom is the QMS reviewed for adequacy and how is its performance quantified and reported?

Who reviews quality objectives to ensure that they are achieved or instigates action in order to implement them?

Is the review effective and how is action monitored?

Are there records that give evidence of the review process?

Who investigates the cause of non-conformity and the subsequent actions taken?

Who is responsible for ensuring that potential causes of non-conformity are identified and action taken to ensure that recurrences do not take place?

(continued)

Typical auditor's questions (improvement)	Remarks
How are customer complaints handled and is there a method of routing them for analysis by the company's nominated authority?	
How are corrective actions controlled and is the method of control adequately defined?	
What system is available to update procedures to ensure that non-conformities are rectified and preventive measures introduced and are all people who need to be aware of it informed?	
How are changes to methods implemented and recorded?	
What procedures control the processes of corrective action and preventive action, and what records are available?	

3.7 Example stage audit checks

The following is a list of the most important questions that an external auditor is likely to ask when evaluating an organisation for their:

- design stage;
- manufacturing stage;
- acceptance stage;
- in-service stage.

3.7.1 Design stage

Item	Related item	Remark
1 Requirements	1.1 Information	Has the customer fully described his requirement?
		Has the customer any mandatory requirements?
		Are the customer's requirements fully

Item	Related item	Remark
		understood by all members of the design team?
		Is there a need to have further discussions with the customer?
		Are other suppliers or subcontractors involved? If yes, who is the prime contractor?
	1.2 Standards	What international standards need to be observed? Are they available?
		What national standards need to be observed? Are they available?
		What other information and procedures are required? Are they available?
	1.3 Procedures	Are there any customer-supplied drawings, sketches or plans? Have they been registered?
2 Quality procedures	2.1 Procedures manual	Is one available?
		Does it contain detailed procedures and instructions for the control of all drawings within the drawing office?
	2.2 Planning implementation and production	Is the project split into a number of work packages? If so:
		• are the various work packages listed? • have work package leaders been nominated? • is their task clear? • is their task achievable?
		Is a time plan available? Is it up to date? Regularly maintained? Relevant to the task?

(continued)

Item	Related item	Remark
3 Drawings	3.1 Identification	Are all drawings identified by a unique number?
		Is the numbering system strictly controlled?
	3.2 Cataloguing	Is a catalogue of drawings maintained?
		Is this catalogue regularly reviewed and up to date?
	3.3 Amendments and modifications	Is there a procedure for authorising the issue of amendments to drawings?
		Is there a method for withdrawing and disposing of obsolete drawings?
4 Components	4.1 Availability	Are complete lists of all the relevant components available?
	4.2 Adequacy	Are the selected components currently available and adequate for the task? If not, how long will they take to procure? Is this acceptable?
	4.3 Acceptability	If alternative components have to be used are they acceptable to the task?
5 Records	5.1 Failure reports	Has the design office access to all records, failure reports and other relevant data?
	5.2 Reliability data	Is reliability data correctly stored, maintained and analysed?
	5.3 Graphs, diagrams, plans	In addition to drawings, is there a system for the control of all graphs, tables, plans, etc.? Are CAD facilities available? (If so, go to 6.1)

Item	Related item	Remark
6 Reviews and audits	6.1 Computers	If a processor is being used: • are all the design office personnel trained in its use? • are regular back-ups taken? • is there an anti-virus system in place?
	6.2 Manufacturing division	Is a close relationship being maintained between the design office and the manufacturing division?
	6.3	Is notice being taken of the manufacturing division's exact requirements, their problems and their choices of components, etc.?

3.7.2 Manufacturing stage

Item	Related item	Remark
1 Degree of quality	1.1 Quality control procedures	Are quality control procedures available? Are they relevant to the task? Are they understood by all members of the manufacturing team? Are they regularly reviewed and up to date? Are they subject to control procedures?
	1.2 Quality control checks	What quality checks are being observed? Are they relevant? Are there laid down procedures for carrying out these checks?

(continued)

Item		Related item		Remark
				Are they available?
				Are they regularly updated?
2	Reliability of product design	2.1	Statistical data	Is there a system for predicting the reliability of the product's design?
				Is sufficient statistical data available to be able to estimate the actual reliability of the design, before a product is manufactured?
				Is the appropriate engineering data available?
		2.2	Components and parts	Are the reliability ratings of recommended parts and components available?
				Are probability methods used to examine the reliability of a proposed design? If so, have these checks revealed:
				• design deficiencies such as: − assembly errors? − operator learning, motivational, or fatigue factors? − latent defects? − improper part selection?

3.7.3 Acceptance stage

Item		Related item		Remark
1	Product performance			Does the product perform to the required function? If not what has been done about it?
2	Quality level	2.1	Workmanship	Does the workmanship of the product fully meet the level of

Item		Related item		Remark
				quality required or stipulated by the user?
		2.2	Tests	Is the product subjected to environmental tests? If so, which ones?
				Is the product field tested as a complete system? If so, what were the results?
3	Reliability	3.1	Probability function	Are individual components and modules environmentally tested? If so, how?
		3.2	Failure rate	Is the product's reliability measured in terms of probability function? If so, what were the results?
				Is the product's reliability measured in terms of failure rate? If so, what were the results?
		3.3	Mean time between failures	Is the product's reliability measured in terms of mean time between failure? If so, what were the results?

3.7.4 In-service stage

Item		Related item		Remark
1	System reliability	1.1	Product basic design	Are statistical methods being used to prove the product's basic design? If so, are they adequate? Are the results recorded and available?
				What other methods are used to prove the product's basic design?

(continued)

Item		Related item		Remark
				Are these methods appropriate?
2	Equipment reliability	2.1	Personnel	Are there sufficient trained personnel to carry out the task?
				Are they sufficiently motivated? If not, what is the problem?
		2.1.1	Operators	Have individual job descriptions been developed? Are they readily available?
				Are all operators capable of completing their duties?
		2.1.2	Training	Do all personnel receive appropriate training?
				Is a continuous On The Job training (OJT) programme available to all personnel? If not, why not?
		2.2	Product dependability	What proof is there that the product is dependable?
				How is product dependability proved? Is this sufficient for the customer?
		2.3	Component reliability	Has the reliability of individual components been considered?
				Does the reliability of individual components exceed the overall system reliability?
		2.4	Faulty operating procedures	Are operating procedures available?
				Are they appropriate to the task?
				Are they regularly reviewed?

Item	Related item		Remark
	2.5	Operational abuses	Are there any obvious operational abuses?
			If so, what are they? How can they be overcome?
	2.5.1	Extended duty cycle	Do the staff have to work shifts? If so, are they allowed regular breaks from their work?
			Is there a senior shift worker? If so, are his duties and responsibilities clearly defined?
			Are computers used?
			If so, are screen filters available?
			Do the operators have keyboard wrist rests?
	2.5.2	Training	Do the operational staff receive regular on-the-job training?
			Is there any need for additional in-house or external training?
3	Design capability	3.1 Faulty operating procedures	Are there any obvious faulty operating procedures?
			Can the existing procedures be improved upon?

3.8 Complete index for ISO 9001:2000

The following is a list of all the main topics and subjects covered in ISO 9001:2000.

Unsuitability for use
    customer property   7.5.4

Urgent release of goods   8.2.4

Validation
    changes in design and development   7.3.7
    design and development   7.3.6
    design and development planning   7.3.1b
    in products   7.1c
    partial   7.3.6
    prior to delivery   7.3.6
    production and service processes   7.5.2
    qualification of
        equipment   7.5.2b
        personnel   7.5.2b
        processes   7.5.2a
    records   4.2.4, 7.3.6, 7.5.2d
    revalidation   7.5.2e

Verification
    changes in design/development   7.3.7
    customer property   7.5.4
    design and development   7.3.5
    design and development planning   7.3.1b
    in products   7.1c
    lack of   7.5.2
    of corrective action from internal audits   8.2.2
    purchased product   7.4.3
        at supplier's premises   7.4.3
    records   7.3.5
    reporting of results   8.2.2

Work environment   6.4

Work instructions
    availability of   7.5.1b

Workspace
    identification, provision and maintenance of   6.3a

3.9 ISO 9001:2000 crosscheck and correspondence form

The intention of this form is to show how and where the requirements of ISO 9001:2000 have been met in an organisation's quality management system.

Clause No.	ISO 9001:2000 title	CORRESPONDENCE			
		Quality Manual	Business Process	Quality Procedure	Work Instruction
1	Scope				
1.1	General				
1.2	Application				
2	Normative reference				
3	Terms and definitions				

Clause No.	ISO 9001:2000 title	CORRESPONDENCE			
		Quality Manual	Business Process	Quality Procedure	Work Instruction
4.1	General requirements				
4.2	Documentation requirements (title only)				
4.2.1	General				
4.2.2	Quality Manual				
4.2.3	Control of documents				
4.2.4	Control of records				

Clause No.	ISO 9001:2000 title	CORRESPONDENCE			
		Quality Manual	Business Process	Quality Procedure	Work Instruction
5.1	Management commitment				
5.2	Customer focus				
5.3	Quality policy				
5.4	Planning (title only)				
5.4.1	Quality objectives				
5.4.2	Quality management system planning				
5.5	Responsibility, authority and communication (title only)				
5.5.1	Responsibility and authority				
5.5.2	Management representative				
5.5.3	Internal communication				
5.6	Management review (title only)				
5.6.1	General				
5.6.2	Review input				
5.6.3	Review output				

Clause No.	ISO 9001:2000 title	CORRESPONDENCE			
		Quality Manual	Business Process	Quality Procedure	Work Instruction
6.1	Provision of resources				
6.2	Human resources (title only)				
6.2.1	General				
6.2.2	Competence, awareness and training				
6.3	Infrastructure				
6.4	Work environment				

Clause No.	ISO 9001:2000 title	CORRESPONDENCE			
		Quality Manual	Business Process	Quality Procedure	Work Instruction
7.1	Planning of product realisation				
7.2	Customer-related processes (title only)				
7.2.1	Determination of requirements related to the product				
7.2.2	Review of requirements related to the product				
7.2.3	Customer communication				
7.3	Design and development (title only)				
7.3.1	Design and development planning				
7.3.2	Design and development inputs				
7.3.3	Design and development outputs				
7.3.4	Design and development review				
7.3.5	Design and development verification				
7.3.6	Design and development validation				
7.3.7	Control of design and development changes				
7.4	Purchasing (title only)				
7.4.1	Purchasing process				
7.4.2	Purchasing information				
7.4.3	Verification of purchased product				
7.5	Production and service provision (title only)				
7.5.1	Control of production and service provision				
7.5.2	Validation of processes for production and service provision				
7.5.3	Identification and traceability				
7.5.4	Customer property				
7.5.5	Preservation of product				
7.6	Control of monitoring and measuring devices				

Clause No.	ISO 9001:2000 title	CORRESPONDENCE			
		Quality Manual	Business Process	Quality Procedure	Work Instruction
8.1	General				
8.2	Monitoring and measurement (title only)				
8.2.1	Customer satisfaction				
8.2.2	Internal audit				
8.2.3	Monitoring and measurement of processes				
8.2.4	Monitoring and measurement of product				
8.3	Control of non-conforming product				
8.4	Analysis of data				
8.5	Improvement (title only)				
8.5.1	Continual improvement				
8.5.2	Corrective action				
8.5.3	Preventive action				

3.10 Audit check sheet

A list of the most important questions an auditor should ask.

3.10.1 Systematic requirements

Section No.	ISO 9001:2000 title	Typical auditor's questions	Currently met?	Document	Remarks
4	Quality Management System requirement	• Has a Quality Management System been established in accordance with the requirements of ISO 9001:2000?			

4.1	General requirements	• Is the QMS:
		  – documented?
		  – implemented?
		  – maintained?
		  – continually improved?
		• Does the organisation have all the documents necessary to ensure the effective operation and control of its processes?			

- **Has the organisation:**
  - identified the sequence of processes and sub-processes needed for the QMS?
  - determined the sequence and interaction of these processes?
  - determined the criteria and methods required to ensure the effective operation and control of these processes?
  - ensured that information necessary to support the monitoring and operation of these processes is available?
  - ensured that resources necessary to support the monitoring and operation of these processes is available?
- **Does the organisation measure, monitor and analyse these processes?**
- **Is the necessary action implemented to achieve planned results and continual improvement of the processes?**
- **Does the organisation manage these processes in accordance with the requirements of ISO 9001:2000?**

3.10.2 Document requirements

Section No.	ISO 9001:2000 title	Typical auditor's questions	Currently met?	Document	Remarks
4.2	Documentation requirements	• **Have the requirements of ISO 9001:2000 been met?**			
4.2.1	General	• **Does the QMS include:** – a Quality Manual? – statements concerning quality policy and quality objectives? – documented procedures? – quality records?			
4.2.2	Quality Manual	• **Is the Quality Manual:** – controlled? – maintained? • **Does it include details concerning:** – the scope of the QMS? – justifications for any exclusion from the ISO 9001:2000 requirements? – associated documented procedures? – the sequence and interaction of processes?			
4.2.3	Control of documents	• **Has the organisation established a documented procedure to control all of its QMS documents?**			

- **Does this procedure include methods for:**
  - controlling their distribution?
  - approving documents prior to issue?
  - reviewing, updating and reapproving documents?
  - identifying the current revision status of documents?
  - ensuring that documents fulfil a useful purpose in the organisation?
  - ensuring that relevant versions of all applicable documents are available at points of use?
  - ensuring that documents remain legible, readily identifiable and retrievable?
  - ensuring that information is kept up to date?
  - identifying, distributing and controlling of documents received from an external source?
  - ensuring that classified information is restricted to those who are authorised to receive it?
  - the identification and control of obsolete documents that have been retained for any purpose?

4.2.4 **Control of records**

- **Does the organisation have a documented procedure for records covering:**
  - control, maintenance and identification?
  - storage and retrieval?
  - protection and retention?
- **Do these records provide evidence of:**
  - the organisation's conformance to the ISO 9001:2000 requirements?
  - the effective operation of the QMS?

3.10.3 Management requirements

Section No.	ISO 9001:2000 title	Typical auditor's questions	Currently met?	Document	Remarks
5	Management responsibility	• **Is the organisation committed to developing, establishing and improving its QMS?**			

5.1	Management commitment	• **Does the organisation demonstrate its commitment to developing, establishing and improving the organisation's QMS through:**
		  – management commitment?
		  – an established quality policy?
		  – determining customer requirements and achieving customer satisfaction?
		  – a quality policy?
		  – regularly reviewing the QMS documentation?
		• **Does the organisation:**
		  – ensure that all personnel are aware of the importance of meeting customer, regulatory and legal requirements?
		  – establish the quality policy and quality objectives?
		  – conduct internal management reviews?
		  – ensure the availability of necessary resources to administer the QMS?			

5.2	Customer focus	• **Does the organisation ensure that customer needs and expectations are recognised and established?** • **Are these customer needs and expectations converted into requirements?** • **Does the organisation ensure that customer requirements are fulfilled?**			

5.3	Quality policy	• **Is the organisation's quality policy:**
		   – controlled?
		   – appropriate?
		   – regularly reviewed for continued suitability?
		   – committed to meeting requirements?
		   – communicated and understood throughout the company?
		   – capable of continual improvement?
		   – capable of providing a framework for establishing and
		     reviewing quality objectives?

5.4	Planning	• **Does the organisation have planned quality objectives?**

5.4.1	Quality objectives	• **Is the organisation's quality planning documented?**
		• **Does it include:**
		   – quality objectives?
		   – resources?
		• **Has the organisation established quality objectives for each relevant function and level within the company?**
		• **Are the organisation's quality objectives measurable and consistent with quality policy?**
		• **Do they include:**
		   – a commitment for continual improvement?
		   – product requirements?

5.4.2	Quality Management System planning	• **Does the organisation's quality planning cover:**
		   – the processes required for a QMS (as mentioned in
		     Section 4)?

(continued)

Section No.	ISO 9001:2000 title	Typical auditor's questions	Currently met?	Document	Remarks
		– the identification and availability of resources and information?			
		– any permissible exclusion (to the requirements of ISO 9001:2000)?			
		– the requirements for continual improvement?			
		– the requirements for change control?			
		• **Does the organisation's quality planning ensure that the QMS is maintained during planned changes?**			
5.5	Responsibility and authority and communication	• **Has the organisation defined and implemented a QMS that addresses its quality objectives?**			
		• **Is the administration of the organisation's QMS documented?**			
		• **Does it cover:**			
		– responsibilities and authorities?			
		– management representative's duties?			
		– internal communication?			
		– the Quality Manual?			
		– control of documents?			
		– control of quality records?			

5.5.1	Responsibility and authority	• Are the functions and interrelationships of all staff defined? • Are staff responsibilities and authorities defined?

5.5.2	Management representative	• Has the organisation appointed a Quality Manager who (regardless of all other duties) has sole responsibility for the implementation and management of the QMS?
		• Is the administration of the organisation's QMS documented?
		• Does the organisation's QMS adequately cover:
		  – responsibilities and authorities?
		  – management representative's duties?

5.5.3	Internal communication	• Does the organisation ensure that there are lines of communication between all members of staff to ensure the effectiveness of the QMS processes? • Is there a procedure for internal communication?
5.6	Management review	• Does the organisation's top management regularly review the QMS at planned intervals?

5.6.1	General	• Does the QMS review cover the continuing suitability, adequacy and effectiveness of the QMS?
		• Does the review evaluate the:
		  – need for changes?
		  – quality policy?
		  – quality objectives?

(continued)

Section No.	ISO 9001:2000 title	Typical auditor's questions	Currently met?	Document	Remarks

5.6.2	Review input	● **Does the management review include:**
		  – internal audit results?
		  – external and third party audit results?
		  – customer feedback?
		  – process performance?
		  – product conformance?
		  – implemented preventive and corrective actions?
		  – outstanding preventive and corrective actions?
		  – results from previous management reviews?
		  – changes that could affect the QMS?			

5.6.3	Review output	● **Do the outputs of management reviews include recommendations for:**
		  – the improvement of the QMS and its processes?
		  – the improvement of the product related to customer requirements?
		  – confirming and establishing resource needs?
		● **Are the results of management reviews recorded?**
		● **Are the results (e.g. minutes and action sheets) circulated?**			

3.10.4 Resource requirements

Section No.	ISO 9001:2000 title	Typical auditor's questions	Currently met?	Document	Remarks
6	Resource management	• **Does the organisation plan and provide necessary resources?**			
6.1	Provision of resources	• **Does the organisation provide the resources required to:** – implement and improve the QMS processes? – ensure customer satisfaction? – meet customer requirements?			
6.2	Human resources	• **Has the organisation established procedures for:** – the assignment of personnel? – training? – awareness? – competency?			
6.2.1	General	• **Has the organisation established procedures for the assignment of personnel on the basis of:** – competency? – qualification? – training? – skill and experience?			

(continued)

Section No.	ISO 9001:2000 title	Typical auditor's questions	Currently met?	Document	Remarks

6.2.2	Competence, awareness and training	● **Does the organisation:**
		  – identify training requirements?
		  – provide appropriate training?
		  – evaluate the training provided?
		● **Does the organisation ensure that all their staff appreciates the relevance and importance of their activities and how they contribute towards achieving quality objectives?**
		● **Does the organisation keep staff records covering education, experience, qualifications, training, etc.?**			

6.3	Infrastructure	● **Does the organisation identify, provide and maintain the necessary:**
		  – workspace and associated facilities?
		  – equipment, hardware and software?
		  – supporting services?**			

6.4	Work environment	**Does the organisation identify and manage the work environment (including human and physical factors) to ensure conformity of product?**			

3.10.5 Product requirements

Section No.	ISO 9001:2000 title	Typical auditor's questions	Currently met?	Document	Remarks
7	Product realisation	**Has the organisation established the processes necessary to achieve the product?**			
7.1	Planning and realisation	● **Has the organisation:**			
		– identified the sequence of processes and subprocesses needed for the QMS?			
		– determined the sequence and interaction of these processes?			
		– determined the criteria and methods required to ensure the effective operation and control of these processes?			
		– ensured that information necessary to support the monitoring and operation of these processes is available?			
		– ensured that resources necessary to support the monitoring and operation of these processes is available?			
		● **Within this sequence of processes and subprocesses, has the following been determined:**			
		– the quality objectives for the product, project or contract?			
		– product-specific processes, documentation, resources and facilities?			

(continued)

Section No.	ISO 9001:2000 title	Typical auditor's questions	Currently met?	Document	Remarks
		– verification and validation activities? – criteria for acceptability? – required records? **● Does the organisation have a documented procedure for records covering:** – control, maintenance and identification? – storage and retrieval? – protection and retention? **● Do these records provide evidence of:** – the organisation's conformance to the ISO 9001:2000 requirements?			
7.2	Customer-related processes	**● Has the organisation established procedures for the:** – identification of customer requirements? – review of product requirements? – customer communication?			
7.2.1	Determination of requirements related to product	**● Has the organisation established a process for identifying customer requirements?** **● Does this process determine:** – customer-specified product requirements (e.g. availability, delivery and support)? – non-specified customer requirements (e.g. those affecting the product)? – mandatory requirements (such as regulatory and legal obligations)?			

(continued)

7.2.2 — **Review of requirements related to product**

- **Has the organisation established a process for ensuring that product requirements have been fully established?**
- **Does the process ensure that (prior to submission of tender or acceptance of contract):**
  - all customer requirements have been defined and can be met?
  - where no written requirements are available, that verbal customer requirements are confirmed?
  - any contract or order requirements differing from those previously expressed (e.g. in a tender or quotation) are resolved?
  - the organisation has the ability to meet the defined requirements?

7.2.3 — **Customer communication**

- **Has the organisation an established process for:**
  - providing customers with product information?
  - handling customer enquiries, contracts or orders (including amendments)?
  - customer feedback and customer complaints?

7.3 — **Design and development**

Has the organisation a process and adequate procedures for their design and development activities?

7.3.1 — **Design and development planning**

- **Does the organisation plan and control design and development of the product?**
- **Do these processes include:**
  - stage review, verification and validation activities?
  - identification of responsibilities and authorities?

Section No.	ISO 9001:2000 title	Typical auditor's questions	Currently met?	Document	Remarks
		– management of the interfaces between different groups that may be involved?			
		– provision of effective communication and clarity of responsibilities?			
		– product and planning reviews?			
		● **Are these processes adequate?**			
7.3.2	**Design and development inputs**	● **Does the organisation have a process for developing project plans?**			
		● **Does the organisation define and document product requirement inputs?**			
		● **Do these input requirements include:**			
		– function and performance requirements?			
		– applicable regulatory and legal requirements?			
		– applicable standards, specifications and tolerances?			
		– applicable requirements derived from previous similar designs?			
		– any other requirements essential for design and development?			
		● **Are inadequate, incomplete, ambiguous or conflicting input requirements resolved?**			
7.3.3	**Design and development outputs**	● **Are all products approved prior to release?**			
		● **Does the organisation define and document their product outputs?**			

- **Do these critical requirements ensure that the product:**
  - meets the design and development input requirements?
  - provides appropriate information for production and service operations?
  - contains or makes reference to product acceptance criteria?
  - defines the characteristics of the product that are essential to its safe and proper use?

| 7.3.4 | Design and development review |

- **Are systematic reviews of the design and development carried out at suitable stages? Do they:**
  - evaluate the ability of the product to fulfil the requirements?
  - include representatives from the functions concerned with the design and development stage being reviewed?
- **Are follow-up actions from the reviews recorded?**

| 7.3.5 | Design and development verification |

- **Does the organisation verify that the design output meets the design and development input?**
- **Are the results of this verification (and any necessary subsequent follow-up actions) recorded?**

| 7.3.6 | Design and development validation |

- **Does the organisation validate that the product is capable of meeting the requirements of intended use?**
- **Are these results and any necessary subsequent follow-up actions recorded?**

(continued)

Section No.	ISO 9001:2000 title	Typical auditor's questions	Currently met?	Document	Remarks
		• Wherever applicable, is the validation completed prior to the delivery or implementation of the product? • If full validation is impractical prior to delivery or implementation of the product, is a partial validation performed to the maximum extent applicable?			
7.3.7	Control of design and development changes	• Does the organisation have a procedure that identifies the need for a design and development change? • Are these results of implementing this procedure (and any necessary subsequent follow-up actions) recorded? • Are the effects of these changes reviewed, verified and validated before implementation?			

7.4	Purchasing	• Does the organisation have processes for:
		  – purchasing control?
		  – purchasing information?
		  – verification of purchased product?			

7.4.1	Purchasing process	• Does the organisation have processes for:
		  – purchasing control?
		  – purchasing information?
		  – verification of purchased product?			

(continued)

7.4.2   Purchasing information

- **Does the organisation have documentation describing:**
  - the product to be purchased?
  - requirements for approval or qualification (i.e. product, procedures, processes, equipment and personnel)?
  - QMS requirements?
- **Does the organisation ensure the adequacy of the specified requirements contained in the purchasing documents prior to their release?**

7.4.3   Verification of purchased product

- **Does the organisation identify (and implement) the activities necessary for the verification of a purchased product?**
- **Are these verification arrangements specified by the organisation or its customer (particularly if verification is to be carried out at the supplier's premises)?**
- **Is the method of product release specified in the purchasing documents (particularly if verification is to be carried out at the supplier's premises)?**

7.5   Production and service operations

- **Does the organisation have procedures for the control of:**
  - production and service operations?
  - identification and traceability?
  - customer property?
  - preservation of product?
  - validation of processes?

Section No.	ISO 9001:2000 title	Typical auditor's questions	Currently met?	Document	Remarks
7.5.1	Control of production and service provision	• **Does the organisation plan and control production and service operations?** • **Is this achieved through:** – information concerning the characteristics of the product? – appropriate work instructions? – the use and maintenance of suitable equipment for production and service operations? – the availability and use of measuring and monitoring devices?			
7.5.2	Validation of processes for production and service provision	• **Where the resulting output cannot be verified by subsequent measurement or monitoring, does the organisation validate production and service processes to demonstrate the ability of the processes to achieve planned results?** • **Does this validation demonstrate the ability of the processes to achieve planned results?** • **Does the validation include:** – qualification of processes? – qualification of equipment and personnel? – use of defined methodologies and procedures? – requirements for records? – revalidation?			

- Does this validation include any processes where deficiencies may become apparent only after the product is in use or the service has been delivered?

7.5.3 | **Identification and traceability**
- Does the organisation have procedures available to identify the product throughout production and service operations?
- Is the product status identifiable with respect to measurement and monitoring requirements?
- When traceability is a requirement, does the organisation control and record the unique identification of a product?

7.5.4 | **Customer property**
- Does the organisation exercise care with customer property?
- Does the organisation verify, protect and maintain customer property provided for use or incorporated into a product?
- Are records maintained of any customer property that is lost, damaged or otherwise found to be unsuitable for use?

7.5.5 | **Preservation of product**
- Does the organisation have set procedures for the identification, handling, packaging, storage and protection of products during internal processing and delivery to the intended destination?

(continued)

Section No.	ISO 9001:2000 title	Typical auditor's questions	Currently met?	Document	Remarks

7.6	Control of measuring and monitoring devices	• **Where applicable, are measuring and monitoring devices:**
		  – calibrated and adjusted periodically or prior to use, against devices traceable to international or national standards?
		  – safeguarded from adjustments that would invalidate the calibration?
		  – protected from damage and deterioration during handling, maintenance and storage?
		• **Are the results of the calibration recorded?**
		• **Is the validity of previous results reassessed if they are subsequently found to be out of calibration, and corrective action taken?**
		• **If software is used for measuring and monitoring, has it been validated prior to use?**			

3.10.6 Measurement analysis and improvement requirements

Section No.	ISO 9001:2000 title	Typical auditor's questions	Currently met?	Document	Remarks
8	Measurement, analysis and improvement	● **Does the organisation define the activities needed to measure and monitor:** – product conformity? – product improvement?			
8.1	General	● **Does the organisation define the activities needed to measure and monitor:** – product conformity? – product improvement? ● **Does the organisation continually strive to improve the effectiveness of its QMS?**			
8.2	Monitoring and measurement	● **Has the organisation procedures available to:** – ensure customer satisfaction? – control internal audits? – ensure effective measurement and monitoring of products and processes?			
8.2.1	Customer satisfaction	● **Does the organisation monitor information regarding customer satisfaction?** ● **Does the organisation monitor information regarding customer dissatisfaction?** ● **Are the methods and measures for obtaining such information defined?**			

(continued)

Section No.	ISO 9001:2000 title	Typical auditor's questions	Currently met?	Document	Remarks
		• Is there an agreed change control procedure? • Is there an agreed customer complaints procedure? • Are these methods and measures utilised as part of the performance measurements of the QMS?			
8.2.2	Internal audit	• Does the organisation conduct periodic internal audits? • Do these audits determine whether the QMS: – conforms to the requirements of ISO 9001:2000? – has been effectively implemented and maintained? • Are audits only carried out by personnel who are not associated with the activity or department being audited? • Are the audits planned to take into account: – the status and importance of the activities and areas to be audited? – the results of previous audits? • Are the audit scope, frequency and methodologies defined? • Does the organisation have a documented procedure for audits that includes: – the responsibilities and requirements for conducting audits? – the method for recording results? – the method for reporting to management?			

- Does management take timely corrective action on deficiencies found during an audit?
- Do these follow-up actions include the verification of the implementation of corrective action and the reporting of verification results?

| 8.2.3 | Monitoring and measurement of processes | - Does the organisation apply suitable methods for the measurement and monitoring of processes:
  – to meet customer requirements?
  – to confirm the process's continuing ability to satisfy its intended purpose? |
| 8.2.4 | Monitoring and measurement of product | - Does the organisation apply suitable methods to measure and monitor the characteristics of the product at appropriate stages of the product realisation process?
- Is there documented evidence of conformity with the acceptance criteria?
- Are the responsibilities and authorities defined with regard to release of product?
- Does the organisation ensure that the product is not released or the service delivered until all the specified activities have been satisfactorily completed (unless otherwise approved by the customer)? |

(continued)

Section No.	ISO 9001:2000 title	Typical auditor's questions	Currently met?	Document	Remarks

8.3	Control of non-conforming product	• **Has the organisation defined a procedure for the control of non-conformities?**
		• **Does this procedure ensure that:**
		  – products which do not conform to requirements are prevented from unintended use or delivery?
		  – non-conforming products that have been corrected are subject to reverification to demonstrate conformity?
		  – non-conforming products detected after delivery or use are either corrected or removed from service?
		• **Is there provision for the notification of the customer, end user, regulatory or other body when required?**			

8.4	Analysis of data	• **Does the organisation collect and analyse data to determine suitability and effectiveness of the QMS?**
		• **Does the organisation analyse the data to provide information regarding:**
		  – possible improvement that can be made to the QMS?
		  – customer satisfaction and dissatisfaction?
		  – conformance to customer requirements?
		  – the characteristics of processes, products and their trends?
		  – suppliers?			

(continued)

8.5	Improvement	• **Does the organisation have procedures available for:**
		– planning continual improvement?
		– corrective action?
		– preventive action?
8.5.1	Continual improvement	• **Does the organisation plan and manage the processes necessary for the continual improvement of the QMS?**
		• **Is the continual improvement of the QMS facilitated by the use of:**
		– the quality policy?
		– quality objectives?
		– audit results?
		– analysis of data?
		– corrective and preventive action?
		– management reviews?
		– concessions and approvals?
		– concession scheme?
		– defects and defect reports?
		– bonded store?
8.5.2	Corrective action	• **Has the organisation a documented procedure to enable corrective action to be taken to eliminate the cause of non-conformities and prevent recurrence?**
		• **Does this procedure define the requirements for:**
		– identification of non-conformities (including customer complaints)?

Section No.	ISO 9001:2000 title	Typical auditor's questions	Currently met?	Document	Remarks
		– determining the causes of non-conformities? – evaluating the need for action to ensure that non-conformities do not recur? – determining and implementing the corrective action needed? – ensuring results of action taken are recorded?			
8.5.3	Preventive action	• **Has the organisation a documented procedure to enable corrective action to be taken to eliminate the cause of non-conformities and prevent recurrence?** • **Does this procedure define the requirements for:** – identification of non-conformities (including customer complaints)? – determining the causes of non-conformities? – evaluating the need for action to ensure that non-conformities do not recur? – determining and implementing the corrective action needed? – ensuring results of action taken are recorded? – reviewing the corrective action taken?			

3.11 Comparison between ISO 9001:2000 and ISO 9001:1994

Clause No.	ISO 9001:2000 title	ISO 9001:1994 correspondence
1	Scope	1
1.1	General	
1.2	Application	
2	Normative reference	2
3	Terms and definitions	3
4	Quality Management System (title only)	
4.1	General requirements	4.2.1
4.2	Documentation requirements (title only)	
4.2.1	General	4.2.2
4.2.2	Quality Manual	4.2.1
4.2.3	Control of documents	4.5.1, 4.5.2, 4.5.3
4.2.4	Control of records	4.16
5	Management responsibility (title only)	
5.1	Management commitment	4.1.1
5.2	Customer focus	4.3.2
5.3	Quality policy	4.1.1
5.4	Planning (title only)	
5.4.1	Quality objectives	4.1.1
5.4.2	Quality management system planning	4.2.3
5.5	Responsibility, authority and communication (title only)	
5.5.1	Responsibility and authority	4.1.2.1
5.5.2	Management representative	4.1.2.3
5.5.3	Internal communication	
5.6	Management review (title only)	
5.6.1	General	4.1.3
5.6.2	Review input	
5.6.3	Review output	
6	Resource management (title only)	
6.1	Provision of resources	4.1.2.2
6.2	Human resources (title only)	
6.2.1	General	4.1.2.2
6.2.2	Competence, awareness and training	4.18
6.3	Infrastructure	4.9
6.4	Work environment	4.9
7	Product realisation (title only)	
7.1	Planning of product realisation	4.2.3, 4.10.1
7.2	Customer-related processes (title only)	
7.2.1	Determination of requirements related to the product	4.3.2, 4.4.4

(continued)

Clause No.	ISO 9001:2000 title	ISO 9001:1994 correspondence
7.2.2	Review of requirements related to the product	4.3.2, 4.3.3, 4.3.4
7.2.3	Customer communication	4.3.2
7.3	Design and development (title only)	
7.3.1	Design and development planning	4.4.2, 4.4.3
7.3.2	Design and development inputs	4.4.4
7.3.3	Design and development outputs	4.4.5
7.3.4	Design and development review	4.4.6
7.3.5	Design and development verification	4.4.7
7.3.6	Design and development validation	4.4.8
7.3.7	Control of design and development changes	4.4.9
7.4	Purchasing (title only)	
7.4.1	Purchasing process	4.6.2
7.4.2	Purchasing information	4.6.3
7.4.3	Verification of purchased product	4.6.4, 4.10.2
7.5	Production and service provision (title only)	
7.5.1	Control of production and service provision	4.9, 4.15.6, 4.19
7.5.2	Validation of processes for production and service provision	4.9
7.5.3	Identification and traceability	4.8, 4.10.5, 4.12
7.5.4	Customer property	4.7
7.5.5	Preservation of product	4.15.2, 4.15.3, 4.15.4, 4.15.5
7.6	Control of monitoring and measuring devices	4.11.1, 4.11.2
8	Measurement, analysis and improvement (title only)	
8.1	General	4.10.1, 4.20.1, 4.20.2
8.2	Monitoring and measurement (title only)	
8.2.1	Customer satisfaction	
8.2.2	Internal audit	4.17
8.2.3	Monitoring and measurement of processes	4.17, 4.20.1, 4.20.2
8.2.4	Monitoring and measurement of product	4.10.2, 4.10.3, 4.10.4, 4.10.5, 4.20.1, 4.20.2
8.3	Control of non-conforming product	4.13.1, 4.13.2
8.4	Analysis of data	4.20.1, 4.20.2
8.5	Improvement (title only)	
8.5.1	Continual improvement	4.1.3
8.5.2	Corrective action	4.14.1, 4.14.2
8.5.3	Preventive action	4.14.1, 4.14.3

3.12 Counter-comparison between ISO 9001:1994 and ISO 9001:2000

ISO 9001:1994		ISO 9001:2000
1	Scope	1
2	Normative reference	2
3	Definitions	3
4	Quality system requirements (title only)	
4.1	Management responsibility (title only)	
4.1.1	Quality policy	5.1, 5.3, 5.4.1
4.1.2	Organisation (title only)	
4.1.2.1	Responsibility and authority	5.5.1
4.1.2.2	Resources	6.1, 6.2.1
4.1.2.3	Management representative	5.5.2
4.1.3	Management review	5.6.1, 8.5.1
4.2	Quality system (title only)	
4.2.1	General	4.1, 4.2.2
4.2.2	Quality system procedures	4.2.1
4.2.3	Quality planning	5.4.2, 7.1
4.3	Contract review (title only)	
4.3.1	General	
4.3.2	Review	5.2, 7.2.1, 7.2.2, 7.2.3
4.3.3	Amendment to a contract	7.2.2
4.3.4	Records	7.2.2
4.4	Design control (title only)	
4.4.1	General	
4.4.2	Design and development planning	7.3.1
4.4.3	Organisational and technical interfaces	7.3.1
4.4.4	Design input	7.2.1, 7.3.2
4.4.5	Design output	7.3.3
4.4.6	Design review	7.3.4
4.4.7	Design verification	7.3.5
4.4.8	Design validation	7.3.6
4.4.9	Design changes	7.3.7
4.5	Document and data control (title only)	
4.5.1	General	4.2.3
4.5.2	Document and data approval and issue	4.2.3
4.5.3	Document and data changes	4.2.3
4.6	Purchasing (title only)	
4.6.1	General	
4.6.2	Evaluation of subcontractors	7.4.1
4.6.3	Purchasing data	7.4.2
4.6.4	Verification of purchased product	7.4.3
4.7	Control of customer-supplied product	7.5.4

(continued)

ISO 9001:1994		ISO 9001:2000
4.8	Product identification and traceability	7.5.3
4.9	Process control	6.3, 6.4, 7.5.1, 7.5.2
4.10	Inspection and testing (title only)	
4.10.1	General	7.1, 8.1
4.10.2	Receiving inspection and testing	7.4.3, 8.2.4
4.10.3	In-process inspection and testing	8.2.4
4.10.4	Final inspection and testing	8.2.4
4.10.5	Inspection and test records	7.5.3, 8.2.4
4.11	Control of inspection, measuring and test equipment (title only)	
4.11.1	General	7.6
4.11.2	Control procedure	7.6
4.12	Inspection and test status	7.5.3
4.13	Control of non-conforming product (title only)	
4.13.1	General	8.3
4.13.2	Review and disposition of non-conforming product	8.3
4.14	Corrective and preventive action (title only)	
4.14.1	General	8.5.2, 8.5.3
4.14.2	Corrective action	8.5.2
4.14.3	Preventive action	8.5.3
4.15	Handling, storage, packaging, preservation and delivery (title only)	
4.15.1	General	
4.15.2	Handling	7.5.5
4.15.3	Storage	7.5.5
4.15.4	Packaging	7.5.5
4.15.5	Preservation	7.5.5
4.15.6	Delivery	7.5.1
4.16	Control of quality records	4.2.4
4.17	Internal quality audits	8.2.2, 8.2.3
4.18	Training	6.2.2
4.19	Servicing	7.5.1
4.20	Statistical techniques (title only)	
4.20.1	Identification of need	8.1, 8.2.3, 8.2.4, 8.4
4.20.2	Procedures	8.1, 8.2.3, 8.2.4, 8.4

3.13 A selection of audit forms

The following is a small selection of forms, typically used by auditors.

FUNCTION/ DEPARTMENT	JAN	FEB	MAR	APR	MAY	JUN	JULY	AUG	SEPT	OCT	NOV	DEC
Administration and finance	x				x				x			
Drawing office		x				x				x		
Workshops			x				x				x	
Stores				x				x				x

Annual quality audit schedule

Audit Reference No.:	File No.: ....
Purpose of audit:	
Scope of audit:	
Lead auditor assigned:	
Location(s) of audit:	
Unit or area to be audited:	
Reference documents:	
Team members:	
Date of audit:	Anticipated duration of audit: ....
Time of opening meeting:	Anticipated time of closing meeting: ....
Facilities requested:	

Internal audit plan

AUDIT CHECKLIST	FUNCTION/PROCESS AUDITED: .... DOCUMENT REFERENCES:		AUDIT NO.: .... AUDIT DATE:	
ITEM NO.	AUDIT QUESTIONS	REFERENCE	RESULT	NOTES/OBSERVATIONS
	PREPARED BY:	PAGE ... OF ...		DATE PREPARED: ....

Audit checklist

TIMETABLE	TEAM A	TEAM B	AUDITEE PARTICIPATION
0900–0930	Opening meeting		Senior management and department heads
0930–1030	Managing director Quality policy Management review	Laboratory 1	Technical director
1030–1100	Review of: Document control Non-conformity	Laboratory 2	Department heads
1100–1200	Purchasing	Laboratory 2	Department heads
1200	Lunch		
1330–1500	Purchasing	Laboratory 2 (cont.)	Department heads
1500–1600	Personnel training	Electrical test house	Department heads
1600–1700	Commercial/Sales	Calibration service	Department heads

Audit programme

Section or project to be audited:	
Reason for audit:	
Audit No.:	Date:
Auditor:	Sheet ... of ...

Serial No.	Observation/supporting evidence	
	Action required	Yes/No

Circulation:	
Attached sheets:	

Signed:		Name:		Date:	

Audit observation sheet

Section or project audited:			
Reason for audit:			
Audit No.:		Date:	
Auditor:		Sheet ... of ...	
Audit area(s):			
Reference document(s):			
Summary:			
Audit observation sheet number	Observation number	Comments	Corrective action requirement
Prepared:	Name:	Date:	
Agreed:	Name:	Date:	
Circulation:		Attached sheets	

Audit report form

Section or project audited:			
Reason for audit:			
Audit No.:		Audit date:	
Auditor(s):		Auditee(s):	
Audit area(s):			
Reference document(s):			
Non-conformance details:			
Signed: (Auditor)		Name:	Date:
Agreed corrective action:			
Signed: (Auditee)		Name:	Date:
Agreed time limit:			
Signed: (Actionee)		Name:	Date:
Progress		Signed	Date

Corrective action request

3.14 ISO 9001:2000 elements covered and outstanding

The following is a checklist used by auditors to confirm that the client's QMS fully covers the requirements (i.e. clauses) of ISO 9001:2000.

Clause No.	ISO 9001:2000 title	Covered (Yes/No)
4	Quality Management System (title only)	
4.1	General requirements	
4.2	Documentation requirements (title only)	
4.2.1	General	
4.2.2	Quality Manual	
4.2.3	Control of documents	
4.2.4	Control of records	
5	Management responsibility (title only)	
5.1	Management commitment	
5.2	Customer focus	
5.3	Quality policy	
5.4	Planning (title only)	
5.4.1	Quality objectives	
5.4.2	Quality management system planning	
5.5	Responsibility, authority and communication (title only)	
5.5.1	Responsibility and authority	
5.5.2	Management representative	
5.5.3	Internal communication	
5.6	Management review (title only)	
5.6.1	General	
5.6.2	Review input	
5.6.3	Review output	
6	Resource management (title only)	
6.1	Provision of resources	
6.2	Human resources (title only)	
6.2.1	General	
6.2.2	Competence, awareness and training	
6.3	Infrastructure	
6.4	Work environment	
7	Product realisation (title only)	
7.1	Planning of product realisation	
7.2	Customer-related processes (title only)	
7.2.1	Determination of requirements related to the product	
7.2.2	Review of requirements related to the product	
7.2.3	Customer communication	
7.3	Design and development (title only)	
7.3.1	Design and development planning	

Clause No.	ISO 9001:2000 title	Covered (Yes/No)
7.3.2	Design and development inputs	
7.3.3	Design and development outputs	
7.3.4	Design and development review	
7.3.5	Design and development verification	
7.3.6	Design and development validation	
7.3.7	Control of design and development changes	
7.4	Purchasing (title only)	
7.4.1	Purchasing process	
7.4.2	Purchasing information	
7.4.3	Verification of purchased product	
7.5	Production and service provision (title only)	
7.5.1	Control of production and service provision	
7.5.2	Validation of processes for production and service provision	
7.5.3	Identification and traceability	
7.5.4	Customer property	
7.5.5	Preservation of product	
7.6	Control of monitoring and measuring devices	
8	Measurement, analysis and improvement (title only)	
8.1	General	
8.2	Monitoring and measurement (title only)	
8.2.1	Customer satisfaction	
8.2.2	Internal audit	
8.2.3	Monitoring and measurement of processes	
8.2.4	Monitoring and measurement of product	
8.3	Control of non-conforming product	
8.4	Analysis of data	
8.5	Improvement (title only)	
8.5.1	Continual improvement	
8.5.2	Corrective action	
8.5.3	Preventive action	

3.15 Abbreviations and acronyms common to quality management and auditing

The following list, whilst not all-inclusive, typically shows the acronyms and abbreviations normally encountered by auditors.

ABBS	Antigua and Barbuda Bureau of Standards
ABCB	Association for British Certification Bodies Ltd
ABNT	Associacao Brasileira de Normas Tecnicas (ISO member for Brazil)

AECMA	European Association of Aerospace Industries
AENOR	Asociación Espanola de Normalización y Certificación (Spanish Association for Standardisation and Certification)
AFNOR	Association Française de Normalisation (French Standards Association)
ANSI	American National Standards Institute
AOQ	Average Outgoing Quality
AOQL	Average Outgoing Quality Limit
AP	NATO Allied Publications
APA	Assessed Process Average Procedure
AQAP	Allied Quality Assurance Publications (NATO)
AQL	Acceptable Quality Level
AQMC	Association of Quality Management Consultants International
AS 9000	Quality system standard for the aerospace industry, issued by SAE (USA)
ASA	American Standards Association (old name for ANSI)
ASQ	American Society for Quality (was ASQC)
ASQC	American Society for Quality Control (now ASQ)
ASTM	American Society for Testing and Materials
AU	Automobile standards, issued by BSI
BABT	British Approvals Board for Telecommunications
BBA	British Board of Agreement
BEC	British Electrotechnical Committee (part of BSI)
BEC	Belgisch Elektrotechnisch Comité (Belgian Electrotechnical Committee)
BIS	Bureau of Indian Standards
BITS	BSI Information Technology Service
BNSI	Barbados National Standards Institution
BOBS	Botswana Bureau of Standards
BPS	Bureau of Product Standards (Philippines)
BQF	British Quality Foundation
BS	British Standard, issued by BSI
BSI	British Standards Institution
BSMD	Directorate of Standards and Metrology (Bahrain)
BSN	Badan Standardisasi Nasional (National Standardisation Agency, Indonesia)
BSS	British Standards Society
BSTI	Bangladesh Standards and Testing Institution
BTAS/Q	Business and Technical Advisory Service on Quality
c:cure	Certification scheme for information security (BS 7799)
CAD	Computer Aided Design
CASCO	ISO Committee on Conformity Assessment

CB	Certification Body
CCIR	International Radio Consultative Committee
CCITT	The International Telegraph and Telephone Consultative Committee
CDR	Critical Design Review
CE	Comité de Coordination de Qualité
CEB	Comité Electrotechnique Belge (Belgian Electrotechnical Committee)
CECC	CENELEC Electronic Components Committee
CEE	International Commission on rules for the approval of Electrical Equipment (now mostly replaced by IEC publications)
CEI	Comitato Elettrotecnico Italiano (Italian Electrotechnical Standards Committee), but note that CEI is also the French abbreviation for the IEC)
CEN	European Committee for Standardisation. European equivalent of ISO
CENELEC	European Committee for Electrotechnical Standardisation. An impartial body who have the necessary competence and reliability to operate a certification scheme
CGSB	Canadian General Standards Board
CMC	Canadian Standards Association
CNS	Chinese National Standard, issued by NBS (Taiwan)
COGUANOR	Comisión Guatemalteca de Normas (ISO Correspondent member for Guatemala)
CONACYT	Consejo Nacional de Ciencia y Tecnologia (ISO Correspondent member for El Salvador)
COPANIT	Comisión Panamena de Normas Industriales y Tecnicas (ISO member for Panama)
COPOLCO	ISO Committee on consumer policy
COS	Cooperation of Open Systems
COTS	Commercial Off The Shelf
COVENIN	Comisión Venezolana de Normas Industriales (ISO member for Venezuela)
CP	Code of Practice, issued by BSI
CPD	Continuing Professional Development (as in Quality World)
CSA	Canadian Standards Association
ČSN	Czech standard, issued by ČSNI
CSNI	Cesky Normalizační Institut (Czech Standardisation Institute)
CTR	Common Technical Regulation (EU)
CWA	CEN Workshop Agreements, issued by CEN
CYS	Cyprus Organisation for Standards and Control of Quality

DAM	Draft Amendment, issued by ISO
DD	Draft for Development, issued by BSI
DEF	Defence Standard (UK)
Def Spec	Defence Specification (UK)
DEF STAN	Defence Standards (UK)
DGN	Dirección General de Normas (ISO member for Mexico)
DGSM	Directorate General for Specifications and Measurements (Oman)
DIGENOR	Direccion General de Normas y Sistemas de Calidad (ISO subscriber member for Dominican Republic)
DIN	Deutsches Institut für Normung (German Institute for Standardisation)
DIN V	German pre-standard, issued by DIN
DIN-TAB	DIN Handbook
DIS	Draft International Standard, issued by ISO
DOA	Dictionary of Abbreviations
DOR	Date of Ratification/Implementation (EN Standards)
DOW	Date of Withdrawal (EN Standards)
DPA	Defence Procurement Agency
DPQC	Direction de la Promotion de la Qualité et du Conditionnement des Produits (ISO Subscriber member for Benin)
DR	Draft Australian Standard
DS	Dansk Standard (Denmark)
DSC	Dretjtoria e Standardizimit dhe Cilesise (ISO member for Albania)
DSF	Draft standard, issued by Dansk Standard (Denmark)
DSM	Department of Standards Malaysia
DSTU	State Committee of Ukraine for Standardisation, Metrology and Certification (Ukraine)
DTI	Department of Trade and Industry (UK)
DTU	Documents Techniques Unifiés (unified technical document, issued by CSTB)
DZNM	State Office for Standardisation and Metrology (ISO member for Croatia)
E	Draft (Standard)
EA	Environmental Assessment
EAC	European Accreditation of Certification
EAL	European co-operation for the Accreditation of Laboratories
EARA	Environmental Auditors Registration Association (UK)
EC	European Communities
ECE	United Nations Economic Commission for Europe
ECQR	Electronic Component Quality and Reliability Service

EEA	European Economic Area (EU and EFTA countries except Switzerland)
EEC	European Economic Community
EFQM	European Foundation for Quality Management
EFTA	European Free Trade Association (Iceland, Norway, Switzerland and Liechtenstein)
EG	ETSI Guide, issued by ETSI
EMC	Electromagnetic Compatibility directive (EU directive 89/336/EEC)
EMI	Electromagnetic Interference
EMP	Electromagnetic Pulse
EMS	Environmental Management System
EN	European Standard (Norm), issued by CEN, CENELEC and ETSI
ENV	European Pre-Standard (Norm), issued by CEN or CENELEC
EO	Eichordnung (German Calibration Order)
EOQ	European Organisation for Quality
EOQC	European Organisation for Quality Control (now EOQ)
EOS	Egyptian Organisation for Standardisation and Quality Control
EOTC	European Organisation for Testing and Certification
EPA	Environmental Protection Act 1990 (UK)
EPA	Environmental Protection Agency (USA)
EQD	Electrical Quality Assurance Directorate
EQFM	European Foundation of Quality Management
EQV	Indication that a standard is technically equivalent to an international standard
ES	ETSI Standard
ES	European Specification, issued by CENELEC
ETR	ETSI Technical Report
ETS	European Telecommunications Standard, issued by ETSI
ETSI	European Telecommunications Standards Institute
EU	European Union
EUROCODES	A series of documents issued mainly as ENVs by CEN (on the subject of buildings and structures)
EURONORM	A series of European standards issued by ECISS, now largely replaced by the CEN EN 10000 series
EVS	National Standards Board of Estonia
EWOS	European Workshop for Open Systems
EXP	Experimental standard, issued by AFNOR
FDIS	Final Draft International Standard (ISO)
FMEA	Failure Mode and Effect Analysis
FMECA	Failure Mode, Effect and Criticality Analysis

FTA	Fault Tree Analysis
FTZ	Fernmeldetechnisches Zentralamt der Deutschen Bundespost (telecommunications standards issued by the German Federal Post Office)
G7	Canada, France, Germany, Italy, Japan, UK, USA
GB	Mandatory Chinese national standard, issued by CSBTS
GB/T	Recommended Chinese national standard, issued by CSBTS
GDBS	Grenada Bureau of Standards
GNBS	Guyana National Bureau of Standards
GOST R	Committee of the Russian Federation for Standardisation, Metrology and Certification (Russian:OSTP)
GQA	General Quality Assessment Schemes (UK National Rivers Authority)
GS	Ghana standard, issued by GSB
GS	'GS' Mark for Equipment complying with German Equipment Safety Law (GSG)
GS	Gulf Standard, issued by the Standardisation and Metrology Organisation for GCC Countries
GSB	Ghana Standards Board
HD	Harmonisation Document, issued by CENELAC
HMSO	Her Majesty's Stationery Office
HN	Specifications issued by Electricité de France (EDF)
HRN	Croatian standard, issued by DZNM
HSC	Health and Safety Commission (UK)
HSE	Health and Safety Executive (UK)
IAF	International Accreditation Forum
IANOR	Institut Algerian de Normalisation (Algerian Standards Institute)
IAS	International Approval Services, US Inc.
IATCA	International Auditor and Training Certification Association
IBN	Institut Belge de Normalisation (Belgian Standards Institute)
IBNORCA	Instituto Boliviano de Normalización y Calidad (ISO Correspondent member for Bolivia)
ICONTEC	Instituto Columbiano de Normas Técnicas y Certificación (Colombian Institute for Technical Standards and Certification)
ICS	International Classification for Standards (a subject classification scheme using numbers, issued by ISO)
IDT	Indication that a standard is identical with an international standard
IEA	International Energy Agency

IEA	Institute of Environmental Assessment
IEC	International Electrotechnical Commission – Quality Assessment System for Electronic Components
IECC	International Electrotechnical Commission Council
IECEE	IEC System for Conformity Testing and Certification of Electrical Equipment
IECQ	IEC Quality Assessment System for Electronic Components
IEE	Institution of Electrical Engineers
IEEE	Institute of Electrical and Electronics Engineers (USA)
IEEM	Institute for Ecology and Environmental Management (UK)
IEM	Institute of Environmental Management (UK)
IEPG	Independent European Programme Group
IES	Institution of Environmental Sciences (UK)
IES	Institute of Environmental Services (USA)
IIE	Institute of Industrial Engineers (USA)
IIED	International Institute for Environment and Development
IIOC	Independent Organisation for Certification
IIP	Investors in People (UK)
ILU	Integrated Logistic Unit
IMQ	Instituto Italiano del Marchio di Qualita (Italian Institute for the Quality Mark)
IMS	Integrated Management System
INDECOPI	Instituto Nacional de Defensa de la Competencia y de la Protección de la Propiedad Intelectual (ISO Correspondent member for Peru)
INEN	Instituto Ecuatoriano de Normalización (Ecuadorian Institute for Standardisation)
INFCO	ISO Committee on information systems and services
INM	Institut de Normalisation et de Métrologie (ISO Correspondent member for Guinea)
INN	Instituto Nacional de Normalisatión (National Institute for Standardisation, Chile)
INNOQ	National Institute of Standardisation and Quality (Mozambique)
INNORPI	Institut National de la Normalisation et de la Propriété Industrièlle (ISO member for Tunisia)
INSTA	Inter-Nordic Standardisation (Denmark, Iceland, Norway, Sweden, Finland)
INTECO	Instituto de Normas Técnicas de Costa Rica (Costa Rica Institute for Technical Standards)
INTN	Instituto Nacional de Tecnologia y Normalización (ISO Correspondent member for Paraguay)
INTRANET	Internal Network

IOS	Iraq Organisation for Standardisation
IPQ	Instituto Português da Qualidade (Portuguese Institute for Quality) (the national standards organisation for Portugal)
IQA	Institute of Quality Assurance (UK)
IRAM	Instituto Argentino de Normalizaciòn (Argentinian Standards Institute)
IRCA	International Register of Certified Auditors
IRS	Institut Român de Standardizare (Romanian Institute for Standardisation)
IS	Indian Standard, issued by BIS
IS	Irish Standard, issued by NSAI
ISA	Instrument Society of America
ISA	International Federation of the National Standardising Associations (forerunner to ISO, active 1926 to 1942)
ISBN	International Standard Book Number
ISDN	Integrated Service Digital Network
ISIS	Information Society Initiative for Standardisation (EU)
ISO	International Organisation for Standardisation
ISO/IEC	Joint standard of ISO and IEC
ISO/R	ISO Recommendation (now standards)
ISO/TC176	The ISO Technical Committee responsible for the ISO 9000 series standards
ISO/TR	ISO Technical Report
ISONET	ISO Information Network
ISP	Internet Service Provider
ISRC	International Standard Recording Code
ISRN	International Standard
ISSN	International Standard Serial Number
ISSS	Information Society Standardisation System (of CEN)
IST	Icelandic standard, issued by STRI
IT	Information Technology
ITU	International Telecommunications Union
ITU-R	Radiocommunication standardisation
ITU-T	Telecommunication standardisation sector of ITU
J	SAEJ, automotive standards issued by SAE
JAS	Japanese Agricultural Standard, issued by JETRO
JASO	Standards issued by Society of Automotive Engineers of Japan
JBS	Jamaica Bureau of Standards
JCSEE	Joint Committee on Standards for Educational Evaluation (USA)
JIS	Japanese Industrial Standard, issued by JSA
JISC	Japanese Industrial Standards Committee
JISM	Jordanian Institution for Standards and Metrology

JS	Jamaican Standard, issued by JBS
JSA	Japanese Standards Association
JTC	Joint ISO/IEC Technical Committee
JUS	Yugoslavian standard, issued by SZS
KAZMEST	Committee for Standardisation, Metrology and Certification (Kazakhstan)
KEBS	Kenya Bureau of Standards
KEMA	Keuring van Elektrotechnishe Materialen (association for the testing of electrical equipment, Netherlands)
KEMAN-V	Kema (Netherlands NSI)
KNITQ	Korean National Institute of Technology and Quality (South Korea)
KS	Kenyan Standards, issued by KEBS
KS	Korean Standard, issued by KSA
KSA	Korean Standards Association (South Korea)
KSS	Kuwait Standard
KTA	Kerntechnischer Ausschuß (German Nuclear Technical Commission)
LAN	Local Area Network
LAS	Local Area Subsystem
LCA	Life Cycle Assessment
LCC	Life Cycle Costing
LCIA	Life Cycle Impact Assessment
LCR	Life Cycle Review
LCSEA	Life Cycle Stressor-Effects Assessment
LIBNOR	Lebanese Standards Institution
LNCSM	Libyan National Centre for Standardisation and Metrology
LQL	Limiting Quality Level
LST	Lithuanian Standards Board
LVS	Latvian National Centre of Standardisation and Metrology
MA	Marine standard, issued by BSI
MBNQA	Malcolm Baldridge National Quality Award (USA)
MBS	Malawi Bureau of Standards
MD	Managing Director
MDD	Medical Devices Directive (EU directive 93/42/EEC)
MIL	Military Standards (USA)
Mil-Spec	Military Specification
Mil-Std	Military Standard
MOD	Ministry of Defence (UK)
MOU	Memorandum of Understanding
MS	Malaysian Standard, issued by DSM
MS	Mauritius Standard, issued by MSB
MSA	Malta Standardisation Authority
MSB	Mauritius Standards Bureau

MSD	Management Systems Document
MSIT	Major State Inspection of Turkmenistan (ISO Correspondent member)
MSZ	Hungarian standard, issued by MSZT
MSZT	Magyar Szabványügyi Testület (Hungarian Standards Institution)
MTBF	Mean Time Between Failures
MTTF	Mean Time To Failure
NACCB	National Accreditation Council for Certification Bodies (UK), now UKAS
NAD	National Application Document (used with EUROCODES)
NAEM	National Association for Environmental Management (USA)
NATO	North Atlantic Treaty Organisation
NBN	Belgian standard, issued by IBN
NBR	Brazilian standard, issued by ABNT
NBS	National Bureau of Standards (Taiwan)
NBS	National Bureau of Standards (USA, now NIST)
NC	Oficina Nacional de Normalización (National Office for Standardisation, Cuba)
NCB	National Certification Body
NCh	Chilean standard, issued by INN
NCIQ	National Centre for Information Quality
NDT	Non-Destructive Testing
NEC	Nederland's Elektrotechnish Comité (Netherlands Electrotechnical Committee)
NEK	Norsk Elektroteknisk Komite (Norwegian Electrotechnical Committee)
NEMKO	Norges Elektriske Materiellkontrol (Norwegian Board for Testing and Approval of Electrical Equipment)
NEN	Netherlands standard, issued by NNI
NEQ	Indication that a standard is not equivalent to an international standard, but may cover the same subject area
NF	Norme Française, French standard, issued by AFNOR
NISIT	National Institute of Standards and Industrial Technology (Papua New Guinea)
NISO	National Information Standards Organisation (USA)
NM	Moroccan standard, issued by SNIMA
NNI	Nederlands Normalisatie-institut (Netherlands Standards Institute)
NoBo	Notified Body (EU)
NOM	Mexican standard, issued by DGN
NP	Norma Portuguesa (Portuguese standard, issued by IPQ)

NP	Paraguayan standard, issued by INTN
NQA	Niveau de Qualité Acceptable (French for Acceptable Quality Level)
NQAA	National Quality Assurance Authority
NQIC	National Quality Information Centre, part of IQA (UK)
NS	Norsk Standard, issued by NSF, Norway
NSA	National Supervising Authority
NSAI	National Standards Authority of Ireland
NSF	Norges Standardiseringsforbund (ISO member for Norway)
NSI	National Supervising Inspectorate
NSIQO	Namibia Standards Information and Quality Office
NSO	National Standards Organisation
NT	Tunisian standard, issued by INNOrpi
NTC	Colombian standard, issued by ICONTEC
NVN	Netherlands preliminary standard, issued by NNI
NVQ	National Vocational Qualification
NZS	New Zealand Standard, issued by SNZ
OCC	Office Congolais de Controle (ISO subscriber member for Congo)
ODBC	Open DataBase Connectivity
OECD	Organisation for Economic Co-operation and Development
OHS	Occupational Health and Safety
OHSAS	Occupational Health and Safety Assessment Series, available from BSI
OJ	Official Journal of the European Communities
ÖN	Österreichisches Normungsinstitut (Austrian Standards Institution)
ÖN(ORM)	Austrian standard, issued by ÖN
ONN	Organism National de Normalisation (another acronym for NSA)
ONS	Organism National de Surveillance (CECC acronym for NSI)
Ontw.	Draft standard issued by NNI (Netherlands)
OS	Oman Standard, issued by DGSM
OSI	Open Systems Interconnection
ÖVE	Österreichischen Verbandes für Elektrotechnik (Austrian Institution for Electrical Engineering)
PD	Published Document, issued by BSI
PDCA	Plan Do Check Act
PKN	Polish Committee for Standardisation
PN	Polish standard, issued by PKN
PNGS	Papua New Guinea Standard, issued by NISIT

prEN	Designation for draft European Standards (French *projét*) used by CEN, CENELEC and ETSI
PS	Pakistan Standard, issued by PSI
PSI	Pakistan Standards Institution
QA	Quality Assurance
QAI	Quality Assurance Inspector
QAMIS	Quality Assurance Management Information Systems
QASAR	Quality Management Systems Assessment and Registration
QASS	Quality Assurance Support Scheme
QC	Quality Control
QDMC	QDesign Media Codec
QFD	Quality Function Deployment
QMS	Quality Management System
QOS	Quality of Service
QP	Quality Procedure
QPL	Qualified Products List
QS-9000	Quality System requirements based on ISO 9001 issued by Chrysler, Ford and General Motors
QSAE	Quality and Standards Authority of Ethiopia
R&D	Research and Development
RA	Risk Assessment
RAL	Reichsausschub für Lieferbedingungen Deutsches Institut für Gütesicherung (German Institute for Quality Assurance)
REMCO	ISO Committee on reference materials
RGIE	Règlement Générale sur les Installations Electriques (Regulation for electrical installations, Belgium, also known as AREI in Flemish)
RGPT	Règlement Générale pour la Protection du Travail (Regulation for safety at work, Belgium, also known as ARAB in Flemish)
ROOT	A technical thesaurus, issued by BSI (ROOT is not an abbreviation for anything)
RTF	Request For Tender
RTOS	Real Time Operating System
SA 8000	Social Accountability standard, issued by CEP
SAA	Standards Association of Australia/Standards Australia
SABS	South African Bureau of Standards
SANZ	Standards Association of New Zealand
SAS	Swiss Association for Standardisation
SASMO	Syrian Arab Organisation for Standardisation and Metrology
SASO	Saudi Arabian Standards Organisation
SAZ	Standards Association of Zimbabwe

SBS	Seychelles Bureau of Standards
SC	Subcommittee
SCC	Standards Council of Canada
SEA	Strategic Environmental Assessment
SEE	Service de l'Energie de l'Etat (CENELEC member for Luxembourg)
SEK	Svenska Elektriska Kommissionen (Swedish Electrotechnical Commission)
SEM	Single European Market
SEMKO	Svenska Elektriska Materielkontrollanstalten (Swedish Institute for Testing and Approval of Electrical Equipment)
SEN	Swedish standard, issued by SEK
SEPA	Scottish Environmental Protection Agency
SES	Standards Engineering Society (USA)
SEV	Schweizerischer Elektrotechnischererein (Swiss NAI and NSI)
SFS	Suomen Standardisoimisliitto (Finnish Standards Association)
SI	Israeli standard, issued by SII
SI	Statutory Instrument (UK)
SI	Système International d'Unités (the International System of Units)
SIA	Société Suisse des Ingénieurs et des Architects (Swiss Society of Engineers and Architects)
SII	Standards Institution of Israel
SIS	Standardiseringen I Sverige (Swedish Standards Institution)
SIS	Swedish standard, issued before 1 January 1978 by SIS
SIST	Slovenian standard, issued by SMIS
SLBS	Saint Lucia Bureau of Standards
SLSI	Sri Lanka Standards Institution
SME	Small and Medium-sized Enterprises
SMIS	Standards and Metrology Institute of the Republic of Slovenia
SMS	Svensk Material and Mekanstandard (Swedish Material and Mechanical Standards)
SN	Schweizer Norm (Swiss standard, issued by SNV)
SNCT	Syndicat National de la Chaudronnerie, de la Tolerie et de la Tuyauterie Industrielle (National Syndicate for the Boiler, Sheet Metal and Piping Industry, France)
SNI	Indonesian standard, issued by BSN
SNIMA	Service de Normalisation Industrièlle Marocaine (ISO member for Morocco)

SNQ	Service National de la Qualité des Composants Éléctroniques (French NSI)
SNS	Syrian standard, issued by SASMO
SNV	Schweizerische Normen-Vereinigung (Swiss Association for Standardisation)
SNZ	Standards New Zealand
SON	Standards Organisation of Nigeria
SPC	Statistical Process Control
SS	Singapore Standard, issued by PSB
SS	Swedish Standard, issued by SIS after 1 January 1978
SSA	Saudi Arabian Standard, issued by SASO
SSMO	Sudanese Standards and Metrology Organisation
SSUAE	Directorate of Standardisation and Metrology (United Arab Emirates)
STAS	Romanian standards
STN	Slovakian standard, issued by UNMS
STP	Special Technical Publication, issued by ASTM
STRÍ	Icelandic Council for Standardisation
SUVA	Schweizerische Unfallversicherungsanstalt (Swiss Accident Insurance Association)
SZS	Savezni zavod za standardizaciju (ISO member for Yugoslavia)
TAG	Technical Advisory Group
TBS	Tanzania Bureau of Standards
TC	Technical Committee
TCVN	Directorate for Standards and Quality (Vietnam)
THE	Technical Help to Exporters (a BSI/DTI scheme, see TIG)
TIA	Telecommunications Industry Association (USA standards often published jointly with EIA)
TickIT	A certification scheme for software (UK)
TIG	Technical Information Group (part of BSI)
TIS	Thai standard, issued by TISI
TISI	Thai Industrial Standards Institute (Thailand)
TL	Technische Lieferbedingungen (German technical delivery conditions)
TL 9000	A version of ISO 9000 for the telecommunications industry
TMB	ISO Technical Management Board
TPR	Third Party Registrar
TQC	Total Quality Control
TQM	Total Quality Management
TR	Technical Report, issued by ETSI
TS	Technical Specifications, issued by ETSI
TS	Technical Specification, issued by ISO

TS	Turkish Standard, issued by TSE
TSE	Türk Standardlari Enstitüsü (Turkish Standards Institution)
TTA	Technology Trend Assessment, issued by IEC
TTBS	Trinidad and Tobago Bureau of Standards
TTS	Trinidad and Tobago Standard, issued by TTBS
TZS	Tanzanian standard, issued by TBS
UIC	Union International des Chemins de fer
UK	United Kingdom
UKAEA	United Kingdom Atomic Energy Authority
UKAS	United Kingdom Accreditation Service
UN	United Nations
UNBS	Uganda National Bureau of Standards
UNCED	United Nations Conference on Environment and Development
UNE	Designation for Spanish Standards, issued by AENOR
UNEP	United Nations Environment Programme
UNI	Ente Nazionale Italiano di Unificazione (Italian National Standards Institute)
UNIT	Instituto Uruguayo de Normas Técnicas (ISO member for Uruguay)
UNMS	Slovak Office of Standards Metrology and Testing
URN	Series of documents issued by the DTI (UK)
USE	Union des Syndicats de l'Electricité
UTE	Union Technique de l'Électricité (France)
VDE	Verband Deutscher Elektrotechniker (German NSI)
VG	Verteidigungsgeräte-Normen (defence equipment standard, issued by BWB) (Germany)
VIP	Virtual Internet Protocol
VTA	Visual Tree Assessment method
WAN	Wide Area Network
WAP	Wireless Application Protocol
WAUILF	Workplace Applied Uniform Indicated Low Frequency (Application)
WBS	Work Breakdown Structure
WI	Work Instruction
WTO	World Trade Organisation
XP	Experimental standard, issued by AFNOR
YFL	Yearly Functional Logistics
YFR	Yearly Functional Rules
ZS	Zambian Standard
ZSM	Zavod za Standardizacija I Metrologija (ISO member for the former Yugoslav Republic of Macedonia)

3.16 Glossary of terms used in quality

As international trade increases, it is becoming more important than ever to know the exact meaning of some of the basic definitions when referred to the quality of a product or service – especially when used in the vernacular. To overcome this problem an international standard (ISO 8402:1994 – Quality management and quality assurance – vocabulary) was published in three languages (English, French and Russian).

ISO 9000:2000 was then developed within ISO/TC 176. It was developed by first screening existing quality standards (e.g. ISO 8402:1994) and publications that were available to determine the quality terms that could be included and then producing internationally acceptable definitions of them. Because of this 'international acceptability' many of these definitions and terms have specific meanings and applications as opposed to generic definitions that are normally to be found in dictionaries.

Acceptance: Agreement to take a product or service as offered.
Accreditation: Certification, by a duly recognised body, of facilities, capability, objectivity, competence and integrity of an agency, service or operational group or individual to provide the specific service/s or operation/s as needed.
Audit: Systematic, independent and documented process for obtaining evidence and evaluating it objectively to determine the extent to which audit criteria are fulfilled.
Audit client: Person or organisation requesting an audit.
Audit conclusions: Outcome of an audit decided by the audit team after consideration of all the audit findings.
Audit criteria: Set of policies, procedures or requirements against which collected audit evidence is compared.
Audit evidence: Records, verified statements of fact or other information relevant to the audit.
Audit findings: Results of the evaluation of the collected audit evidence against audit criteria.
Audit programme: Set of audits to be carried out during a planned time frame.
Audit scope: Extent and range of a given audit.
Audit team: One or more auditors conducting an audit, one of whom is appointed as leader.
Auditee: Organisation being audited.
Auditor: Person qualified and competent to conduct audits.
Bonded store: A secure place in which only supplies that have been accepted as satisfactory by the inspection staff are held.
Calibration: The operation that is required to determine the accuracy of measuring and test equipment.

Capability: Ability of an organisation, system or process to realise a product that fulfils the requirements for that product.

Cen (European Committee for Standardisation): European equivalent of ISO.

Cenelec (European Committee for Electrotechnical Standardisation)
Certification Body: An impartial body who have the necessary competence and reliability to operate a certification scheme.

Censored test: A test carried out on a number of items which is terminated before all the tested items have failed.

Certification: The procedure and action by a duly authorised body of determining, verifying and attesting in writing to the qualifications of personnel, processes, procedures, or items in accordance with applicable requirements.

Certification body: An impartial body, governmental or non-governmental, possessing the necessary competence and reliability to operate a certification system, and in which the interests of all parties concerned with the functioning of the system are represented.

Certification system: A system having its own rules of procedure and management for carrying out certification.

Chief inspector: An individual who is responsible for the manufacturer's Quality Management System (also referred to as the Quality Manager).

Company: Term used primarily to refer to a business first party, the purpose of which is to supply a product or service.

Compliance: The fulfilment of a Quality Management System or quality procedure of specified requirements.

Concession: Authorisation to use or release a product that does not conform to specified requirements.

Concession/waiver: Written authorisation to use or release a quantity of material, components or stores already produced but which do not conform to the specified requirements.

Consignment: Products (or goods) that are issued or received as one delivery and covered by one set of documents.

Contract: Agreed requirements between a supplier and customer transmitted by any means.

Corrective action: Action taken to eliminate the cause of a detected nonconformity or other undesirable situation.

Customer: Ultimate consumer, user, client, beneficiary or second party.

Customer complaint: Any written, electronic, or oral communication that alleges deficiencies related to the identity, quality, durability, reliability, safety or performance of a device that has been placed on the market.

Customer dissatisfaction: Customer's opinion of the degree to which a transaction has failed to meet the customer's needs and expectations.

Customer organisation: Customer organisation or person that receives a product.

Customer satisfaction: Customer's opinion of the degree to which a transaction has met the customer's needs and expectations.

Defect: Non-fulfilment of a requirement related to an intended or specified use.

Design and development: Set of processes that transforms requirements into specified characteristics and into the specification of the product realisation process.

Design authority: The approved firm, establishment or branch representative responsible for the detailed design of material to approved specifications and authorised to sign a certificate of design, or to certify sealed drawings.

Design capability: The ability of a manufacturer to translate a customer requirement into a component that can be manufactured by their particular technology.

Design failure: A failure due to an inadequate design of an item.

Design review: A formal, documented, comprehensive and systematic examination of a design to evaluate the design requirements and the capability of the design to meet these requirements and to identify problems and propose solutions.

Document: Information and its support medium.

Effectiveness: Measure of the extent to which planned activities are realised and planned results achieved.

Efficiency: Relationship between the result achieved and the resources used.

Environment: All of the external physical conditions that may influence the performance of a product or service.

Environmental condition: The characteristics (such as humidity, pressure, vibration etc.) of the environment in which the product is operating.

Equipment: Machines, apparatus, fixed or mobile devices, control components and instrumentation thereof and detection or prevention systems which, separately or jointly, are intended for the generation, transfer, storage, measurement, control and conversion of energy for the processing of material and which are capable of causing an explosion through their own potential sources of ignition.

Evaluation: The systematic evaluation of the effectiveness of a contractor's Quality Management System.

Failure: The termination of the ability of an item to perform a required function.

Failure mode, effect and criticality analysis (FMECA): FMEA together with a consideration of the probability of occurrence and a ranking of the seriousness of the failure.

Failure mode/fault mode: One of the possible states of a failed (faulty) item, for a given required function.

Failure mode and effect analysis (FMEA): A qualitative method of reliability analysis which involves the study of the failure modes which can exist in every sub-item of the item and the determination of the effects of each failure mode on other sub-items of the item and on the required function of the item.

Failure rate (instantaneous): The limit, if this exists, of the conditional probability that the instant of time of a failure of an item falls within a given time interval to the length of this interval, when given that the item is in an up state at the beginning of the time interval.

Failure tree analysis (FTA): The study, with the use of diagrammatic algorithms, of the possible sequence of events leading up to the failure of a product.

Fault: The state of an item characterised by inability to perform a required function, excluding the inability during preventive maintenance or due to lack of external resources or other planned action.

Fault tree: A logic diagram showing how a given fault mode of an item is related to possible fault modes of sub-items or to external events, or combinations thereof.

Fault tree analysis: An analysis in the form of a fault tree in order to determine how a stated fault mode of the item may be the result of the fault modes of the sub-items or of external events, or combinations thereof.

Final inspection: The last inspection by a manufacturer or supplier before delivery.

In-process inspection: Inspection carried out at various stages during processing.

In-progress inspections: QA Inspectors perform these on a random basis or while assisting the technician. They may also be considered as 'training' inspections and are meant to help the technician perform better maintenance whilst actually learning about the equipment.

Inspection: Activities such as measuring, examining, testing, gauging one or more characteristics of a product or service and comparing these with specified requirements to determine conformity.

Interested party: Person or group having an interest in the performance or success of an organisation.

Maintenance: The combination of technical and administrative actions that are taken to retain or restore an item to a state in which it can perform its stated function.

Management: Co-ordinated activities to direct and control an organisation.

Management system: To establish policy and objectives and to achieve those objectives.

Manufacturer: The natural or legal person with responsibility for the design, manufacture, packaging and labelling of a device before it is placed on the market under his own name, regardless of whether these operations are carried out by that person himself or on his behalf by a third party.

May: This auxiliary verb indicates a course of action often followed by manufacturers and suppliers.

Measurement: Set of operations having the object of determining the value of a quantity.

Nonconformity: Non-fulfilment of a requirement.

Operational cycle: A repeatable sequence of functional stresses.

Operational requirements: All the function and performance requirements of a product.

Organisation: A company, corporation, firm or enterprise, whether incorporated or not, public or private.

Group of people and facilities with an orderly arrangement of responsibilities, authorities and relationships.

Organisational structure: Orderly arrangement of responsibilities, authorities and relationships between people.

Outgoing inspections: These are performed after a job or task has been completed to verify that everything has been done correctly on a repaired equipment that is ready for return to the customer. The Quality Assurance Inspector is normally required to check the item to see how it compares against the manufacturer's specification. Any item failing an outgoing inspection has to be returned to the Technician or his Section Manager for corrective action. It will then be subject to a further outgoing inspection by the QA Inspector.

Procedure: Describes the way to perform an activity or process.

Product: Result of a process.

 Note: There are four agreed generic product categories:

- hardware (e.g. engine mechanical part);
- software (e.g. computer program);
- services (e.g. transport);
- processed materials (e.g. lubricant).

Hardware and processed materials are generally tangible products, while software or services are generally intangible.

Most products comprise elements belonging to different generic product categories. Whether the product is then called hardware, processed material, software or service depends on the dominant element.

Project: Unique process, consisting of a set of co-ordinated and controlled activities with start and finish dates, undertaken to achieve an objective conforming to specific requirements, including the constraints of time, costs and resources.

Quality: Ability of a set of inherent characteristics of a product, system or process to fulfil requirements of customers and other interested parties.

Quality assurance: Part of quality management, focused on providing confidence that quality requirements are fulfilled.

Quality audit: A systematic and independent examination to determine whether quality activities and related results comply with planned arrangements and whether these arrangements are implemented effectively and are suitable to achieve objectives.

Quality control: Part of quality management, focused on fulfilling quality requirements.

Quality costs: The expenditure incurred by the producer, by the user and by the community, associated with product or service quality.

Quality level: A general indication of the extent of the product's departure from the ideal.

Quality loop: Conceptual model of interacting activities that influence the quality of a product or service in the various stages ranging from the identification of needs to the assessment of whether these needs have been satisfied.

Quality manager: A person who is responsible for the manufacturer's Quality Management System (also sometimes referred to as the Chief Inspector).

Quality management: That aspect of the overall management function that determines and implements the quality policy.

NOTE The terms 'quality management' and 'quality control' are considered to be a manufacturer/supplier (or 1st party) responsibility. 'Quality Assurance' on the other hand has both internal and external aspects which in many instances can be shared between the manufacturer/supplier (1st party), purchaser/customer (2nd party) and any regulatory/certification body (3rd party) that may be involved.

Quality Management System: System to establish a quality policy and quality objectives and to achieve those objectives.

Quality Management System review: A formal evaluation by top management of the status and adequacy of the Quality Management System in relation to quality policy and new objectives resulting from changing circumstances.

Quality manual: Document specifying the quality management system of an organisation.

Quality plan: Document specifying the quality management system elements and the resources to be applied in a specific case.

Quality policy: The overall quality intentions and direction of an organisation as regards quality, as formally expressed by top management.

Quality procedure: A description of the method by which quality system activities are managed.

Quality records: Records should provide evidence of how well the Quality System has been implemented.

Quality system: The organisational structure, responsibilities, procedures, processes and resources for implementing quality management.

Quarantine store: A secure place to store supplies that are awaiting proof that they comply with specified requirements.

Receiving inspection/incoming inspection: Inspection by a customer (or department) of materials and manufactured products as received.

Record: Document stating results achieved or providing evidence of activities performed.

Reliability: The ability of an item to perform a required function under stated conditions for a stated period of time.

Repair: Action taken on a nonconforming product to make it acceptable for the intended usage.

Requirement: Need or expectation that is stated, customarily implied or obligatory.

Review: Activity undertaken to ensure the suitability, adequacy, effectiveness and efficiency of the subject matter to achieve established objectives.

Risk: The combined effect of the probability of occurrence of an undesirable event, and the consequence of the event.

Sample: A group of items or individuals, taken from a larger collection or population that provides information needed for assessing a characteristic (or characteristics) of the population, or which serves as a basis for action on the population, or the process that produced it.

Shall: This auxiliary verb indicates a course of action that must be followed by manufacturers and suppliers.

Should: This auxiliary verb indicates that a certain course of action is preferred but not necessarily required.

Specification: The document that describes the requirements with which the product, material or process has to conform.

Supplier: The organisation that provides a product to the customer (EN ISO 8402:1995).

 Notes:

1. In a contractual situation, the supplier may be called the contractor.
2. The supplier may be, for example, the producer, distributor, importer, assembler or service organisation.
3. The supplier may be either external or internal to the organisation.
4. With regard to MDD the term supplier is NOT used. The Directive instead refers to 'manufacturer'.

Supplier evaluation: Assessment of a supplier's capability to control quality.

Supplier rating: An index related to the performance of a supplier.

Top management: Person or group of people who direct and control an organisation at the highest level.

User requirement: The documented product or service requirements of a customer or user.

Validation: Confirmation and provision of objective evidence that the requirements for a specific intended use or application have been fulfilled.

Verification: The act of reviewing, inspecting, testing, checking, auditing or otherwise establishing and documenting whether items, processes, services, or documents conform to specified requirements.

Work instruction: A description of how a specific task is carried out.

References

The following is intended as a guide to the most common publications and references for quality management.

Standards

Number	Date	Title
ANSI 90 series		American quality standards
ASC Q9000 series	various	Quality management and quality assurance standards
AS/EN/JIS Q 9100	2001	Quality management systems – aerospace – requirements
BS 0	1997	A standard for standards
BS 2011	various	Basic environmental testing procedures
BS 3934 series	various	Dimensions of semiconductor devices
BS 4778	1979	Quality vocabulary
BS 4891	1972	A guide to quality assurance (now withdrawn)
BS 5701	1980	Guide to number of defective charts for quality control
BS 5703		Superseded by BS 5703:PT1
BS 5703:PT1	1980	Guide to data analysis and quality control using cusum techniques – introduction to cusum charting
BS 5750	1987	Superseded by ISO 9000:1994
BS 5760	various	Reliability of systems, equipment and components
BS 6000	1972	Superseded by BS 6001:PT0(1996)
BS 6001:PT0	1996	Sampling procedures for inspection by attributes
BS 6001:PT1	1991	Sampling procedures for inspection by attributes – specification for sampling plans by acceptable quality level (AQL) for lot-by-lot inspection
BS 6002		Superseded by BS 6002:PT1(1993)

Number	Date	Title
BS 6002:PT1	1993	Sampling procedures for inspection by variables – specification for single sampling plans indexed by acceptable quality level (AQL) for lot-by-lot inspection
BS 6143		Superseded by BS 6143:PT2(1990)
BS 6143:PT2	1990	Guide to the economics of quality – prevention, appraisal and failure model
BS 6548 series		Maintainability of equipment
BS 7000 series	various	Design management systems
BS 7750		Superseded by ISO 14001:1994
BS 7799	1995	Information security management system recommendations
BS 7850 series	1992	Total quality management
BS 8800	2004	Guide to occupational health and safety management systems
BS 9000 series	various	General requirements for a system of electronic components of assessed quality
EN 540	1993	Clinical investigation of medical devices for human subjects
EN 724	1994	Guidance on the application of EN 29001 and EN 46001 and of EN 29002 and EN 46002 for non-active medical devices
EN 928	1994	In vitro diagnostic systems – guidance on the application of EN 29001 and EN 46001 and of EN 29002 and EN 46002 for in vitro diagnostic medical devices
EN 1041	1998	Information supplied by the manufacturer with medical devices
EN 29000	1987	Renumbered as ISO 9000/1
EN 46001	1996	Quality systems – medical devices – particular requirements for the application of EN ISO 9001
EN 46002	1996	Quality systems – medical devices – particular requirements for the application of EN ISO 9002
EN 50103	1995	Guidance on the application of EN 29001 and EN 46001 and of EN 29002 and EN 46002 for the active (including active implantable) medical device industry
IEC 271	1974	Guide on the reliability of electronic equipment and parts used therein – terminology
IEC 729	1982	Concerning abbreviations

Number	Date	Title
ISO 3534 series	1977	Statistical terminology Part 1: Glossary of terms relating to probability and general terms relating to statistics
ISO 8402	1994	Quality management and quality assurance – vocabulary
ISO 8800	No data	Health and safety management system recommendations
ISO 9000	1994 series	Replaced by the ISO 9001:2000 series of standards
ISO 9000	2000	Quality management systems – fundamentals and vocabulary
ISO 9000/1	1994	Quality management and quality assurance standards – guide to their selection and use
ISO 9000/2	1997	Quality management and quality assurance standards – generic guidelines for the application of ISO 9001, 9002 and 9003
ISO 9000/3	1997	Quality management and quality assurance standards – guidelines for the application of ISO 9001 to the development, supply and maintenance of software
ISO 9000/4	1993	Quality management and quality assurance standards – guide to dependability programme management
ISO 9001	1994	Quality management systems – model for quality assurance in design, development, production, installation and servicing
ISO 9001	2000	Quality management systems – requirements
ISO 9002	1994	Quality management systems – model for quality assurance in production and installation
ISO 9003	1994	Quality management systems – model for quality assurance in final inspection and test
ISO 9004	2000	Quality management systems – guidance for performance improvement
ISO 9004/1	1994	Quality management and quality management system elements – guide to quality management and quality management system elements
ISO 9004/2	1991	Quality management and quality management system elements – guidelines for service
ISO 9004/3	1993	Quality management and quality management system elements – guidelines for processed materials

Number	Date	Title
ISO 9004/4	1994	Quality management and quality management system elements – guidelines for quality improvement
ISO 10005	1995	Quality management – guidelines for quality plans
ISO 10011/1	1990	Guidelines for auditing quality systems – auditing
ISO 10011/2	1991	Guidelines for auditing quality systems – qualification criteria for quality systems auditors
ISO 10011/3	1991	Guidelines for auditing quality systems – management of audit programmes
ISO 10012	2003	Measurement management systems. Requirements for measurement processes and measuring equipment
ISO 10012/1	1992	Quality assurance requirements for measuring equipment – metrological confirmation system for measuring equipment
ISO 10012/2	1997	Quality assurance for measuring equipment – guidelines for control of measuring processes
ISO 10013	1995	Guidelines for developing quality manuals
ISO 11134	1994	Sterilisation of health care products – requirements for validation and routine control – industrial moist heat sterilisation
ISO 11135	1994	Medical devices – validation and routine control of ethylene oxide sterilisation
ISO 11137	1995	Sterilisation of healthcare products – requirements for validation and routine control
ISO 13485	1996	Quality systems – medical devices – particular requirements for the application of ISO 9001 (replaced by ISO 13485:2003)
ISO 13485	2003	Medical devices – quality management systems – requirements for regulatory purposes
ISO 13488	1996	Quality systems – medical devices – particular requirements for the application of ISO 9002
ISO 14001	1996	Environmental management systems – specifications with guidance for use
ISO 14004	1996	Environmental management systems – general guidelines on principles, systems and supporting techniques
ISO 14010	1996	Guidelines for environmental auditing – general principles
ISO 14011	1996	Guidelines for environmental auditing – auditing procedures

Number	Date	Title
ISO 14012	1996	Guidelines for environmental auditing – qualification criteria for environmental auditors
ISO 14015	2001	Environmental management – environmental assessment of sites and organisations (EASO)
ISO 14031	1999	Environmental management – environmental performance evaluation – guidelines
ISO 14040	1997	Environmental management – life cycle assessment – principles and framework
ISO 14041	1998	Environmental management – life cycle assessment – goal and scope definition and inventory analysis
ISO 14042	2000	Environmental management – life cycle assessment – life cycle impact assessment
ISO 14043	2000	Environmental management – life cycle assessment – life cycle interpretation
ISO 19011	2002	Guidelines for quality and/or environmental management systems auditing
ISO/TR 10013	2001	Guidelines for quality management documentation
ISO/TR 13352	1997	Guidelines for the interpretation of ISO 9001:2000 for application within the iron ore industry
ISO/TR 14032	1999	Environmental management – examples of environmental performance evaluation (EPE)
ISO/TR 14047	2003	Environmental management – life cycle impact assessment – examples of application of ISO 14042
ISO/TR 14049	2000	Environmental management – life cycle assessment – examples of application of ISO 14041 to goal and scope definition and inventory analysis
ISO 14050	2002	Environmental management – vocabulary
ISO 15161	2001	Guidelines for the application of ISO 9001:2000 for the food and drink industry
ISO/IEC guide 66:1999		General requirements for bodies operating assessment and certification/registration of environmental management systems (EMS)
ISO/IEC 17025	2000	General requirements for the competence and testing of calibration laboratories
ISO/IEC 90003	2004	Software engineering – guidelines for the application of ISO 9001:2000 to computer software

Number	Date	Title
ISO/TR 14061	1998	Information to assist forestry organisations in the use of environmental management system standards ISO 14001 and ISO 14004
ISO/TR 14062	2002	Environmental management – integrating environmental aspects into product design and development
ISO/TS 16949	2002	Quality management systems – particular requirements for the application of ISO 9001:2000 for automotive production and relevant service part industries
ISO 19011	2002	Guidelines for quality and/or environmental management system auditing
IWA 2	2003	Quality management systems – guidelines for the application of ISO 9001:2000 in education
PD ISO/TS 29001	2003	Petroleum, petrochemical and natural gas industries – sector special quality management systems – requirements for product and service supply organisations
QS 9000	1998	Quality system requirements of the automotive industry
TL 9000		Quality management systems for the telecommunications sector

Other publications

Title	Details
An Executive Guide to the Use of UK National Standards and International Standards for Quality Management Systems	A British Standards Institution publication
BSI in Europe	A British Standards Institution newsletter
BSI Inspectorate	A British Standards Institution publication
BSI's Quality Management Handbook	(formally Handbook no. 22 'Quality Management System')
Comd 8621	'Standards, Quality and International Competitiveness'. A White Paper in support of the statement made by the Secretary of State

Title	Details
DEF STAN 13-131/2:1997	Ordinance Board safety guidelines for weapons and munitions
ISO 9000 for Small Businesses (Third edn)	Tricker, Ray. Published by Elsevier Butterworth-Heinemann. 2005
ISO 9000 in Brief (Second edn)	Tricker, Ray and Sherring-Lucas, Bruce. Published by Elsevier Butterworth-Heinemann. 2005
ISO Guide 2:1996	General terms and their definitions concerning standardisation and certifications
Loss of quality through poor maintenance	A paper by Herne Consultancy Group. 1994
NAO Targets for Excellence	General Motors Company quality standard
Operating degradations during the in-service stage	A paper by Herne Consultancy Group. 1994
Q101	Ford Motor Company quality standard
Standards in Electronics	Tricker, Ray. Butterworth-Heinemann. 1996
Standards, Quality and International Competitiveness	Division of Trade and Industry. Oct. 1986
Statistical Process Control	Oakland, John S. Elsevier Butterworth-Heinemann. 2002
Suppliers' Quality Assurance Manual	Chrysler Motor Company quality standard
The History of Quality Assurance and EQD	By Peter Tennyson from material researched by Dick Peal *et al.*
The Work and Significance of ANSI	Davis, Nancy M. *Standards Express.* Spring 1989
Total Quality Management	Oakland, John S. Butterworth-Heinemann. 1994
Working for Quality	A British Standards Institute pamphlet
'New Approach' Web	A new website representing the joint efforts of CEN, CENELEC and ETSI, together with the European Commission and EFTA, has recently been developed, enabling 24-hour access to online information about European standards.

Title	Details
	The 'New Approach' website provides SMEs with a facility for determining the appropriate standards for the products they manufacture, irrespective of which of the three European standards organisations is responsible for the applicable standards.
	Additionally, all of the European standards referred to are available from BSI Customer Services on 0181 996 9001, while further information on particular products or markets may be obtained from BSI's Technical Help for Exporters advice service on 0181 996 7111. To access the 'New Approach' website, go to www.NewApproach.org

 Note: Extracts from British Standards are reproduced in this book with the kind permission of the British Standards Institute. Complete copies of all British Standards can be obtained, by post, from Customer Services, BSI Standards, 389 Chiswick High Road, London W4 4AL.

The ISO 9001 Auditing Practices Group

The ISO 9001 Auditing Practices Group (APG) (an informal group of quality management system experts, auditors and practitioners drawn from the ISO Technical Committee 176 and the International Accreditation Forum (IAF)) has developed a number of guidance papers and presentations. These papers are primarily aimed at QMS auditors, consultants and quality practitioners and contain ideas, examples and explanations about the auditing of QMSs and are intended to provide additional assistance to ISO 9001:2000 users, without modifying any of the requirements of the standard.

Guidance notes are available on the APG website at: http://isotc176sc2. elysium-ltd.net/APG index.html and include:

- The need for a two-stage approach to auditing.
- Measuring QMS effectiveness and improvements.
- Identification of processes.
- Understanding the process approach.

- Determination of the 'where appropriate' processes
- Auditing the 'where appropriate' requirements
- Demonstrating conformity to the standard
- Linking an audit of a particular task, activity or process to the overall system
- Auditing continual improvement
- Auditing a QMS which has minimum documentation
- How to audit top management processes
- The role and value of the audit checklist
- Scope of ISO 9001:2000, scope of QMS and defining scope of certification
- Value-added auditing
- Auditing competence and the effectiveness of actions taken
- Effective use of ISO 19011:2002, *Guidelines for quality and/or environmental management systems auditing*
- Auditing statutory and regulatory requirements
- Auditing quality policy and quality objectives
- Auditing the control of monitoring and measuring devices
- Auditing customer satisfaction
- Writing non-conformities that are understandable, useful and therefore add value
- Reviewing responses to non-conformities to assure correction and corrective action that is effective.

A link to the documents on the APG website is also provided in the ISO 9000 section on ISO's main website www.iso.org. This section also includes the latest versions of the free-of-charge documents comprising the *ISO 9000:2000 Introduction and support package* – another initiative by ISO to facilitate the understanding and implementation of its quality system standards. In addition, the section has a wide choice of free sample articles from ISO's bimonthly magazine *ISO Management Systems* which provides a worldwide overview of the ISO 9000 and ISO 14000 families of quality and environmental management standards, including implementation case studies, surveys, analyses, viewpoints and debates.

Press contact

Roger Frost
Press and Communication Manager
Public Relations Services
Tel +41 22 749 01 11
Fax +41 22 733 34 30
E-mail frost@iso.org

Books by the same author

Title	Details	Publisher
ISO 9001:2000 for Small Businesses (Third edn) 	A guide to cost-effective compliance with the requirements of ISO 9001:2000	Elsevier Butterworth-Heinemann ISBN: 0 7506 6617 X
ISO 9001:2000 in Brief (Second edn) 	A 'hands-on' book providing practical information on how to cost effectively set up an ISO 9001:2000 Quality Management System	Elsevier Butterworth-Heinemann ISBN: 0 7506 6616 1
Building Regulations in Brief (Second edn) 	Handy reference guide to the requirements of the Building Act and its associated Approved Documents. Aimed at experts as well as DIY enthusiasts and those undertaking building projects	Elsevier Butterworth-Heinemann ISBN: 0 7506 5367 1

Title	Details	Publisher
Optoelectronic and Fiber Optic Technology	An introduction to the fascinating technology of fiber optics	Butterworth-Heinemann ISBN: 0 7506 5370 1
CE Conformity Marking	Essential information for any manufacturer or distributor wishing to trade in the European Union. Practical and easy to understand	Butterworth-Heinemann ISBN: 0 7506 4813 9
Environmental Requirements for Electromechanical and Electronic Equipment	Definitive reference containing all the background guidance, ranges, test specifications, case studies and regulations worldwide	Butterworth-Heinemann ISBN: 0 7506 3902 4

Title	Details	Publisher
MDD Compliance using Quality Management Techniques	Easy to follow guide to MDD, enabling the purchaser to customise the Quality Management System to suit his own business	Butterworth-Heinemann ISBN: 0 7506 4441 9
Quality and Standards in Electronics	Ensures that manufacturers are aware of all the UK, European and international necessities, and know the current status of these regulations and standards, and where to obtain them	Butterworth-Heinemann ISBN: 0 7506 2531 7

Useful addresses

Members of the International Organisation for Standardisation (ISO) located within the EEC.

Austria (ON)   Österreichisches Normungsinstitut
                          Austrian Standards Institute
                          Heinestrasse 38
                          AT-1020 Wien
                          Tel   +43 1 213 00 610
                          Fax   +43 1 213 00 609
                          E-mail iro@on-norm.at
                          Web   http://www.on-norm.at/

Belgium (IBN)   Institut belge de normalisation
                          Av. de la Brabançonne 29
                          BE-1000 Bruxelles
                          Tel   +32 2 738 01 11
                          Fax   +32 2 733 42 64
                          E-mail voorhof@ibn.be
                          Web   http://www.ibn.be

Cyprus (CYS)   Cyprus Organization for the Promotion of Quality
                          Ministry of Commerce, Industry and Tourism
                          CY-Nicosia 1421
                          Tel   +357 22 40 93 06
                          Fax   +357 22 75 41 03
                          E-mail ikaris@cys.mcit.gov.cy

Czech Republic (CSNI) Czech Standards Institute
                          Biskupsky dvur 5
                          CZ-110 02 Praha 1
                          Tel   +420 2 21 80 21 11
                          Fax   +420 2 21 80 23 11
                          E-mail extrel@csni.cz
                          Web   http://www.csni.cz

Denmark (DS)

Dansk Standard
(Danish Standards Association)
Kollegievej 6
DK-2920 Charlottenlund
Tel   +45 39 96 61 01
Fax   +45 39 96 61 02
E-mail   dansk.standard@ds.dk
Web   http://www.ds.dk/

Finland (SFS)

Finnish Standards Association SFS
P.O. Box 116
FI-00241 Helsinki
Tel   +358 9 149 93 31
Fax   +358 9 146 49 25
E-mail   sfs@sfs.fi
Web   http://www.sfs.fi/

France (AFNOR)

Association française de normalisation
11, avenue Francis de Pressensé
FR-93571 Saint-Denis La Plaine Cedex
Tel   +33 1 41 62 80 00
Fax   +33 1 49 17 90 00
E-mail   uari@afnor.fr
Web   http://www.afnor.fr/

Germany (DIN)

DIN Deutsches Institut für Normung
Burggrafenstrasse 6
DE-10787 Berlin
Tel   +49 30 26 01-0
Fax   +49 30 26 01 12 31
E-mail   directorate.international@din.de
Web   http://www.din.de

Greece (ELOT)

Hellenic Organisation for Standardisation
313, Acharnon Street
GR-111 45 Athens
Tel   +30 210 21 20 100
Fax   +30 210 21 20 131
E-mail   info@elot.gr
Web   http://www.elot.gr/

Hungary (MSZT)

Magyar Szabványügyi Testület
Üllöi út 25
Pf. 24.
HU-1450 Budapest 9
Tel   +36 1 456 68 00
Fax   +36 1 456 68 23
E-mail isoline@mszt.hu
Web   http://www.mszt.hu/

Ireland (NSAI)

National Standards Authority of Ireland
Glasnevin
IE-Dublin-9
Tel   +353 1 807 38 00
Fax   +353 1 807 38 38
E-mail nsai@nsai.ie
Web   http://www.nsai.ie

Italy (UNI)

Ente Nazionale Italiano di Unificazione
Via Battistotti Sassi 11/b
IT-20133 Milano
Tel   +39 02 70 02 41
Fax   +39 02 70 10 61 49
E-mail uni@uni.com
Web   http://www.uni.com

Luxembourg (SEE)

Service de l'Energie de l'Etat
Organisme Luxembourgeois de Normalisation
34 avenue de la Porte-Neuve
B.P. 10
LU-2010 Luxembourg
Tel   +352 46 97 46 1
Fax   +352 46 97 46 39
E-mail see.normalisation@eg.etat.lu
Web   http://www.see.lu

Malta (MSA)

Malta Standards Authority
Second Floor, Evans Building
Merchants Street
MT-Valletta VLT 03
Tel   +356 21 24 24 20
Fax   +356 21 24 24 06
E-mail info@msa.org.mt
Web   http://www.msa.org.mt

Netherlands (NEN)   Nederlands Normalisatie-instituut
Vlinderweg 6
NL-2623 AX Delft
Postal Address   P.O. Box 5059
NL-2600 GB Delft
Tel   +31 15 2 69 03 90
Fax   +31 15 2 69 01 90
E-mail   info@nen.nl
Web   http://www.nen.nl

Poland (PKN)   Polish Committee for Standardisation
ul. Swietokrzyska 14
PL-00-0050 Warszawa
Tel   +48 22 556 75 91
Fax   +48 22 556 77 86
E-mail   pl.isonb@pkn.pl
Web   http://www.pkn.pl

Portugal (IPQ)   Instituto Português da Qualidade
Rua António Gião, 2
PT-2829-513 Caparica
Tel   +351 21 294 81 00
Fax   +351 21 294 81 01
E-mail   ipq@mail.ipq.pt
Web   http://www.ipq.pt/

Slovakia (SUTN)   Slovak Standards Institute
P.O. Box 246
Karloveská 63
SK-840 00 Bratislava 4
Tel   +421 2 60 29 44 74
Fax   +421 2 65 41 18 88
E-mail   ms_post@sutn.gov.sk
Web   http://www.sutn.gov.sk

Slovenia (SIST)   Slovenian Institute for Standardisation
Smartinska 140
SI-1000 Ljubljana
Tel   +386 1 478 30 13
Fax   +386 1 478 30 94
E-mail   sist@sist.si
Web   http://www.sist.si

Spain (AENOR)   Asociación Española de Normalización y Certificación
Génova, 6
ES-28004 Madrid
Tel   +34 91 432 60 00
Fax   +34 91 310 49 76
E-mail   aenor@aenor.es
Web   http://www.aenor.es/

Sweden (SIS)   SIS, Swedish Standards Institute
Sankt Paulsgatan 6
SE- Stockholm
Postal Address
SE-118 80 Stockholm
Tel   +46 8 55 55 20 00
Fax   +46 8 55 55 20 01
E-mail   info@sis.se
Web   http://www.sis.se

United Kingdom British Standards Institution
(BSI)   389 Chiswick High Road
GB-London W4 4AL
Tel   +44 208 996 90 00
Fax   +44 208 996 74 00
E-mail   standards.international@bsi-global.com
Web   http://www.bsi-global.com

Other useful addresses

American National Standards   American National Standards Institute
Institute (ANSI)   1819 L Street, NW
US-Washington, DC 20036
Tel   +1 212 642 49 00
Fax   +1 212 398 00 23
E-mail   info@ansi.org
Web   http://www.ansi.org

American Society for Quality   611 East Wisconsin Avenue
Control (ASQ)   P.O. Box 3005
Milwaukee WI 53201-3005, USA
Tel   00 1 414 272 8575 or 800 248 1946
Fax   00 1 414 272 1734
E-mail   cs@asq.org
Web   http://www.asq.org

Canada (SCC)	Standards Council of Canada 270 Albert Street, Suite 200 CA-Ottawa, Ontario K1P 6N7 *Tel* +1 613 238 32 22 *Fax* +1 613 569 78 08 *E-mail* info@scc.ca *Web* http://www.scc.ca
Comission Europeen de Normalisation (CEN)	36, rue de Stassart 1050 Bruxelles, Belgium *Tel* 0032 2 550 08 11 *Fax* 0032 2 550 08 19 *E-mail* infodesk@cenclcbel.be *Web* http://www.cenorm.be
Croatia (DZNM)	State Office for Standardisation and Metrology Ulica grada Vukovara 78 HR-10000 Zagreb *Tel* +385 1 610 63 20 *Fax* +385 1 610 93 20 *E-mail* ured.ravnatelja@dznm.hr *Web* http://www.dznm.hr
ETSI	Route des Lucioles – Sophia Antipolis – Valbonne 06921 Sophia Antipolis, France *Tel* 0033 4 92 94 42 00 *Fax* 0033 4 93 65 47 16 *E-mail* infocentre@etsi.fr *Web* http://www.etsi.org
European Committee for Electrotechnical Standardisation (CENELEC)	35, rue de Stassart 1050 Bruxelles, Belgium *Tel* 0032 2 519 68 71 *Fax* 0032 2 519 69 19 *E-mail* general@cenelec.be *Web* http://www.cenelec.be
European Organisation for Testing and Certification (EOTC)	Egmont House Rue d'Egmont 15 1000 Bruxelles, Belgium *Tel* 0032 2 502 4141 *Fax* 0032 2 502 4239

Iceland (IST)	Icelandic Standards Laugavegi 178 IS-105 Reykjavik *Tel* +354 520 71 50 *Fax* +354 520 71 71 *E-mail* stadlar@stadlar.is *Web* http://www.stadlar.is
ILI (America)	60 Winters Avenue Paramus, NJ 07652, USA *E-mail* sales@ili-info.com
Infornorme London Information (ILI)	Index House Ascot Berkshire SL5 7EU, UK *Tel* 01344 636400 *Fax* 01344 291194 *E-mail* databases@ili.co.uk *Web* http://www.ili.co.uk
International Electrotechnical Commission (IEC)	Rue de Varembe 3 Case Postale 131 1211 Geneva 20, Switzerland *Tel* 0041 22 919 0211 *Fax* 0041 22 919 0300 *Web* http://www.iec.ch
International Standards Organisation ISO Central Secretariat:	International Organisation for Standardisation (ISO) 1, rue de Varembé, Case postale 56 CH-1211 Geneva 20, Switzerland *Tel* +41 22 749 01 11 *Fax* +41 22 733 34 30 *Web* http://www.iso.org
National Center for Standards and Certification Information	US Department of Commerce Building 820, Room 164 Gaithersburg, MD 20899, USA *Tel* 00 1 301 9754040 *EU Hotline* 00 1 301 921-4164 *Fax* 00 1 301 926 1559

Norway (SN)

Standards Norway
Strandveien 18
NO-1366 Lysaker
Postal Address PO Box 242
NO-1326 Lysaker
Tel +47 67 83 86 00
Fax +47 67 83 86 01
E-mail info@standard.no
Web http://www.standard.no

Office of the Official
Publications of the EC

2 Rue Mercier
2144 Luxembourg
Tel 00352-29291
Fax 00352 292942763
E-mail infor.info@opece.cec.be
Web http://www.eur-op.eu.int

Russian Federation (GOST R)

State Committee of the Russian
Federation for Standardisation and
Metrology
Leninsky Prospekt 9
RU-Moscow, V-49, GSP-1, 119991
Tel +7 095 236 40 44
Fax +7 095 237 60 32
E-mail info@gost.ru
Web http://www.gost.ru

Serbia and Montenegro (ISSM)

Institution for Standardisation of
Serbia and Montenegro
Stevana Brakusa 2
Post. fah 2105
CS-11030 Belgrade
Tel +381 11 54 70 96
Fax +381 11 35 41 258
E-mail jus@jus.org.yu
Web http://www.jus.org.yu

Switzerland (SNV)

Swiss Association for Standardisation
Bürglistrasse 29
CH-8400 Winterthur
Tel +41 52 224 54 54
Fax +41 52 224 54 74
E-mail info@snv.ch
Web http://www.snv.ch/

VDE-Verlag GmbH
Bismarkstrasse 33
10625 Berlin, Germany
Tel   0049 30 348001-0
Fax   0049 30 3417093
E-mail service@vde.com
Web   http://www.vde.de

And not forgetting – www.direct.gov.uk

Whatever your public service information need, you will probably find it here. Beneath the banners of employment, health and well-being, home and community, learning, motoring and transport you will find information on everything from having a baby and paying your road tax to employment for the over 50s. The website has a number of services including a job database for public sector workers, online tax return forms, foreign travel advice – and most fun of all – a message service which allows you to report suspect activity to MI5. Impressively interactive, with information and advice that is helpful and straightforward, this is a one stop shop for all your public service requirements.

Index